Physical Level
Interfaces and Protocols

Uyless Black

The Computer Society Order Number 824
Library of Congress Number 88-70541
IEEE Catalog Number EHO275-8
ISBN 0-8186-8824-6

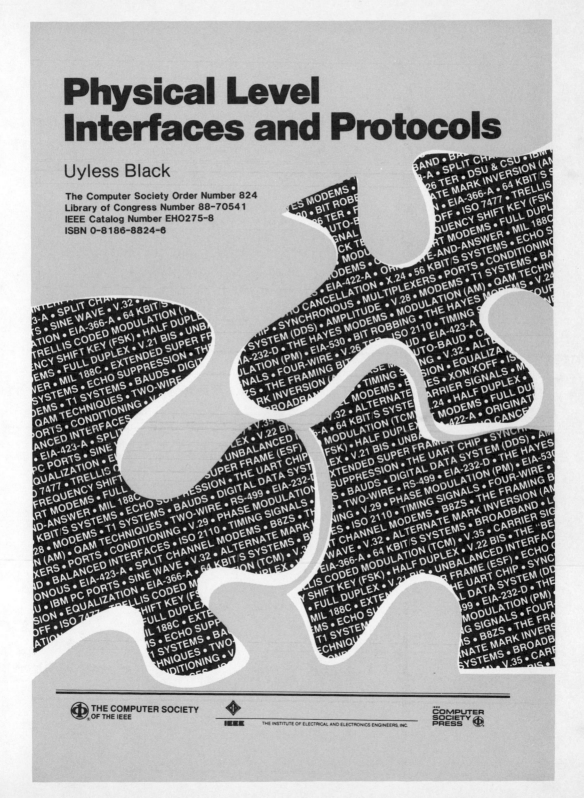

THE COMPUTER SOCIETY OF THE IEEE

IEEE THE INSTITUTE OF ELECTRICAL AND ELECTRONICS ENGINEERS, INC.

COMPUTER SOCIETY PRESS

PHYSICAL LEVEL INTERFACES AND PROTOCOLS

Uyless Black
Information Engineering, Inc.
and
Information Engineering Institute

Published by Computer Society Press
1730 Massachusetts Avenue, N.W.
Washington, D.C. 20036-1903

Cover designed by Jack I. Ballestero

Computer Society Order Number 824
Library of Congress Number 88-70541
IEEE Catalog Number EH0275-8
ISBN 0-8186-8824-6 (casebound)
ISBN 0-8186-4824-4 (microfiche)
SAN 264-620X

Order from:

The Computer Society	IEEE Service Center	The Computer Society
Terminal Annex	445 Hoes Lane	13, Avenue de l'Aquilon
P.O. Box 04699	P.O. Box 1331	B-1200 Brussels
Los Angeles, CA 90051	Piscataway, NJ 08855-1331	BELGIUM

 THE INSTITUTE OF ELECTRICAL AND ELECTRONICS ENGINEERS, INC.

Dedication

To my parents Ruby and Jim
and my friends Ray and Susan

Preface

A recurring frustration for the data communications user is the difficulty or inability to decipher vendors' descriptions of their physical level products such as modems and multiplexers. For example, typical sales brochures or specification sheets describe a modem in such terms as, ". . . conforms to EIA-232-D/V.24 and V.28 recommendations . . . uses ISO 2110 mechanical connector interface . . . may operate on switched lines in which case CCITT recommendation V.25 or EIA-366 is employed . . . full duplex channel separation on a two-wire circuit is achieved by frequency division . . . subchannels employ four-phase (dibit) shifts of 45°, 135°, 225°, and 315° . . . signaling rate is 1200 bauds with a 2400 bit/s line speed. . . ."

Such a description almost sounds like a foreign language. Indeed it is, if the user does not take the time to understand what the terms actually mean. As we shall see, most of them are relatively easy to grasp.

The experienced and practiced data communications professional may understand all these terms but does not have a ready reference to compare and equate the many physical level interfaces available today. These references and standards are published in separate documents by several different organizations.

The purpose of this book is (1) to explain the concepts and ideas associated with physical level protocols and (2) to provide the reader with a convenient summary of the industry's most widely used physical level interface standards.

This book focuses primarily on the physical interfaces between a user device (e.g., computer, terminal) and a communications line interface device (modem, data service unit, multiplexer). The book also emphasizes the systems used on the public telephone network and, therefore, serial communications. However, much of the material is applicable to private-wired systems as well.

Several of the interfaces are used on either analog or digital lines. Indeed, many of these protocols make no distinction between the signaling techniques because they describe only the user side of the physical level interface and do not describe the communications (line) side. The book concentrates on the user device side of the interface since many data communications users are tasked with the cabling and connector selection between the user device and the communications line termination equipment (such as a modem or multiplexer). Where applicable, the line side is also described.

A considerable portion of the book is devoted to the CCITT V series recommendations. Until the past few years, the V series were of limited interest in North America although they are used extensively in Europe. The CCITT interfaces are now widely used in North America. In several instances, they have surpassed the Bell standards in acceptance by vendors. For example, several of the Hayes modems use the V series recommendations.

A section is devoted to digital interfaces. The T1 carrier system and the digital data system (DDS) are examined because of their wide use.

While this guide explains many physical level interfaces in some detail, the reader should obtain vendor descriptions or the specific standards manual for a more thorough examination of a product or standard (see Appendix A for addresses).

Notes for the Reader

The standards organizations usually describe their specifications with a prefix. For example, the CCITT uses the term recommended standard (RS). As another example, until 1987 the Electronics Industries Association (EIA) used the letters RS (for recommended standard) for several of its communications interfaces. It now uses EIA as its prefix. For purposes of brevity, this book does not use the term recommended standard as a prefix to each CCITT specification. For example, V.22 bis is used instead of (1) recommended standard V.22 bis or (2) recommendation V.22 bis.

The EIA is in the process of changing its prefix from RS to EIA. To simplify matters, this book uses EIA, unless RS is specifically used by another standard (such as the Bell modem specifications). Also, the ubiquitious RS-232-C has been changed and designated as EIA-232-D. This book uses the term EIA-232 if either RS-232-C or EIA-232-D are applicable. If only one of the standards is applicable, the notation will so indicate with either RS-232-C or EIA-232-D.

In several instances, the various specifications use more than one term to describe one concept. For example, the terms "carrier detect" and "received line signal detector" describe the same process. A glossary is provided at the end of the book to assist the reader in learning about these terms. Indeed, since this book is intended as a reference guide, the glossary should be consulted for specific definitions.

Acknowledgments

I would like to express my appreciation to the CCITT, ISO, EIA, IEEE, and ANSI organizations for providing the foundations for this book. These organizations have gone through the laborious and time-consuming process of developing and publishing many physical level interfaces and protocols (several of which are described in this book). My task has been much simpler: to summarize the results of their efforts.

I would also like to express my gratitude to Holly Velez, who continues to provide support well beyond the call of duty.

I wish to thank several people for providing me the opportunity and motivation over the past several years to write and lecture in this exciting field: Jim Opperman, Warren Minami, Walter Kennevan, and Ken Sherman. I also want to acknowledge my friends at the Center for Advanced Professional Education and wish them good fortune in the future.

I also want to thank the staff, instructors, and consultants who have worked with me at the Information Engineering Institute in Falls Church, Virginia. Their contributions have been quite important to my efforts.

The reader should remember that a general reference (such as this book) is intended to provide an overview or a selected view of physical level standards. The actual document from the standards groups should be obtained if a detailed discourse on all attributes of the interface is required.

Several tables in this book are derived from the CCITT Standards (see the V series and X series recommendations). CCITT is the copyright holder for these tables.

Table of Contents

PHYSICAL LEVEL INTERFACES
AND PROTOCOLS

Section 1:
Introduction

BLACK

Section 1: Introduction

Since this document is designed primarily as a reference guide, it assumes that the reader has a basic level of understanding of data communications systems. A tutorial is provided in this section on physical level interfaces and protocols, with the assumption that the reader understands the basic ideas of data communications. The tutorial also assumes that the reader has a rudimentary knowledge of electronics.

Terms and Concepts

Computers and terminals communicate with each other through many kinds and levels of protocols. One level is called the physical level because it defines the procedures and conventions for physically connecting computers and terminals to each other and to communications channels such as telephone lines and other links. The term protocol describes an agreement about how to communicate. A protocol permits the interconnection of different vendors' systems, one hopes, with little conversion or reconfiguration. The term protocol is borrowed from social parlance to describe a common convention for communications.

A physical level protocol (also called a physical level interface) defines the following attributes of a data communications system:

- the wiring connections between the devices (if wires are used)
- the electrical, electromagnetic, or optical characteristics of the signals between the communicating devices
- the provision for mechanical connectors (such as the dimensions and numbers of the plugs and pins)
- the stipulation of the types of clocking signals that will enable the devices to synchronize onto each other's signals
- the provisions for electrical grounding in some instances
- the provisions for describing how the physical channels are used

So, the term "physical" is very appropriate as a descriptor of these functions. At this level, the machines are indeed physically communicating.

It will prove useful in this book to divide physical level systems into four major elements: mechanical, electrical, functional, and operational. The mechanical element describes the physical means of connecting devices. The electrical specification describes the voltage and current limitations, the logic conventions, and other electrical specifications. The functional element provides definitions of each circuit, its state, the timing constraints, and its actual method of use. The operational element defines the parameters that may be more device dependent, such as codes and diagnostic routines.

The physical interfaces described in this book are concerned with the communications between the user devices (such as terminals and computers) across a communications path. The industry uses the following terms to describe these components (see Figure 1):

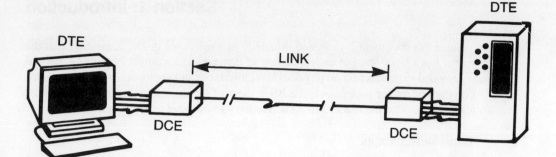

Figure 1: The DTE/DCE Interface

- DTE—data terminal equipment
- DCE—data circuit-terminating equipment (also called data communications equipment)
- circuit—data communications path

The DTE is typically an end-user device. It can be a terminal or a computer, such as a large mainframe computer or a small personal computer. The DTE usually supports the end-user application program, data files, and databases.

The DCE provides the connection of the user DTE into the communications circuit. The actual connections at the DTE and DCE are called "ports," and contain the logic needed to connect the devices. Notice from Figure 1 that a DCE exists at each end of the circuit to provide this function. A few vendors use the term "data set" to describe a DCE although the term is falling into disuse. (This term has nothing to do with a disk data set.)

The data communications circuit is the physical path between the DCEs. There are several names used in the industry to describe the circuit: channel, line, trunk, or link, for example. The terms are usually used interchangeably by vendors and users.

Two Sides to the Physical Level Protocol

The physical level protocols explained in this book may include descriptions for communications on one or both sides of the DCE. For example, the DTE-to-DCE physical side is covered in many of the Electronic Industries Association's (EIA) specifications. However, most of the EIA specifications do not describe the DCE-to-line signaling. In contrast, the majority of the CCITT recommendations describe the physical level signaling on both sides of the DCE. The distinction of where the physical level protocol actually resides in relation to the specification will be discussed as each standard is explained.

Analog and Digital Signals

Our voice signals, as well as the signals on the telephone circuit exhibit three characteristics that are relevant to physical level protocols: amplitude, frequency, and phase.

The amplitude of a signal is its measurement in relation to the voltage level. As Figure 2a indicates, a typical signal alternates between zero, positive, and negative voltage. The amplitude varies continuously, gradually changing from positive to

BLACK

negative voltage. The term "analog" is used to describe this type of signal.

The complete transition of a waveform is called its cycle. A waveform exhibits oscillating characteristics, which are described in cycles per second. Various combinations of these waveforms comprise a person's speech. The term "hertz" (Hz) is generally used instead of cycles per second. The frequency of the signal is a description of the number of cycles per second. A signal can be described as operating at 2400 Hz (i.e., its frequency).

The third major characteristic of the signal is its phase. The phase describes the point the signal has reached in its cycle. In Figure 2, the phase is compared to a 360° circle. When the signal is one-fourth through its cycle (like that of a circle), it is at 90° phase. The use of the phase concept is quite valuable to the design of certain DCEs, as we shall see shortly.

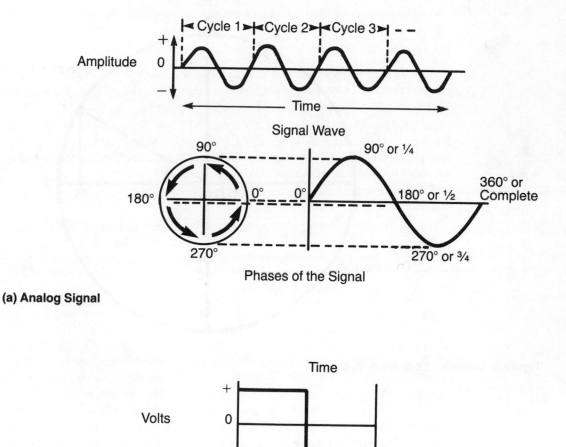

(a) Analog Signal

(b) Digital Signal

Figure 2: Analog and Digital signals

Machines such as computers do not usually represent data with analog signals; instead, digital signals are used. As Figure 2b shows, digital signals are discrete, changing suddenly from one voltage level to another. The computer uses transistor technology to effect these "off/on" changes to represent binary 0s and 1s.

The Sine Wave

The analog waveform is often described in terms of circular motion, and trigonometry is used to define the relationship. In trigonometry, a convenient method of measurement is a cartesian coordinate system. With this method, a grid is used to represent vertical and horizontal positions on a plane. Figure 3 shows the plane as four quadrants with positive or negative ordinates in the planes. A plot (point) on the grid is positive if it is above the x axis and negative if below.

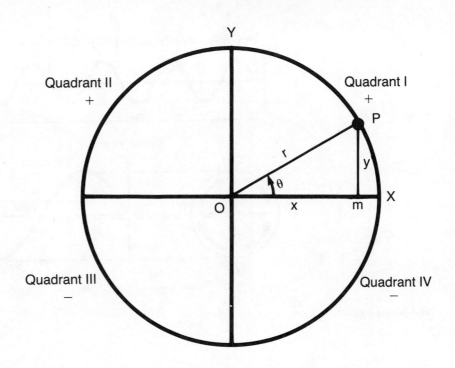

Figure 3: Cartesian Coordinate System

If a line is drawn from the origin (0) to a point on the grid (P), a triangle is formed with OP, PM, and MO representing the three sides of the triangle (see Figure 4). The sides are labeled r, y, and x. From the lengths of r, y, and x, the following ratios can be obtained (four other ratios are possible but not relevant to our discussion): y/r and x/r. The relationships of r, y, and x are determined with the value of the angle (Θ) at 0. The values of the ratios depend upon the size of Θ. The two ratios are defined and labeled as

$$\text{sine } \Theta \quad = y/r; \quad \text{abbreviated as } \sin \Theta$$
$$\text{cosine } \Theta \quad = x/r; \quad \text{abbreviated as } \cos \Theta$$

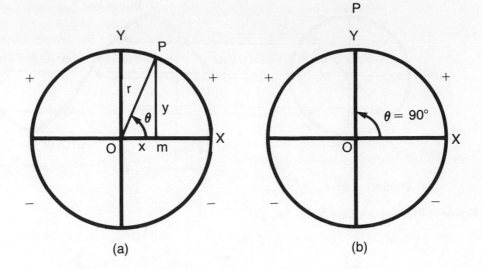

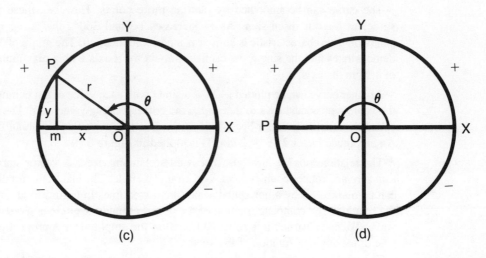

Figure 4: The Sin θ

Sin Θ and cos Θ are called trigonometric functions because the values of the ratios depend upon the value of Θ. This idea is illustrated by comparing Figure 4a with Figure 4b. As Θ increases, y increases, and, therefore, y/r increases.

However, the continuing increase of Θ does not create a continuing increase in y/r. Notice in Figure 4b that Θ is a 90° angle, P coincides with c, and y = 0C = 1. Yet, in Figure 4c, as Θ goes from 90° toward 180°, y becomes smaller, and in Figure 4d sine Θ decreases in value.

The rotation of the line OP into the negative quadrants creates the same (but negative) values of sine Θ as we found in the positive quadrants.

To construct a graph of sine Θ, let Y = sin Θ. Figure 5 is drawn from tables readily available in math books. Each value of sine Θ can be plotted and the curve drawn through the plotted points. The plotted curve is called a sine wave because its shape is

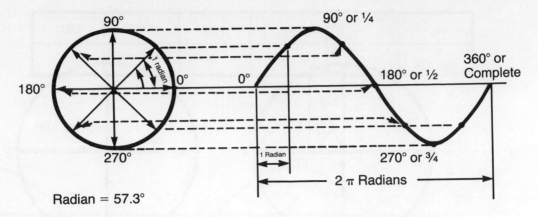

Radian = 57.3°

Figure 5: Plotting the Sine Wave

proportional to the sine and the position within the quadrant.

The curve can be smoothed by plotting more points. However, these points are sufficient for our discussion. As Θ increases beyond 360°, the curve repeats its behavior. This characteristic is known as a periodic function. The graph of Y = sin Θ demonstrates that the sine wave oscillates about the x axis with a maximum distance of 1 from the axis.

Another curve can be plotted as Y = a sin Θ with each value of sin Θ multiplied by the value represented by a to determine the corresponding value of Y. The a value is called the amplitude factor because it determines the curve's swing about the x axis. An amplitude factor 2 (Y = 2 sin Θ) is plotted in Figure 6.

The relationships we have just discussed are summarized. A vector starts at position zero and rotates counter-clockwise around a circle. The end of the rotating vector can be marked off by a horizontal scale (the dotted lines in Figure 5) at any point in the rotation. The complete rotation of the vector around the circle is plotted as a sine wave. We have learned it is so named because the amplitude a is proportional to the sine of the angle of rotation of the vector.

The angles of vectors are expressed in radians (rad = 57.3), which describe the angular part of the vector rotation that includes an arc equal to the radius of the circle. The circumference of a circle equals 2π rad. As Figure 5 demonstrates, the vector goes through 2π radians during one complete revolution. Thus, the length of the cycle is 2π radians, because 2π rad = 360°.

The waveform is subject to varying frequencies. From the context of Figure 5, a rapidly rotating vector produces more cycles per second. This rate of vector rotation is called the angular velocity (AV). A rotation rate of 2π radians per second produces 1 cycle per second, 4π radians per second produces 2 cycles per second, and so on. Angular velocity is a function of the frequency of the waveform

$$AV = 2\pi * f$$

where AV is radians per second, 2 is radians per cycle, and f is cycles per second.

Figure 5 also shows another component of the waveform, the phase which represents the relative position of time within the period of a signal. The phase is usually

θ		90°	180°	270°	360°
Y (sin θ)	0	1	0	−1	0

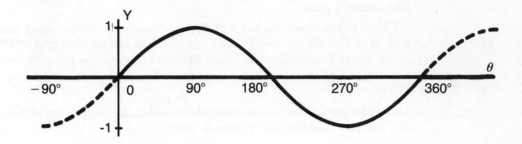

(a) Y = Sin θ

θ	0°	90°	180°	270°	360°
(sin θ)	0	1	0	−1	0
Y (2 sin θ)	0	2	0	−2	0

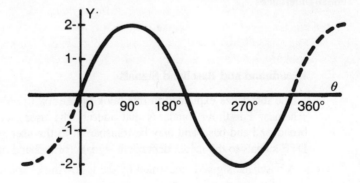

(b) Y = 2 Sin θ

Figure 6: The Amplitude Factor

measured in degree markings, which depict the position in the waveform. For example, a 90° phase describes the vector angle and the point in the waveform of a relative position of 1/4 t; that is, a position of one-fourth through the wave.

A single waveform is represented by the equation

$$a = A \sin(2\pi ft + \Theta)$$

where a is instantaneous amplitude, A is maximum amplitude, f is frequency, t is time, and Θ is phase.

Figure 7 shows two sine waves of the same frequency that are out-of-phase with each other. One wave is described as a = $A \sin(2\pi$ ft) and the other by $a = A \sin(2\pi ft + \Theta)$, where Θ represented the phase difference. Two waves that differ in time Δt have a phase difference of $\Theta = 2\pi\Delta t$ radians. Therefore, the time difference $\Delta T = \Theta/2\pi f$.

From previous discussions, we now know that we can also plot one of these curves as a sine curve and the other as a cosine curve.

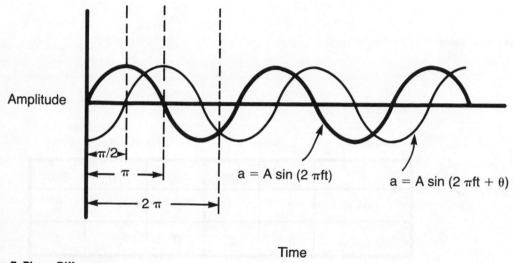

Figure 7: Phase Differences

Broadband and Baseband Signals

The interfaces explained in this book operate with either broadband or baseband schemes. For those standards that address the user side of the DCE, the use of broadband and baseband may be transparent to the user since the DCE converts the DTE signals to the media-dependent signals (broadband or baseband).

A baseband signal is identified by the following characteristics:

- typically uses voltage shifts to represent digital signals
- bandwidth is limited
- does not use modulation
- may use time division multiplexing for channel sharing

A broadband signal is identified by the following characteristics:

- uses analog wave forms
- has a large bandwidth (typically in the megahertz to gigahertz range)
- uses analog modulation
- often uses frequency division multiplexing for channel sharing

Many people use the term "baseband" to describe an unmodulated signal. As explained in the next section, a baseband signal may be used to modulate an analog carrier signal, but the carrier need not be a broadband carrier; it may be a voiceband carrier, which is not considered a broadband signal.

Both approaches are widely used today. Baseband is simple and, conceptually, less expensive than broadband. Baseband systems are also easy to install. However, baseband systems are more limited in capacity. Broadband systems are very high-capacity systems and, with active amplifiers, can be used over a wide geographical area. The broadband technology is more complex and requires an experienced engineer to maintain the system.

Bit Transfer Rate

DCEs transmit bits across the communications line. The bit representations depict user data and control data. The control data are used to manage the communications line and the flow of the user data. The speed of the circuit and transmission is described in bits per second (or bit/s). For example, typical speeds and uses of data communications channels are:

Category	Speed	Typical Uses
Low Speed	600 bit/s	Telegraph Transmissions
Medium Speed	2400 bit/s	Personal Computer Communications
High Speed	9600 bit/s	Large Amounts of Data Transfer
Very High Speed	64000 bit/s	Digital Voice

Modulation

The digitally oriented computers and terminals often communicate with each other through the analog telephone facilities. The modem is the DCE responsible for providing the required translation and interface between the digital and analog worlds. The majority of the DCEs described in this book are modems. Modems are designed around the use of an analog carrier frequency. The carrier has the DTE digital data stream superimposed upon it at the transmitting end of the circuit (modulation). The data signal is called a baseband signal. The carrier signal is changed back to the digital signal at the receiver DCE (demodulation). These DCEs thus transmit and receive the binary bits of user data generated by the DTEs.

Signal Conversion

Previous discussions have explained analog and digital signals. (Digital signals are used in computer systems to represent binary numbers, and analog signals are found in voice-oriented systems.) Many physical level protocols convert analog to digital signals and vice-versa. All four conversions are used for various reasons, but this book addresses digital-to-analog since the DTEs are digital devices and the vast majority of telephone lines use analog signaling. Digital-to-analog is the conversion of digital computer-oriented signals to analog signals in order to use analog-oriented facilities; for example, the telephone loops.

Digital-to-Analog Conversion

This technique is most often used when a user device such as a terminal or computer transmits and receives data through the public switched telephone network (PSTN). The device used to support this type of communications is the familiar modem.

Three basic methods of digital-to-analog modulation exist, and other methods are available that use a combination of the basic techniques. Some modems use more than one of the methods. The three methods are called amplitude, frequency, and phase modulation. Each method impresses the data on a carrier signal, which is altered to carry the properties of the digital data stream.

In this book, each physical level specification and its modulation technique (if used) will be explained in relation to the material in the following sections.

Amplitude Modulation (AM)

AM modems alter the carrier signal amplitude in accordance with the modulating digital bit stream (see Figure 8a). The frequency and phase of the carrier are held constant, and the amplitude is raised or lowered to represent a 0 or a 1. In its simplest form, the carrier signal can be switched on or off to represent the binary state. AM modulation is not often used by itself owing to transmission power problems and sensitivity to distortion. However, it is commonly used with phase modulation to yield a method superior to either FM or AM.

The AM signal is represented as

$$S(t) = A \cos (2\pi f_c t + \Theta_c) \quad \text{for binary 1}$$
$$S(t) = 0 \qquad\qquad\qquad\quad \text{for binary 0}$$

where $S(t)$ = value of carrier at time t, A = maximum amplitude of the carrier voltage, f_c = carrier frequency, and Θ_c = carrier phase.

This approach also shows that binary 0 is represented by no carrier, which is called off/on keying or amplitude shift keying (ASK). These conventional AM data signals are detected at the receiver by envelope detection. The signal is rectified at the receiver and is smoothed to obtain its envelope. This approach does not require the use of a reference carrier. Consequently, ASK is a relatively inexpensive process (since the use of a carrier reference is a more complex and expensive process). However, envelope detection does require both sidebands for accurate detection.

The off/on keying is a popular approach because it is simple. Nonetheless, ASK makes inefficient use of transmission power because the binary 0 signal is not the exact negative of the binary 1. The best use of power is achieved by having one signal the exact opposite of the other.

This problem is overcome with phase reversal keying (PRK). The idea is to produce two identical signals except for a 180° phase reversal—hence the name PRK.

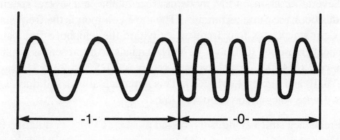

(a) Amplitude Modulation

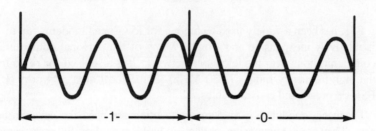

(b) Frequency Modulation

(c) Phase Modulation

Figure 8: Modulation Techniques

It is obvious that PRK uses phase changes, but it is still considered a special form of amplitude modulation.

PRK signals are detected at the receiver by the use of a coherent (or homodyne) carrier reference. A local receiver carrier is synchronized with the phase of the transmitter. With on/off AM systems, no information is contained in the phase; with PRK, the phase contains all the data information and the synchronization information.

The use of AM for data communications has decreased because a multilevel scheme requires the use of several to many signal levels. Very few of the specifications described in this book use AM alone. As the number of signal levels increases, the distance between the levels decreases. AM transmitters often "saturate" the narrow distances and, in some cases, they must be used at less than maximum power to diminish the saturation problem.

Thus, AM modems must be designed (1) with sufficiently long signaling intervals (low baud) to keep the signal on the channel long enough to withstand noise and to be detected at the receiver and (2) with sufficient distances between the AM levels to allow accurate detection and to diminish saturation.

Frequency Modulation (FM)

Figure 8b illustrates frequency modulation. This method changes the frequency of the carrier in accordance with the digital bit stream. The amplitude is held constant. In its simplest form, a binary 1 is represented by a certain frequency and a binary 0 by another.

Several variations of FM modems are available and several specifications described in this book use these techniques. The most common is the frequency shift key (FSK) modem which uses four frequencies within the telephone line bandwidth. The FSK modem transmits 1070 and 1270 Hz signals to represent a binary 0 (SPACE) and binary 1 (MARK), respectively. It receives 2025 and 2225 Hz signals as a binary 0 (SPACE) and binary 1 (MARK). This approach allows full duplex transmission over a two-wire voice-grade telephone line.

Frequency shift keying is expressed as

$$s(t) = A \cos(2\pi f_1 t + \Theta_c) \text{ binary 0}$$
$$s(t) = A \cos(2\pi f_2 t + \Theta_c) \text{ binary 1}$$

FSK has been a widely used technique for low-speed modems (up to 1200 bit/s). It is relatively inexpensive and simple. Many of the personal computers use FSK for communications over the telephone network. It is also used for radio transmission in the high-frequency ranges (3-30 MHz). Some local area networks (LANs) employ FSK on broadband coaxial cables.

Frequency modulation modems quite often are used for asynchronous transmission. They are not expensive modems to build, many can fit on the same circuit card, and they are not very noise sensitive. They are used for many low-speed transmissions, especially for terminals or personal computers, where the software has been designed for generating and transmitting asynchronous characters.

However, its use on voice-grade lines is decreasing as more manufacturers implement DCEs with phase modulation techniques. Phase modulation techniques are almost exclusively used today on high speed digital radio systems, as well as the newer Bell, Hayes, and CCITT modems.

Phase Modulation (PM)

Previous discussions of the sine wave describe how a cycle is represented with phase markings to indicate the point to which the oscillating wave has advanced in its cycle. PM modems alter the phase of the signal to represent a 1 or 0 (see Figure 8c).

The phase modulation method is also called phase shift keying (PSK). A common approach to PSK is to compare the phase of the current signal state to the previous signal state, which is known as differential PSK (DPSK). This technique uses bandwidth more efficiently than FSK because it puts more information into each signal. It also requires more elaborate equipment for signal generation and data representation.

The PSK signal is represented as

$$S(t) = A \cos(2\pi f_c t + \Delta\Theta)$$

where $\Delta\Theta$ = the change in phase.

Phase shift key can be used to provide multilevel modulation. The technique is called quadrature signal modulation. For example, a dibit modem (2 bits per baud) typically encodes the binary data stream as follows:

11:	$\Delta\Theta$	=	45°
10:	$\Delta\Theta$	=	135°
01:	$\Delta\Theta$	=	225°
00:	$\Delta\Theta$	=	315°

Quadrature Signal Representation

To introduce quadrature signaling, examine Figure 9. A common technique to determine impairments and/or signal quality is the use of the ternary "eye" diagram. These diagrams are shown on an oscilloscope by synchronizing the clock frequency to a time base and then superimposing and displaying the states of a long sequence of digits. The eye diagram is so named because a nondistorted signal shows a wide-open eye and a degraded signal shows the eye closing. The smaller the eye opening, the greater the signal degradation and the higher the probability of errors occurring. The eye diagram is also used to show the effects of multilevel signaling with the quadrature and quadrature amplitude modulation methods.

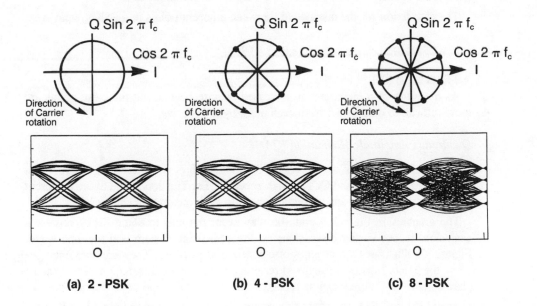

(a) 2 - PSK   (b) 4 - PSK   (c) 8 - PSK

Figure 9: The I and Q Signal

The phase diagram (also called a constellation pattern), is used to represent quadrature modulation. The $\cos 2\pi f_c t$ signal is referred to as in-phase or I signal; the $\sin 2\pi f_c t$ signal is referred to as the out-of-phase or Q signal. This relationship is depicted in Table 1 and Figure 9.

Table 1: Quadrature Coefficients for 4 and 8 PSKs

Data Bits	Quadrature ($\sin 2\pi f_c$)	Coefficients ($\cos 2\pi f_c$)
4 PSK		
01	−0.707	0.707
00	−0.707	−0.707
10	0.707	−0.707
11	0.707	0.707
8 PSK		
011	−0.383	0.924
010	−0.924	0.383
000	−0.924	−0.383
001	−0.383	−0.924
101	0.383	−0.924
100	0.924	−0.383
110	0.924	0.383
111	0.383	0.924

Another PSK modem is a tribit device (3 bits per baud), which uses 8-PSK modulation. The phase diagram for the 8-PSK modem is also shown in Figure 9. The quadrature coefficients for 4-PSK and 8-PSK are depicted in Table 1.

The calculation for the distance (d) between adjacent points in a PSK system is

$$d = 2\,\sin(\pi/n)$$

where n = number of phases.

As the value of n increases, an increased bit rate results, but the close points are more difficult to distinguish from each other by the receiver.

Quadrature Amplitude Modulation (QAM)

A special extension of multiphase PSK modulation is QAM (see Figure 10). It is widely used in the Bell and CCITT high-speed DCEs. The dots in the figure represent composite signal points and amplitude levels in each quadrature channel.

The graphics in Figures 9 and 10a may seem familiar to some. They represent extensions to our earlier discussions on the coordinate system and the sine wave. Figure 10a illustrates the concept of constellation patterns. They are so named because the points (tips of the arrows) resemble points in a constellation. The Q and I planes shown in Figure 9 can be related to the constellation points in Figure 10a.

The QAM and PSK spectrum shapes are identical. For example, a 16-PSK spectrum shape is the same as a 16-QAM spectrum shape. However, a QAM system exhibits considerably better error performance than its PSK counterpart. As evidenced in Figure 10b, the distances between points is smaller in a PSK system.

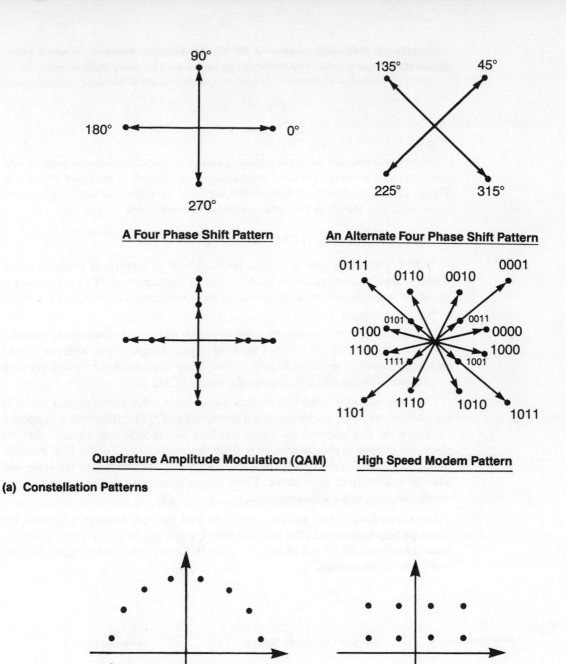

A Four Phase Shift Pattern

An Alternate Four Phase Shift Pattern

Quadrature Amplitude Modulation (QAM)

High Speed Modem Pattern

(a) Constellation Patterns

16-PSK

16-QAM

(b) Distance between Points in 16-PSK and 16-QAM Systems

Figure 10: Multilevel Modulation Constellation Patterns

Moreover, the following expression for QAM distances between adjacent points shows that an n-ary QAM system performs better than an n-ary PSK system:

$$d = \frac{\sqrt{2}}{(L\text{-}1)}$$

where L = power levels on each axis.

QAM systems do not require the I and Q signals to coincide; they are independent. Thus, the signals can be applied to produce a waveform such as the signal depicted in Figure 11. These systems are now widely used and have found several implementations in the Bell and CCITT V series modems discussed later.

Trellis Code Modulation (TCM)

TCM is a relatively new technique now available in high-speed modems and is found in a wide variety of vendor models. A brief explanation of TCM is provided to assist the reader in understanding several of the specifications described in this book.

In data communications systems, error detection and error resolution are typically performed by the data link control protocol logic. (It rests above a physical level protocol.) However, error correction is now being implemented in many physical level protocols, primarily with a technique called TCM.

The many elements involved in a data transmission often create errors. Yet, it is obvious that the signal always starts at a known value within certain limits. Suppose a method is devised whereby the signal (derived and coded from the user data bit stream) is allowed to assume only certain characteristics (states) on the line. Furthermore, suppose the user bits are interpreted such that only certain of the states are allowed to exist from prior states. These suppositions allow a designer to build a modem to perform the following tasks.

The transmitting device accepts a series of user bits and develops additional yet restricted bit patterns from these bits. Moreover, a previous user bit pattern (a state) is used to determine the current bit patterns (states). Certain other states are not allowed and are never transmitted.

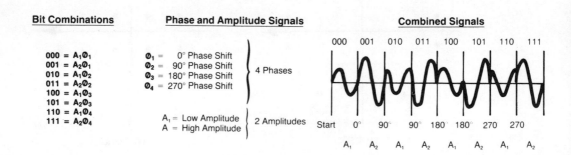

Figure 11: Multilevel Modulation Signals

The transmitter and receiver are programmed to understand the allowable states and the permissible state transitions. If the receiver receives states and state transitions (because of channel impairments) that differ from predefined conventions, it is assumed that an error has occurred on the circuit.

But trellis coding goes further. Since, by convention, the transmitter and the receiver know the transmission states and the permissible state transitions, the receiver analyzes the received signal and makes a "best guess" as to what state the signal should assume. It analyzes current states, compares them to previous states, and makes decisions as to the most relevant state. In effect, it uses a path history to reconstruct damaged bits.

Trellis coding is an error-correction code with a memory. Its encoded values depend on the corresponding Kbit message and also on m previous message blocks. It increases the error performance on a line by two to three orders of magnitude. Later discussions on the CCITT V.32 recommendation explain TCM further.

Baud versus Bit Rate

One of the most confusing terms in the data communications industry is baud (or bauds), which is commonly and mistakenly used to mean bits per second. Bit/s and baud mean the same only with low-speed devices (300, 600, and some 1200 bit/s interfaces). To gain an understanding of the differences between bits per second and baud, let us examine Figure 12.

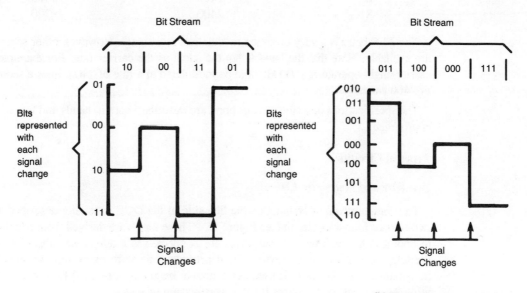

(a) Two Bits Per Signal   (b) Three Bits Per Signal

Figure 12: Multilevel Schemes

A baud is defined as the rate of signaling changes per second on a channel. The terms "signaling change rate" and "modulation rate" are also used to describe the same characteristic. The arrows in Figure 12 indicate when a signal change occurs. The left side of the graphic depicts the possible bit representation with each change (baud).

By allowing more bit combinations to be represented with each baud, it is possible to achieve multiple level transmission; that is to say, each baud represents multiple bits. In Figure 12a, a four-level scheme provides 2 bits per baud ($2^2 = 4$). In Figure 12b, an eight-level scheme provides 3 bits per baud ($2^3 = 8$). It should now be evident that the QAM methods discussed earlier use multilevel modulation techniques.

A modem is usually capable of transmitting or receiving a bit rate (bit/s) that is greater than the signal change (baud) since multiple bits are encoded with each baud. This approach is certainly the case with high-speed devices.

Here are some typical modem encoding and modulation rates:

Bits Encoded	Modulation Rate (Bauds)	Bits Transmitted
1	2400	2400
2	2400	4800
3	2400	7200
4	2400	9600
5	2400	12000
6	2400	14400
8	2400	19200

The 2400 baud is a very common modulation rate signal. However, other schemes are available. Note that the baud is not the same as the carrier rate. For example, a carrier might operate at 1800 Hz, and be modulated at a rate of 2400 times a second, or 2400 bauds.

The specifications described in this book are described both in bauds and bit rate (if appropriate).

Types of Circuits

Two-Wire and Four-Wire Circuits

The communications channel on the line side of the DCE is usually described as a two-wire or four-wire circuit (see Figure 13). These terms are derived from telephone technology, in which two or four wires are connected to a telephone subscriber and the telephone office. A two-wire circuit provides one wire on which the signal is transmitted. The other wire is used as a return or balancing circuit. A two-wire circuit provides only one of the wires for the transmission of data.

A four-wire circuit consists of two pairs of two wires between devices. In this configuration, two wires are available for the transmission of user data. The other two wires are unavailable and are used for balancing the line and/or as return. Typically, one pair of wires is used for transmission of data in each direction. The terms "two-wire" and "four-wire" are often confused with dial-up and leased lines. Telephone companies and other carriers provide various combinations of these offerings. A two-wire circuit does not necessarily mean a dial-up arrangement to the telephone office, nor does a four-wire circuit imply strictly a leased or dedicated path to the telephone office.

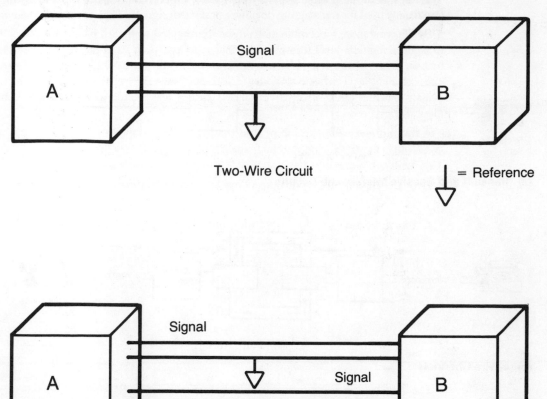

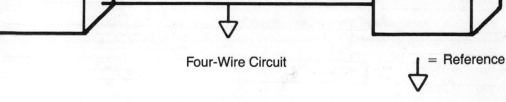

Figure 13: Two-Wire and Four-Wire Circuits

The majority of local loops uses two wires to save copper wire and to be compatible with the two-wire interface systems (see Figure 14a). Owing to numerous problems with two-wire facilities, longer distance voice frequency (VF) circuits employ four wires. A separate transmission path is used for each direction.

The interfaces between the wires is provided by a device called a "hybrid." It is used to interface between the two-wire and four-wire circuits. The hybrid, which is a transformer, is quite useful in providing efficient coupling between circuits having different electrical characteristics.

A simple hybrid, which consists of closely coupled inductive windings wound around magnetic material, is shown in Figure 14b. The device transfers signals through inductance. Figure 14c shows the center tap circuits of the transformer windings. In the past, these circuits were used for speech transmission, but today they are mainly used for transmitting dc power or control signals. They are called phantom circuits.

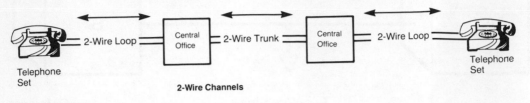

(a) Transmit and Receive Interchange Circuits

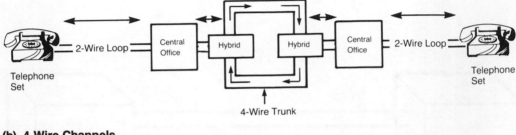

(b) 4-Wire Channels

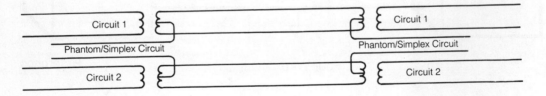

(c) Phantom or Simplex Circuit

Figure 14: Subscriber Loop Connections

Cable between DTE and DCE

The cable connecting the DTE and DCE is available in several different types. One of the more common media is unshielded cable. This type of connection generally presents no problems if the system is not subject to interference or if the FCC does not forbid the use of it because of shielding regulations. The unshielded cable has a tin plating around each copper wire to prevent oxidation and help provide accurate data transmission.

In a noisier environment, shielded cable is advised. Most shielded cable provides considerable protection against radio frequency interference (RFI) and electromagnetic radiation (EMR). Because of FCC regulation requirements, shielded cable usually has a 90 percent tin copper shield with a die casting hood attached.

Another type of shielded cable is known as the double shielded cable. This media consists of a copper shield. In addition, a mylar foil is wrapped around the data cables.

If the user has to connect the terminal with the DCE in a noisy environment for extended distances, the next step is to use shielded low capacitance cables. This system has double shielding with copper and mylar foil and also uses polyethylene insulation, which lowers capacitance of the cable. Most vendors provide these types of connections through a variety of ISO and EIA specified cables. The most common choices are shown in Table 2.

Table 2: DTE/DCE Cable

Type Cable (Assumes 5 Feet Length, Purchase of 1 Cable)	Cost Factor (Unshielded Used as a Bench Mark with a Factor of 1)
Unshielded	1
Shielded	1.75
Double Shielded	2.05
Low Capacitance	2.14

Half Duplex and Duplex Data Flow

Two terms describe how data are transmitted across the channel, regardless of the physical configuration of the circuit itself (see Figure 15). Data flow across a channel and physical level interfaces is described as half duplex or duplex. Half duplex (HDX) defines a transmission in which data are transmitted in both directions but not at the same time. The DCE used to transmit the data alternates between transmit and receive between the devices. The term "duplex" describes the simultaneous transmission of data in both directions. Many vendors also use the term "full duplex" (FDX) to describe this particular type of data flow.

Some people use the term "half duplex" to describe a two-wire circuit and "full duplex" to describe a four-wire circuit. For purposes of clarity, it is preferable to use the terms " two-wire" and "four-wire" to describe the actual physical layout of the circuit and the terms half duplex and full duplex to describe the actual data flow, regardless of the physical layout. The industry now is using the term "two-way alternate" (TWA) to describe a half duplex data flow and "two-way simultaneous" (TWS) to describe a full duplex data flow. These two terms remove some of the ambiguity associated with the dual usage of half duplex and duplex to describe the physical circuit and the data flow on the circuit.

Point-to-Point and Multipoint Schemes

A circuit is also classified point to point or multipoint. As the names imply, a point-to-point circuit connects two devices only and a multipoint circuit connects more than two devices (see Figure 16).

When the DCEs use half duplex schemes, an interval is required for the devices to stabilize and adjust to the signals in the other direction. This stabilization period is called "training time," and the process of reversing the signal is called "line turn around." These factors can be quite significant: 100 to 200 milliseconds for a turn around is not uncommon. Because of this delay, most multipoint systems keep the master device's carrier on constantly (constant carrier) with the slaves configured for switched carrier operation (switched carrier). This approach eliminates half the turn-around delay. Some DCEs use split channel operations (discussed next) to completely eliminate the switched carrier delay.

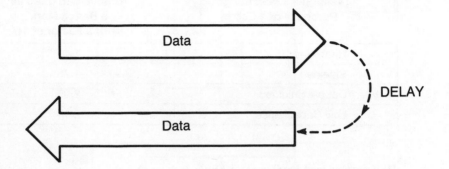

(a) Half Duplex Data Flow

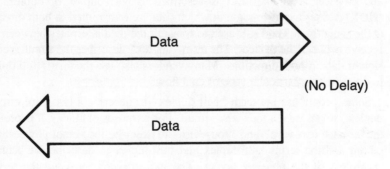

(b) Full Duplex Data Flow

Figure 15: Data Flow across the Circuits

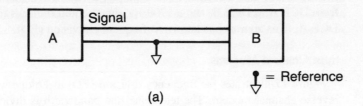

(a)

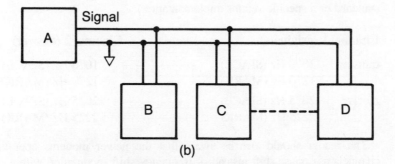

(b)

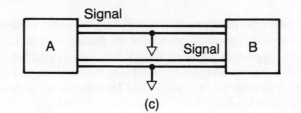

(c)

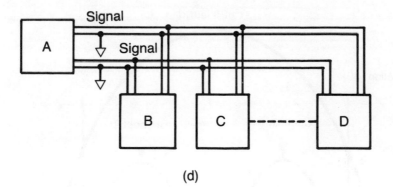

(d)

Figure 16: Point-to-Point and Multipoint Circuits

In some systems, FDX transmission is obtained by using a four-wire circuit. In others, a two-wire circuit is obtained, and different frequencies are used to transmit two signals in both directions. For example, a 1200 Hz signal could transmit traffic from DCE A to DCE B, and a 1700 Hz signal could transmit traffic from DCE B to DCE A. This approach is known as frequency division (FD).

Split Channel Modems

Figure 17 illustrates the frequency division (FD) technique with a split channel or reverse channel modem. The telephone line bandwidth is divided into subchannels, each of a lesser bandwidth than the telephone channel. The signals in each subchannel are modulated by using frequency shift (the actual frequencies vary with a particular standard or a specific vendor implementation):

Channel 1 (originate)		Channel 2 (answer)
transmit	1070 Hz (SPACE) ——————	1070 Hz (SPACE) receive
	1270 Hz (MARK) ——————	1270 Hz (MARK)
receive	2025 Hz (SPACE) ——————	2025 Hz (SPACE) transmit
	2225 Hz (MARK) ——————	2225 Hz (MARK)

The reader should also be aware that the newer modems operating with split channels use phase shift instead of frequency shift modulation within each subchannel.

Also, note that the illustration above designates one modem as originate and the other as answer. This designation does not mean a modem can only do one function (i.e., only originate or answer a signal). It is used to establish a convention by which the transmit and receive functions are reversed at each end of the phone line. The originating modem uses the 1070-1270 frequencies for transmit and the 2025-2225 frequencies for receive.

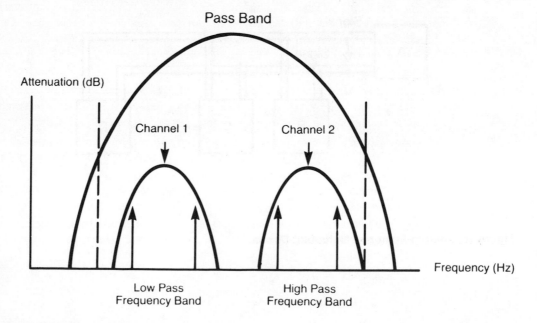

Figure 17: Split Channel Reverse Channel Modems

BLACK

For systems in which the communications originate one way only (for example, a terminal calling a mainframe computer), it is simpler and less expensive to design the frequencies permanently as originate and answer. The modems' receivers, transmitters, and filters do not have to be changed.

The terms "originate" and "answer" came into use because the Bell 103A modems use the originate mode for a call that is originated and the answer mode for a call that is answered.

Several modem types support the split channel but with the bandwidth split divided unequally between the channels. The low capacity backward channel (BC) is usually for low bit transfer rate data signals. This eliminates the need for reversing the direction of transmission (such as on half duplex) to send data between two sites. Typically, the backward channel supports data rates up to 75 bit/s while newer systems support 150 bit/s. In many systems, the backward channel is simply turned ON or OFF to provide flow control or to acknowledge data reception.

The Bell 202 modem is an example of the backward channel modem. It uses a 387 Hz tone that is keyed ON or OFF to acknowledge traffic. Later sections discuss higher speed backward channels that operate at 75 bauds. However, newer technology will eventually replace the backward channel modems.

Split stream modems often employ soft carrier turn-off frequency. The modem shifts the mark carrier frequency from 1200 to 900 Hz, giving a slow turn off. This slow turn off technique eliminates transients that can occur when the 1200 Hz frequency is turned off abruptly. Transients can create erroneous signals at the receiving modem.

Echo Cancelation and Echo Suppression

Another approach to obtain FDX transmission is to cancel out the unwanted signals at the respective DCEs. This approach, called echo cancelation (EC), is widely used on the newer modems (see Figure 18). This technique uses the transmitted signal (say, from modem A) to generate another signal that is a near replica of the returning signal. The replica is inverted and stored for later comparison to the echo. On the return path, the undesired signal is canceled, allowing only the signal from modem B to be received by modem A. The echo cancelation modems have replaced the split channel technique for the newer, higher speed modems.

Echo cancelation is not to be confused with echo suppression, even though both techniques are used to combat echo (the feedback of signals back to the transmitter). An echo suppressor blocks (suppresses) any echoes that may occur.

Echo suppressors cannot be used for data transmission over a voice line. The speech detector in the suppressor has been designed to detect speech signals. Since the telephone network is a primary facility in a data communications network, the echo suppressors must be disabled for data transmissions. The suppressors are disabled by transmitting a tone ranging from 2010 to 2240 Hz for 400 milliseconds. As long as a signal is continuously on the line, the suppressors remain disabled. Once the echo suppressors are disabled, the modems can change to their signaling frequencies and start data transmissions and receptions.

The suppressors reactivate if a signal is removed for 100 milliseconds. Consequently, rapid turnaround is an important aspect of a half duplex operation.

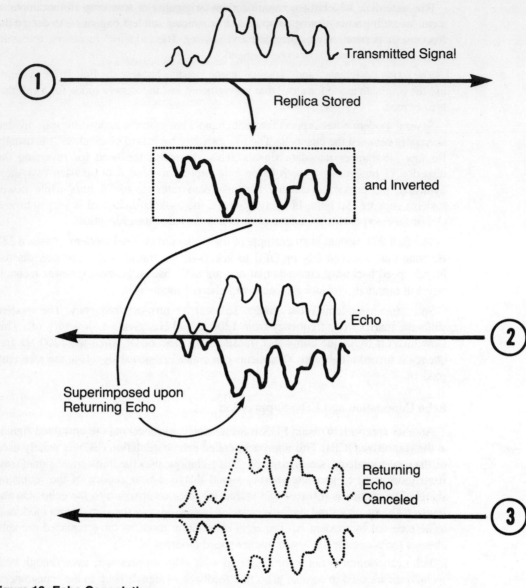

Figure 18: Echo Cancelation

Leased or Dial-up Circuits and Auto-Answer, Auto-Dial Modems

Two options available to the data communications user are dial-up (or switched) lines and leased (or dedicated) lines. The dial-up line requires the user or the DTE and DCE to dial the number of the receiving person or station. The leased line is a different arrangement, which entails a permanent connection from the user's office or home through the telephone network to the final destination.

Modems connected to a dial-up facility usually have automatic dial-up and answer capabilities. As we shall see, these modems employ (sometimes loosely) the CCITT V.25/V.25 bis specification, the Electronic Industries Association (EIA) EIA-366, or the Hayes modem specification for dial and answer operations.

The auto-dial, auto-answer modems must be capable of resolving all the functions (and failures) that exist when dialing and answering a telephone call. As examples, the auto-dial operation must handle the following tasks:

- going off-hook (equivalent to lifting hand set) to initiate a call
- waiting for correct dial tone(s)
- dialing each telephone number in the proper sequence
- waiting for the dialed phone to answer
- hanging up if the line is busy
- possibly redialing later
- going on-hook (equivalent to hanging up the hand set) when the call is completed or abandoned

The auto-dial modem must resolve problems such as

- line busy
- modem answer-tone not returned
- voice answer
- no dial tone
- inability to break the dial tone

The auto-answer part of the modem places the modem in an answer mode automatically upon receiving an incoming call signal. This occurs without human intervention.

Auto-baud dial and answer modems: Many of these modems use auto-baud features. Originally, the term described a device that could adjust to variable signaling speeds. Today, the term also includes the ability to adjust to variable speeds as well as different codes (ASCII/EDCDIC) and parity bit combinations.

Dial and answer modem commands: The foundation for these modems is the use of commands to effect the dial and answer process. The commands can be entered from the DTE keyboard or programmed to executive automatically. A later section in this book illustrates the basic command set of the Hayes modems. Some typical commands are:

- go off-hook
- send signal break
- dial numbers from memory
- list stored numbers
- list log-on messages
- set internal modem options
- ignore ring signal
- give up dialing after n ring-back signals
- set new value in a command parameter
- return modem status
- start/stop modem tests
- set modem to listen to commands (or "unlisten") during data transfer
- go on-hook (hang-up)

Asynchronous and Synchronous Transmission

DTEs and DCEs use two methods for formatting and transmitting user data through the channel (see Figure 19). The first approach, asynchronous transmission, is an older technique. However, owing to its simplicity and relative low cost, it is a very prevalent method today and is found in many systems such as personal computers. Asynchronous transmission is distinguished by the use of timing bits (start/stop bits) surrounding each transmitted character. The purpose of the start/stop bits is to provide for synchronization and timing between the transmitting device and the receiving device. The start bit notifies the receiving device that a character is being transmitted on the channel. The stop bit indicates that all the bits have arrived and provides for other timing functions. In asynchronous transmission, each character is framed by start/stop bits.

The term "asynchronous" also describes a system without a regular time relationship. The "gap" between transmissions is not necessarily fixed in length of time.

The second approach is synchronous transmission. All characters are blocked together and transmitted without the intervening start/stop bits found in asynchronous transmission. Framing codes (called syncs or flags) are placed in front and behind the full data unit (usually called a frame) to indicate to the receiver exactly where the user data begins and ends. The actual timing is achieved by the use of a separate clocking circuit or by changing the data stream (scrambling) in such a manner that it provides timing signals to the receiver. Most modems use scrambling techniques to ensure a proper number of state transitions for accurate timing recovery at the receiver modem.

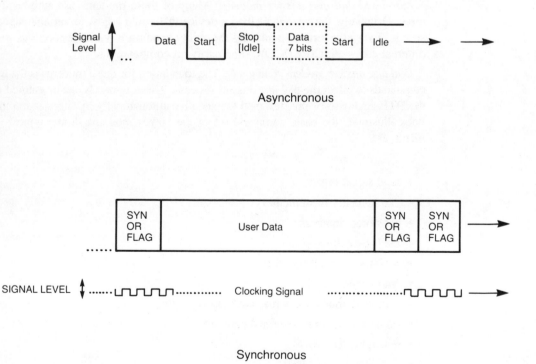

Figure 19: Asynchronous and Synchronous Transmission

The scrambling is usually done by the DCEs. Consequently, scrambling provides modem (DCE-to-DCE) synchronization. However, synchronization of synchronous transmissions between user devices and modems (DTE-to-DCE) must be performed with a separate timing (or clocking) circuit. This circuit is not required for asynchronous devices since the start/stop bits perform this function.

Synchronous transmission can provide timing signals by one of three techniques:

- a separate clocking line
- embedding the clocking signal in the data stream with the data acting as a clock to a simple receiver circuit
- embedding the clocking signal in the data stream and using it to synchronize a receiver clock

A separate clocking line is a widely used technique for short distance connections. In addition to the data line, another line transmits an associated timing signal, which is used to clock the data into the receiver. The clocking line notifies the receiver when a bit is arriving.

The transmitting station does not always provide the clocking signal. Many configurations use the receiver to provide the clocking signal to the transmitting station. The signal dictates the specific time increments for the transmitter to send data.

A separate clocking line is a common technique for synchronous interfaces between terminals/computers and their associated DCEs such as modems and multiplexers. (For example, the EIA-232-D and V.24 specifications provide several options for synchronous transmission and clocking.) However, a separate clocking channel is not practical under certain conditions:

1. Longer distances make the installation of a separate wire prohibitively expensive.
2. Longer distances also increase the probability that the clocking line will lose its synchronization with the data line, since each line has its own unique transmission characteristics.
3. The telephone network does not provide clocking lines for a typical telephone subscriber.

The second approach is to embed the clocking signal in the data and have the receiver extract the clock from the received data stream. The receiver uses relatively simple circuitry for the clock extraction (a delay and rectifier circuit). To embed the clocking signal, the data bits are encoded at the transmitter to provide frequent transitions on the channel.

The third approach is similar to method two, except the receiver has a clock. The line transitions in the incoming bit stream keep the receiver clock aligned (synchronized) onto each bit in the data block.

A digital phase lock-loop (DPLL) is used to maintain bit synchronization with this third method. An oscillator is connected to the DPLL and operates at a rate faster than the bit rate (16 or 32 clock periods per sample, for example). The fast sampling rate is used to detect the 1 to 0 or 0 to 1 transition as soon as possible. If the incoming bit stream and the local clock "drift" from each other, the frequent clock periods still provide an accurate indication of the line transition. Moreover, the DPLL readjusts if line transitions occur more often or less often than the total clock periods per bit cell. The time periods between pulses are shortened or lengthened to keep the sampling close to the center of each bit cell.

The Decibel

The term decibel (dB) (named after the inventor of the telephone, Alexander Graham Bell) is used in communications to express the ratio of two values. The values can represent power, voltage, current, or sound levels. It should be emphasized that the decibel (1) is a ratio and not an absolute value, (2) expresses a logarithmic relationship and not a linear one, and (3) can be used to indicate either a gain or a loss. The logarithmic notation is useful because a signal's strength falls off logarithmically as it passes through the transmission medium.

A decibel is 10 times the logarithm (in base 10) of the ratio; $dB = 10 \log 10 \ P1/P2$, where dB = number of decibels; $P1$ = one value of power and $P2$ = comparison value of the power.

Decibels are often used to measure the gain or loss of a communications signal. These measurements are quite valuable for testing the quality of lines and determining noise and signal losses, all of which must be known in order to design a system (see Table 3). It is a very useful unit because they can be added or subtracted as a signal is cascaded through a communications link. For example, if a line introduces 1 dB of loss in a span of 1 mile, a 3-mile length will produce a loss of 3 dB; if the line is connected to an amplifier with a gain of 10 dB, the total gain is 7 dB.

The dBW (decibel-watt) is used for microwave systems. The measurement is made to a reference and expressed as

$$\text{Power (dBW)} = 10 \log = \frac{\text{Power (W)}}{1W}$$

The dBm is used as a relative power measurement in which the reference power is 1 milliwatt (0.001 watt):

$$dBm = 10 \log 10 \ P/0.001$$

Table 3: Decibels and Signal-to-Noise Ratios

Decibels (dB)	Signal-to-Noise Ratios
0	1:1
+3	2:1
+9	8:1
+10	10:1
+13	20:1
+16	40:1
+19	80:1
+20	100:1
+23	200:1
+26	400:1
+29	800:1
+30	1,000:1
+33	2,000:1
+36	4,000:1
+39	8,000:1
+40	10,000:1

where P = signal power in milliwatts (mW). This approach allows measurements to be taken in relation to a standard. A signal of a known power level is inserted at one end and measured at the other. A 0 dBm reading means 1 mW.

Carriers (such as telephone companies) use a 1004-Hz tone (referred to as a 1-KHz test tone) to test a line. The 1-KHz tone is used as a reference to other test tones of a different level. The test tone is used to establish a zero transmission level point (TLP), which is a convenient concept for relating signal or noise levels at various points in the communications system. It is common practice to consider the outgoing two-wire class 5 system as the 0 dB TLP reference point, and all gains/losses are compared to this value. (Interestingly, a 1000 Hz tone was used in the past, but it created timing problems on digital circuits by creating "perfect" alternating 1s and 0s in every T1 framing bit. This created false framing problems.)

Balanced and Unbalanced Configurations

At the DTE/DCE interface (see Figure 1), the configuration may be either balanced or unbalanced. The balanced setup uses a pair of wires for each interchange circuit (pin). The unbalanced configuration uses one wire for transmitting the signals over each circuit and employs a common return circuit. Another unbalanced approach uses the common return connected to signal ground only at the generator end. Figure 20 summarizes the three configurations.

The telephone companies use balanced pair wires. One significant advantage of this design is that it balances out interferences on the wires. In effect, an interference is induced equally in both wires and is canceled out. The telephone carriers use two terms to describe their balanced systems:

- metallic-circuit currents: currents flowing in opposite directions in the wires of the pair
- longitudinal currents: currents flowing in the same direction in the wires of the pair

Later sections discuss the terms balanced and unbalanced more precisely in relation to the DTE/DCE interface.

Equalization and Conditioning

The decay (attenuation) and delay of a transmitted signal is not equal for all the frequencies that comprise the signal. For attenuation, an equalizer is used in the DCE to flatten the loss across the frequency spectrum. Likewise, equalization is also used to compensate for delay distortion by slowing down the speed of the faster traveling frequencies.

Two options are available to reduce the effects of attenuation and delay distortion. The first option is line conditioning. It can be acquired from the telephone company for leased lines. The carrier adds special equipment to the circuit, such as amplifiers, attenuation equalizers, and delay equalizers.

Conditioning provides a method to diminish the problems of attenuation and delay, but it does not remove the impairments. Rather, it provides for more consistency across the bandwidth. For attenuation, the common carrier introduces equipment that attenuates the frequencies in the signal that tend to remain at a higher level than others. Thus, attenuation still occurs but is more evenly distributed across the channel. The same idea is used in delay. The faster frequencies are slowed so that the signal is more consistent across the band.

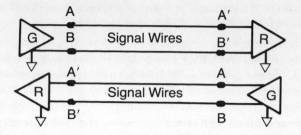

(a) Balanced

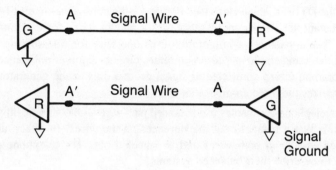

(b) Unbalanced

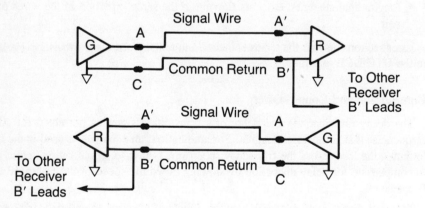

(c) Unbalanced (with Common Return Connected to Signal Ground at G Only)

Figure 20: Balanced and Unbalanced Configurations

An attenuation equalizer adds a loss to the lower frequencies of the signal, since these frequencies decay less than the higher frequencies in the band. The result is that the signal loss is consistent throughout the transmitted signal. After equalization is applied, amplifiers restore the signal back to its original level.

A delay equalizer compensates for total signal delay. The higher frequencies reach the receiver ahead of the lower frequencies. Consequently, the equalizer introduces more delay to these frequencies to make the entire signal propagate into the receiver at the same time.

The second option is to use modems that are equipped with equalizers. Conditioning is not available over the switched telephone network, so these modems may be required, especially for high data rates of transmission.

Most modems that operate with speeds up to 4.8 Kbit/s use fixed equalizers. These devices are designed to compensate for the average conditions on a circuit. However, the fixed equalizers are being replaced with dynamic (or automatic) equalization. The modem analyzes the line conditions and adjusts its equalization accordingly. The adjustments take place without interrupting the flow of traffic. The adjustments occur very rapidly, on the order of 2400 times a second for a 9.6 Kbit/s modem.

The telephone company also provides D conditioning to address harmonic distortion and noise. It is an option that was developed primarily for 9600 bit/s operation. The standard specification requires a signal-to-noise ratio of not less than 24 dB, a second harmonic distortion of not more than -25 dB, and a third harmonic distortion of not more than -30 dB. With conditioning, the carrier gives a S/N ratio specification of 28 dB, a signal to second harmonic distortion ratio of 35 dB, and a signal to third harmonic distortion of 40 dB.

Serial and Parallel Transmission

The majority of long distance data communications systems use serial transmission schemes. With serial transmission, a single channel is used to convey the data. A bit in the data stream is transmitted contiguously behind the preceding bit across the channel. This technique is widely used because the telephone two-wire circuit is inherently serial (and multiple channels are more expensive).

A number of local systems use parallel schemes. Typically, eight separate channels are available to transmit eight bits (an octet or byte) in parallel with each other. As stated in the introduction, this book addresses serial transmission because it is based on physical level protocols that use the telephone channel.

Parallel to Serial Converters

A user may be faced with the problem of interfacing a parallel device with a serial device. For example, it is not uncommon to interface a serial personal computer with a parallel printer. One inexpensive and simple approach to provide this interface is to install a serial to parallel and/or parallel to serial convertor. They are relatively inexpensive and can be plugged into the two ports of the devices. (They are much easier to install than interface cards.) For short distances, the convertors can be installed directly between the two devices as indicated in Figure 21. For longer distances, a common approach is to place serial line drivers on the line side of the convertors. Most of these convertors have a buffer, typically on the order of 64 K (which holds approximately 32 pages). The majority of the convertors are one-way systems designed to work with printers.

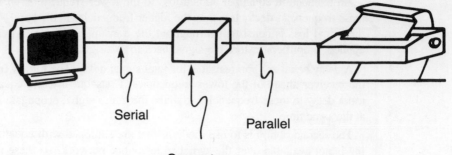

Serial

Parallel

Converter

Figure 21: Parallel/Serial Connectors

Most of the convertors use the EIA-232 25-pin female or Centronix type 36 pin male connectors. They support either XON/XOFF, DTR/DSR, or ETX/STX flow control. (These terms will be explained shortly.) These systems operate from 300 to 38400 bits/s.

Loopbacks

A communications link is often tested by placing the modems in a loopback mode. Practically all modems can be put into loopback tests with a switch on the modem and many modems perform some loopbacks automatically. The loopback signals are analyzed to determine their quality and the bit error rate resulting from the tests. The loopbacks can be sent through the local modem to test its analog and digital circuits; this test is called a local loopback or loop 3. If the bit error rate is not within a specified level, the next step is likely to be a remote line loopback (or loop 2) that tests the carrier signal and the analog circuitry of the remote modem. The remote modem must be placed in the loopback mode in order for this test to be completed. The local DTE/DCE connection can also be tested by looping the DTE transmitted signals back to the DTE. This test is called a local DTE loopback or loop 1. Loopbacks are explained in more detail in the section describing CCITT V.54.

Control at the Physical Level Interface

Many systems employ higher level protocols to control the flow of data between DTEs and DCEs. For example, the level above the physical level is the data link control level (see Figure 22). It usually initiates the line transmissions, provides flow control, performs error detection, and retransmits data in the event of problems.

In a sense, the data link control level "drives" the physical level. The operations of link polling and selection to receive and send data respectively are performed by the link level logic. Typically, the physical level simply reacts in accordance with signals from the link level logic. In turn, the link level logic is controlled by yet another level of protocol. It could be a user's application program, a vendor's package, or the operation system (OS) of the computer.

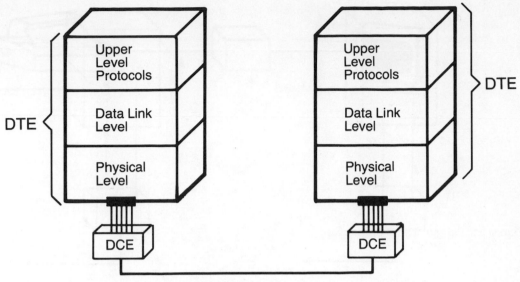

Figure 22: Relationship of Physical Level to Data Link Level

Whatever the higher level protocol may be, the physical level implementation of the upper level control signals is typically accomplished through one of these techniques:

- link level-initiated poll or select commands
- link level-initiated XON or XOFF signals
- physical level-initiated XON or XOFF signals
- link level-initiated use of physical level request to send and clear to send circuits
- physical level-initiated use of physical level request to send and clear to send circuits

Let us briefly examine each possibility, with emphasis on the effect at the physical level interface.

Polling/Selection

The physical connectors between the DTE and DCE consist of a transmit data (TD) and receive data (RD) circuit (see Figure 23a). The data link layer uses the TD and RD circuits to control the flow of data into and out of the machine. Typically, the following operations take place:

1. A poll signal is sent across the TD circuit to elicit data from another station. Any received data are accepted across the RD circuit.

2. A select signal is sent across the TD circuit to notify a station that it is to receive data. The data are also transmitted across the TD circuit.

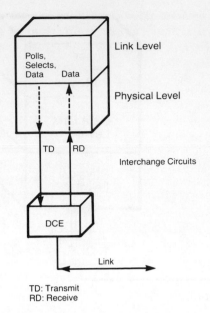

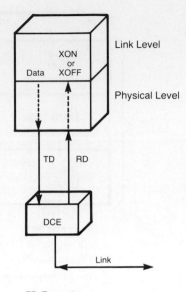

(a) Transmit and Receive Interchange Circuits

(b) XON and XOFF Signals

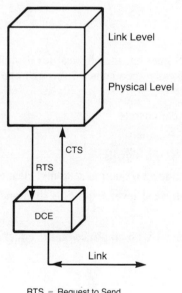

(c) Request to Send and Clear to Send Signals

Figure 23: Physical Level Flow Control

The physical level protocol is unaware of the nature of the data link control signals. They are simply bits to the physical level interface. However, as we shall see in the next section, input/output drivers may use the link level signals to manipulate the physical level interchange circuits.

XON/XOFF Signaling

These signals may be initiated at the physical or data link levels, depending on the specific vendor's systems. XON is an ANSI/IA5 transmission character (see Appendix B for ANSI/IA5 code). The XON character is usually implemented by DC1. The XOFF character, also an ANSI/IA5 character, is represented by DC3. Peripheral devices such as printers, graphics terminals, or plotters can use the XON/XOFF approach to control incoming traffic (see Figure 23b). The station, typically a computer, sends data to the other station on the TD circuit, which prints or graphs the data onto an output media. Since the plotter or printer is slow relative to the transmission speed of the channel and the transmitting computer, its buffers may become full. Consequently, to prevent overflow, it transmits back to the computer an XOFF signal, which is transferred to the computer across the RD circuit. It means to stop transmitting or "transmit off."

On receiving the XOFF, the computer ceases transmission. It "holds" any data until it receives an XON signal. This indicates that the peripheral device is now free (for instance, its buffers now have been cleared) and is ready to receive more data.

Request to Send/Clear to Send Signals

At the risk of getting ahead of ourselves, these signals should now be discussed, even though we have not yet introduced EIA-232-D. They provide continuity to this discussion.

A request to send (RTS) circuit is used by a device at the physical level to request the use of the link for a transmission. If permission is granted, the clear to send circuit is turned on to signify the link is available.

These two circuits are found in many physical level interfaces and are explained in more detail later in the book. For the present, Figure 23c shows that two locally attached devices can control the communications between each other by raising and lowering the RTS/CTS signal on the directly attached channel. A common implementation of this technique is found in the attachment of a terminal to a simple multiplexer. The terminal requests use of the channel by raising its RTS circuit, the multiplexer responds to the request by raising the CTS circuit, and the terminal then sends its data to the multiplexer through the transmitted data circuit (TD).

The Communications Port

The connection of the user device to the modem, data service unit, etc., and the communications link is provided through a component called the communications port. (Other commonly used terms are: communications adapter, serial port, board, UART (univeral asynchronous receiver/transmitter), USART (universal synchronous/asynchronous receiver/transmitter)).

A port is usually a microprocessor with its own separate clock, memory, registers, and a central processing unit (a full-fledged microcomputer). The intelligence of the port is highly variable, depending on the type of interface needed. A computer or other user device may have many ports (see Figure 24).

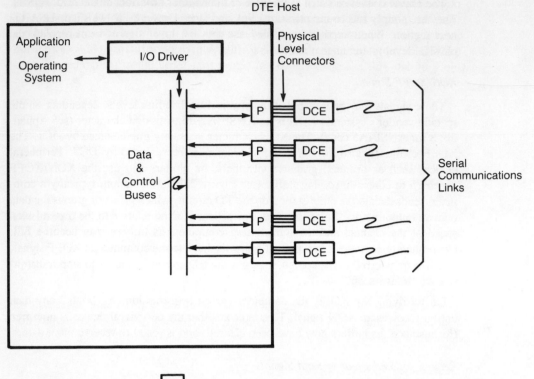

DTE Host

Application or Operating System ⟷ I/O Driver

Physical Level Connectors

Data & Control Buses

P = DCE

P = DCE

P = DCE

P = DCE

Serial Communications Links

P = Communications Port (Data & Control Registers, USART Chip)

Figure 24: The Communications Port

The main purpose of the communications port is to connect the communications channel with the user device and to provide the signals to transfer data into and out of the device. As explained later in the book, it also provides an interface between the data link and the physical level protocols.

Most communications ports in computers and terminals use an input/output (I/O) interface chip called the universal asynchronous receiver/transmitter (UART) or the universal synchronous/asynchronous receiver/transmitter (USART). This large scale integrated (LSI) device performs the following functions:

- accepts parallel data from the DTE and converts it to serial data for the communications link and vice-versa
- performs a limited set of problem detection functions (parity, no stop bit, and character overrun)
- provides for transmitter and/or receiver clocks
- detects a full byte or block of data from the link or from the DTE
- selects the number of stop bits for an asynchronous system
- selects number of bits per character
- selects odd or even parity for error detection

A simple USART interface is shown in Figure 24. Data are received across the physical level connector (such as the EIA-232 connector described in the next section) from the modem and communications link and stored in an 8-bit UART or USART input register. When the register is filled, the data are transferred across a parallel bus to DTE memory for further processing. (Some high-performance chips store a full block of data (for example, 128 bytes) before transferral out of the communications interface.)

The data are transmitted after the DTE I/O driver (an operating system software module, a user written application, or data link level logic) has filled the output register and sent a control signal to instruct the chip to transmit the data. The port logic then transmits the data across a designated conductor to the modem or digital service unit. An I/O driver is usually furnished by the DTE or DCE modem vendor. As shown in Figure 24, it serves as an interface between the DTE software operating sytem (OS) or user application and the port logic.

This simple explanation of the port is sufficient for now. In later sections of this book, the port is explained in considerably more detail and related to the EIA-232 interface and the Hayes modem/IBM personal computer interface.

Standards Organizations

Several standards organizations are actively involved in promoting physical level interface standards. This section provides a brief review of the organizations discussed in this book.

International Standards Organization (ISO)

The ISO is a voluntary organization consisting of national standards committees of each member country. The ISO coordinates its activities with CCITT on common issues. ISO has produced many well-known standards. The organization has a number of subcommittees and groups working with CCITT and the American National Standards Institute (ANSI) to develop standards for encryption, data communications, public data networks, and the well-known open systems interconnection (OSI) model.

Electronic Industries Association (EIA)

The EIA, a trade association, is also very influential in developing standards in North American countries. The EIA work focuses primarily on electrical standards. Its more notable efforts include EIA-232-D and EIA-449, which are discussed later. The EIA work is hardware oriented. The TR-30 Technical Committee, Data Transmission, is responsible for EIA-232 (first issued in 1962). TR-30 meets with ANSI X353 to coordinate their efforts.

The Comite Consultatif Internationale de Telegraphique et Telephonique (CCITT)

The CCITT is a standards body under the International Telecommunications Union, an agency of the United Nations. The CCITT is the primary organization for developing standards on telephone and data communications systems among participating governments. United States membership on CCITT comes from the U.S. Department of State at one level (the only voting level); a second level of membership covers private carriers such as AT&T and GTE; a third level includes industrial and scientific organizations; a fourth level includes other international organizations; and a fifth level includes organizations in other fields that are interested in CCITT's work.

The Institute of Electrical and Electronics Engineers, Inc. (IEEE)

The IEEE, Inc. has been involved for many years in standards activities. It is a well-known professional society with chapters located throughout the world. Its recent efforts in local area networks have received much attention. The IEEE activity addresses local area networks and many other standards as well.

The American National Standards Institute (ANSI)

The ANSI is a national clearing house and coordinating activity for standards implemented in the United States on a voluntary basis. In addition to being the U.S. member of the ISO, ANSI is active in developing standards for data communications for the OSI, as well as for encryption activities and office systems. ANSI tries to adopt the ISO standards, but their specifications may differ, owing to the unique aspects of the North American systems.

The European Computer Manufacturers Association (ECMA)

The ECMA is dedicated to the development of standards applicable to computer and communications technology. It is not a trade organization, as the name might imply, but a standards and technical review group. Several subcommittees within ECMA work actively with CCITT and ISO.

PHYSICAL LEVEL INTERFACES AND PROTOCOLS

Section 2:
Physical Interfaces between the DTE and DCE

BLACK

Section 2: Physical Interfaces between the DTE and DCE

The preceding material has described how signals are transmitted and received between the DCEs (modems) across the communications channel. Let us now focus our attention on how the DCEs and DTEs exchange transmissions with each other.

The standards groups (such as CCITT and the Electronics Industries Association (EIA)), the computer industry and vendors have developed many standards defining the interface of the modems or data service units (DCEs) with the terminals or computers (DTEs). Acceptance of the standards has been instrumental in the ability to use equipment from different vendors.

As stated earlier, this type of connection is called a physical level interface or protocol because the DTE and DCE are physically connected with wires and/or cables; they also exchange electrical signals directly. Recall from Section 1 that physical level interfaces perform these functions:

- control of data transfer across the interface
- provisions for control of signals across interface
- provision for clocking signals to synchronize data flow and regulate the bit rate
- provision for electrical ground
- provision for mechanical connectors

An Overview of V Series Recommendations, ISO Connectors, and EIA-232-D

Many of the standards for the operations of modems and other DCE type components are published by the CCITT and the EIA. In addition, the International Standards Organization (ISO) also publishes specifications on the mechanical connectors that connect DCEs with DTEs. In the United States, the AT&T/Bell specifications are also de facto standards, although the "Bell Specs" are usually part of (or forerunners to) the other organizations' standards. This section introduces these organizations and their standards. Subsequent sections examine all the major V series, EIA-232-D, other EIA recommendations, and the Bell modems in more detail.

The vast majority of our data communications take place over the telephone line. In recognition of this fact, the standards organizations publish many recommended standards (RS) to define how the connections and communications are made on telephone systems.

The CCITT V series are the most widely used recommendations in the world. These recommendations are updated every four years; the latest release was made in 1984. The formal title for these recommended standards is "Data Communications over the Telephone Network."

Table 4 and Box 1 summarize the most widely used V series interfaces. Most of the terms and concepts contained in the table have been explained in the introduction of this book. The other terms will be explained in subsequent material. Also, a brief summary of the table is provided for the reader in Box 1.

Most of these interfaces use several of the "foundation" V series specifications. They are explained in the next section.

The ISO also publishes many standards, some of which describe the mechanical

Table 4: Major V Series Interfaces

Series Number	Line Speed	Channel Separation	Modulation Rate	Carrier Frequency	Use of V.2	FDX or HDX	Synchronous or Asynchronous	Modulation Technique	Bits Encoded
V.21	300	FD	300	1080 & 1750	Yes	FDX	Either	FS	1:1
V.22	1200	FD	600	1200 & 2400	Yes	FDX	Either	PS	2:1
V.22	600	FD	600	1200 & 2400	Yes	FDX	Either	PS	1:1
V.22bis	2400	FD	600	1200 & 2400	ND	FDX	Either	QAM	4:1
V.22bis	1200	FD	600	1200 & 2400	ND	FDX	Either	QAM	2:1
V.23	600	NA	600	1300 & 1700	ND	HDX	Either	FM	NA
V.23	1200	NA	1200	1300 & 2100	ND	HDX	Either	FM	NA
V.26	2400	4-wire	1200	1800	Yes	FDX	Synchronous	PS	2:1
V.26bis	2400	NA	1200	1800	Yes	HDX	Synchronous	PS	2:1
V.26bis	1200	NA	1200	1800	Yes	HDX	Synchronous	PS	1:1
V.26ter	2400	EC	1200	1800	Yes	Either	Either	PS	2:1
V.26ter	1200	EC	1200	1800	Yes	Either	Either	PS	1:1
V.27	4800	4-wire[1]	1600	1800	Yes	Either	Synchronous	PS	3:1
V.27bis	4800	4-wire[2]	1600	1800	Yes	Either	Synchronous	PS	3:1
V.27bis	2400	4-wire[2]	1200	1800	Yes	Either	Synchronous	PS	2:1
V.27ter	4800	None	1600	1800	Yes	HDX	Synchronous	PS	3:1
V.27ter	2400	None	1200	1800	Yes	HDX	Synchronous	PS	2:1
V.29	9600	4-wire	2400	1700	Yes	Either	Synchronous	QAM	4:1
V.29	7200	4-wire	2400	1700	Yes	Either	Synchronous	PS[3]	3:1
V.29	4800	4-wire	2400	1700	Yes	Either	Synchronous	PS	2:1
V.32	9600	EC	2400	1800	Yes	FDX	Synchronous	QAM	4:1
V.32	9600	EC	2400	1800	Yes	FDX	Synchronous	TCM	5:1
V.32	4800	EC	2400	1800	Yes	FDX	Synchronous	QAM	2:1
V.35	48000	4-wire	NA	100000	ND	FDX	Synchronous	AM-FM	NA

Table 4: Major V Series Interfaces (Continued)

Series Number	Backward Channel	Switched Lines	Leased Lines	Use of V.25	Use of V.28	ISO Pin Connector	Equalization	Scrambler
V.21	ND	Yes	O	Yes	Yes	2110	ND	ND
V.22	ND	Yes	PP 2W	Yes	Yes	2110	Fixed	Yes
V.22	ND	Yes	PP 2W	Yes	Yes	2110	Fixed	Yes
V.22bis	ND	Yes	PP 2W	Yes	Yes	2110	Fixed/Adaptive	Yes
V.22bis	ND	Yes	PP 2W	Yes	Yes	2110	Fixed/Adaptive	Yes
V.23	Yes	Yes	O	Yes	Yes	2110	ND	ND
V.23	Yes	Yes	O	Yes	Yes	2110	ND	ND
V.26	Yes	No	PP MP 2W	ND	Yes	2110	ND	ND
V.26bis	Yes	Yes	No	Yes	Yes	2110	Fixed	ND
V.26bis	Yes	Yes	No	Yes	Yes	2110	Fixed	ND
V.26ter	ND	Yes	PP 2W	Yes	Yes	2110	Either	Yes
V.26ter	ND	Yes	PP 2W	Yes	Yes	2110	Either	Yes
V.27	Yes	No	4W[3]	ND	Yes	2110	Manual	Yes
V.27bis	Yes	No	2W 4W	ND	Yes	2110	Adaptive	Yes
V.27bis	Yes	No	2W 4W	ND	Yes	2110	Adaptive	Yes
V.27ter	Yes	Yes	No	Yes	Yes	2110	Adaptive	Yes
V.27ter	Yes	Yes	No	Yes	Yes	2110	Adaptive	Yes
V.29	ND	No	PP 4W	ND	Yes	2110	Adaptive	Yes
V.29	ND	No	PP 4W	ND	Yes	2110	Adaptive	Yes
V.29	ND	No	PP 4W	ND	Yes	2110	Adaptive	Yes
V.32	ND	Yes	PP 2W	Yes	Yes	2110	Adaptive	Yes
V.32	ND	Yes	PP 2W	Yes	Yes	2110	Adaptive	Yes
V.32	ND	Yes	PP 2W	Yes	Yes	2110	Adaptive	Yes
V.35	ND	No	Yes	ND	ND	ND	ND	Yes

Note 1: 4-wire not stipulated; must be assumed.
Note 2: For HDX, 2-wire is used.
Note 3: Amplitude is constant on a relative basis.

Box 1: Summary of Table 4

A V Series number may be entered into the table more than once. This means the recommended standard permits more than one option. The initials *ND* means not defined in the specification. The initials *NA* means not applicable.

Entries	Explanation
Line Speed	Speed in bits per second (bit/s).
Channel Separation	If the recommended standard permits multiple channels, the method of deriving the channels is noted as: FD: Frequency Division Four-wire: Each set of wires carries a channel EC: Echo Cancellation Note that the standard may also use a backward channel.
Modulation Rate	The rate of the signal change of the carrier on the channel; in bauds.
Carrier Frequency	The frequency of the carrier or carriers used on the channel(s). The carrier(s) may be altered to yield different modulated frequencies. For example, the V.21 modem uses two mean frequencies of 1080 and 1750. Each carrier is then modulated with a frequency shift of + 100 Hz for binary 1 and − 100 Hz for a binary 0.
Use of V.2	A CCITT specification, which establishes specified power ranges and levels.
Full Duplex or Half Duplex	FDX: Full Duplex HDX: Half Duplex
Synchronous or Asynchronous	"Either" means the specification will work with one or the other.
Modulation Technique	The description of the modulation technique where FS: Frequency Shift PS: Phase Shift QAM: Quadrature Amplitude Modulation AM: Amplitude Modulation TCM: Trellis Coded Modulation
Bits Encoded	Describes the number of bits encoded per signal change (baud). For example, 2:1 means two bits encoded per baud.
Backward Channel	Describes an alternate channel used for transmission in a reverse direction, at a lower rate, usually 75 bauds. Its absence does not imply that the modem is only HDX, because a FDX modem may not use a backward channel.
Switched Lines	Describes the use of conventional dial-up circuits.
Leased Lines	O: Optional 2W: Two-wire PP: Point-to-point 4W: Four-wire MP: Multipoint

Entries	Explanation
V.25	A CCITT specification that describes the procedures for automatic dial-and-answer. May also offer features on call and answer beyond that of V.25.
V.28	A CCITT specification that describes the electrical characteristics of unbalanced circuits.
ISO Pin Connector	Specifications from the International Standards Organization that describe the actual connector (dimensions, etc.) between the DTE and DCE.
Equalization	A technique to improve signal quality where Fixed: Established when modem left the factory Adaptive: Changes and adjusts to received signal Either: Can be fixed or adaptive
Scrambler	A technique for altering the data stream to enhance the timing and synchronization between the two modems on the circuit.

connectors used by computers, terminals, modems, and other devices. Figure 18 depicts some of the major connectors that are used. These types of connectors will eventually be replaced by a recently approved connector (by CCITT). This "new" connector is really not new; it is the familiar telephone jack that you see in your home and office telephones. The electrical characteristics and number of wires will be changed. However, for the immediate future, the ISO connectors will be the most prevalent type of interface for our computers and terminals.

EIA-232, which is one of the most widely used physical interfaces in the world, is sponsored by the EIA and is most prevalent in North America. It specifies 25 circuits for DTE/DCE use. These circuits are actually 25 pin connections and sockets. The terminal pins plug into the modem sockets. All the circuits are rarely used; most devices use 12 or fewer pins.

The CCITT publishes the V.24 specification, from which the ISO and EIA-232 pin assignments are derived. The ISO establishes the specification for the mechanical dimensions of the pins and connector. EIA-232 uses ISO 2110 as well as some of the V series standards, such as V.28. It can also use others, such as V.24 and V.24 bis.

Let us now focus our attention in Section 3 on the basic V specifications from which EIA-232, the V series in Table 4 and most vendors' modems derive their characteristics and functions. Be aware that this material is an overview; the specific recommended standard should be obtained if more detail is needed.

PHYSICAL LEVEL INTERFACES AND PROTOCOLS

Section 3:
The "Foundation" V Series Recommendations

Section 3: The "Foundation" V Series Recommendations

This section provides an overview of several important V series recommendations from CCITT. The reader should obtain the specific CCITT recommendation for a more detailed explanation.

V.1: Equivalence between Binary Notation Symbols and the Significant Conditions of a Two-Condition Code

This recommendation provides definitions and descriptions of signals, signal states, and binary symbols. Table 5 summarizes this information.

Table 5: V.1 Binary Notation Symbols

	Digit 0 "Start Signal in Start-Stop Code Line Available Condition in Telex Switching "Space" Element of Start-Stop Code Condition A	Digit 1"Stop Signal in Start-Stop Code Line Idle Condition in Telex Switching "Mark" Element of Start-Stop Code Condition Z
Amplitude Modulation	Tone-off	Tone-on
Frequency Modulation	High Frequency	Low Frequency
Phase Modulation with Reference Phase	Opposite Phase to the Reference	Reference Phase
Differential Two-Phase Modulation Where the Alternative Phase Changes Are 0 Degree or 180 Degrees	No Phase Inversion	Inversion of the Phase
Perforations	No Perforation	Perforation

V.2: Power Levels for Data Transmission over Telephone Lines

V.2 establishes the permissible power levels on the telephone lines. The summary of V.2 follows.

Data Transmission over Leased Telephone Circuits (Private Wires) Set up on Carrier Systems

The maximum power output of the subscriber's equipment into the line shall not exceed 1 mW at any frequency. For systems transmitting tones continuously, such as frequency modulation (FM) systems, the maximum power level at the zero relative point shall be -13 dBm0. When transmission of data is discontinued for any appreciable time, the power level should be reduced to -20 dBm0 or lower.

For systems not transmitting tones continuously, such as amplitude modulation

(AM) systems, the signal characteristics should meet all of the following requirements:

1. The maximum value of the 1-minute mean power shall not exceed -13 dBm0.

2. The maximum value of the instantaneous power shall not exceed a level corresponding to that of a 0 dBm0 sine wave signal.

3. The maximum signal power determined for a 10-Hz bandwidth centered at any frequency shall not exceed -10 dBm0.

Data Transmission over the Switched Telephone System

The maximum power output of the subscriber's equipment interface into the line shall not exceed 1 mW. For systems transmitting tones continuously, the level of the subscriber's equipment should be fixed at installation time to allow for loss between the equipment and the point of entry to an international circuit to the extent that the corresponding level of the signal at the international circuit input shall not exceed -13 dBm0.

For systems not transmitting tones continuously, such as amplitude modulation (AM) systems, the signal characteristics should meet all of the following requirements:

1. The maximum value of the 1-minute mean power shall not exceed -13 dBm0.

2. The maximum value of the instantaneous power shall not exceed a level corresponding to that of a 0 dBm0 sine wave signal.

3. The maximum signal power determined for a 10 Hz bandwidth centered at any frequency shall not exceed -10 dBm0.

V.5: Standardization of Data Signaling Rates for Synchronous Data Transmission in the General Switched Telephone Network

This brief recommendation describes the synchronous signaling rates for the telephone network (dial-up). Permissible speeds are as follows: 600, 1200, 2400, 4800, and 9600 bit/s. Also, V.5 stipulates the following V series modems for these speeds on either half duplex or duplex lines:

Half Duplex	Duplex
V.23	V.22
V.26 bis	V.22 bis
V.27 ter	V.26 ter
	V.32

(Note: for 300 bit/s, V.21 applies)

V.6: Standardization of Data Signaling Rates for Synchronous Data Transmission on Leased Telephone-Type Circuits

This recommendation describes the synchronous signaling rates for leased circuits. Signaling rates are described as preferred or supplementary

Preferred		Supplementary	
600*	4800*	3000	7200*
1200*	9000*	6000	12000
2400*	14400		

(*Note: includes V.22, V.22 bis, V.23, V.26, V.26 ter, V.27, V.27 bis, V.29, V.32)

V.10: Electrical Characteristics for Unbalanced Double-Current Interchange Circuits for General Use with Integrated Circuit Equipment in the Field of Data Communications

This recommendation explains the electrical characteristics of the generator, receiver, and interconnecting leads of an unbalanced interchange circuit. For this recommendation, an unbalanced interchange circuit consists of an unbalanced generator connected to a receiver by an interconnecting lead and a common return lead.

V.10 uses the unbalanced configuration depicted in Figure 20b. In addition, V.10 specifies the electrical characteristics of the complete circuit, including the generator, the receiver, the load characteristics, the binary waveform, signal common return, and other aspects.

V.10 supports two categories of receivers (shown later in Figure 32). Category I circuits connect the A′ and B′ terminations of each receiver with a pair of wires to the generator. A balanced or unbalanced generator can be directly connected in a category I circuit for data rates of 20 Kbit/s and below.

Category II circuits use a shared communications circuit from the B′ lead of each receiver device on only one side of the interface to signal ground on the generator side.

V.11: Electrical Characteristics for Balanced Double-Current Interchange Circuits for General Use with Integrated Circuit Equipment in the Field of Data Communications

This recommendation describes the electrical characteristics of the generator, receiver, and interconnecting leads of a differential signaling (balanced) interchange circuit. The balanced generator and load components are intended to cause minimum mutual interference with adjacent balanced or unbalanced interchange circuits if waveshaping is used on the unbalanced circuits.

In the context of V.11, a balanced interchange circuit consists of a balanced generator connected by a balanced interconnecting pair to a balanced receiver. For a balanced generator, the algebraic sum of both the outlet potentials, with respect to earth, is constant for all signals transmitted: The impedances of the outlets with respect to earth are equal.

The electrical characteristics specified in V.11 apply to interchange circuits operating with data signaling rates up to 10 Mbit/s, and are intended to be used primarily in data terminal equipment (DTE) and data circuit-terminating equipment (DCE) implemented in integrated-circuit technology.

This recommendation is not intended to apply to equipment implemented in discrete component technology. The electrical characteristics covered by recommendation V.28 are more appropriate for discrete component technology.

V.11 uses the balanced configuration depicted in Figure 20a. Like V.10, it specifies the electrical characteristics of the generator, the receiver, the load character, the binary waveform, and other aspects. Also, V.11 uses the category I circuit (shown later in Figure 32).

V.24: List of Definitions for Interchange Circuits between Data Terminal Equipment and Data-Circuit Terminating Equipment

This recommendation describes the connecting circuits between the DTE and DCE. The V series modems use V.24, as do standards such as EIA-232. In a sense, it is a "superset" standard. Vendors select the appropriate V.24 circuits for their product, as do the standards groups that publish the V series interfaces. V.24 does not describe the electrical characteristics of the interchange circuits; it describes their functions.

V.24 is applicable to the following:

- synchronous and asynchronous communications
- leased or switched lines
- two-wire or four-wire circuits
- point-to-point or multipoint operation
- certain public data networks

V.24 describes the 100 and 200 interchange circuits. The 100 series are shown in Table 6 and the 200 series are shown in Table 7. The 200 series is used for automatic calling (see V.25 and V.25 bis). The various values for the telephone dialing are established in conformance to the rules in Table 8. The functions of the 100 and 200 series circuits are explained below.

The columns labeled "Data," "Control," and "Timing" describe the functions of the interchange circuits. Each circuit is also noted as to whether the DCE transmits ("from DCE") or receives ("to DCE") the signal.

Note that the explanations to the V.24 circuits are rather brief. Since the most frequently used V.24 circuits are applicable to EIA-232-D, the detailed circuit descriptions and a tutorial explanation of their uses are provided in Section 4 under the EIA-232-D subsection of this book. The reader is encouraged to compared the V.24 and EIA-232-D circuits, and several tables are provided later to assist your exmaination of these interfaces.

100 Series

Circuit 102—Signal ground or common return: This conductor establishes the common return for unbalanced circuits according to recommendation V.28 and the DC reference for circuits according to recommendations V.10, V.11, and V.35.

Circuit 102a—DTE common return: This conductor is used as the reference potential for the unbalanced V.10-type circuit receivers within the DCE.

Circuit 102b—DCE common return: This conductor is used as the reference potential for the unbalanced V.10-type circuit receivers within the DTE.

Circuit 102c—Common return: This conductor establishes the signal common return for single-current circuits with electrical characteristics according to V.31.

Circuit 103—Transmitted data: The data signals originated by the DTE, for transmittal to one or more stations, are transferred on this circuit to the DCE.

Table 6: V.24 100-Series Interchange Circuits

Interchange Circuit No.	Interchange Circuit Name	Ground	Data		Control		Timing	
			From DCE	To DCE	From DCE	To DCE	From DCE	To DCE
102	Signal Ground or Common Return	X						
102a	DTE Common Return	X						
102b	DCE Common Return	X						
102c	Common Return	X						
103	Transmitted Data			X				
104	Received Data		X					
105	Request to Send					X		
106	Ready for Sending				X			
107	Data Set Ready				X			
108/1	Connect Data Set to Line					X		
108/2	Data Terminal Ready					X		
109	Data Channel Received Line Signal Detector				X			
110	Data Signal Quality Detector				X			
111	Data Signal Rate Selector (DTE)						X	
112	Data Signal Rate Selector (DCE)				X			
113	Transmitter Signal Element Timing (DTE)							X
114	Transmitter Signal Element Timing (DCE)						X	
115	Receive Signal Element Timing (DCE)						X	
116	Select Standby					X		
117	Standby Indicator				X			
118	Transmitted Backward Channel Data			X				
119	Received Backward Channel Data		X					
120	Transmit Backward Channel Line Signal					X		
121	Backward Channel Ready				X			
122	Backward Channel Received Line Signal Detector				X			
123	Backward Channel Signal Quality Detector				X			
124	Select Frequency Groups					X		
125	Calling Indicator				X			
126	Select Transmit Frequency					X		
127	Select Receive Frequency					X		
128	Receiver Signal Element Timing (DTE)							X
129	Request to Receive					X		
130	Transmit Backward Tone					X		
131	Received Character Timing						X	
132	Return to Nondata Mode					X		
133	Ready for Receiving					X		
134	Received Data Present				X			
136	New Signal					X		
140	Loopback/Maintenance Test					X		
141	Local Loopback					X		
142	Test Indicator				X			
191	Transmitted Voice Answer					X		
192	Received Voice Answer				X			

Table 7: V.24 200-Series for Automatic Calling

Interchange Circuit No.	Interchange Circuit Name	From DCE	To DCE
201	Signal Ground or Common Return	X	X
202	Call Request		X
203	Data Line Occupied	X	
204	Distant Station Connected	X	
205	Abandon Call	X	
206	Digit Signal 2^0		X
207	Digit Signal 2^1		X
208	Digit Signal 2^2		X
209	Digit Signal 2^3		X
210	Present Next Digit	X	
211	Digit Present		X
213	Power Indication	X	

Table 8: V.24 Digit Signal Circuits

Information	Binary States			
	209	208	207	206
Digit 1	0	0	0	1
Digit 2	0	0	1	0
Digit 3	0	0	1	1
Digit 4	0	1	0	0
Digit 5	0	1	0	1
Digit 6	0	1	1	0
Digit 7	0	1	1	1
Digit 8	1	0	0	0
Digit 9	1	0	0	1
Digit 0	0	0	0	0
Control Character EON (Note 1)	1	1	0	0
Control Character SEP (Note 2)	1	1	0	1

Note 1—The control character EON (end of number) causes the DCE to take appropriate action to await an answer from the called data station.

Note 2—The control character SEP (separation) indicates the need for a pause between successive digits or in front of the digit series, and causes the automatic calling equipment to insert the appropriate time interval.

Circuit 104—Received data: The data signals generated by the DCE are transferred on this circuit to the DTE in response to data channel signals received from a data station or in response to the DTE maintenance test signals.

Circuit 105—Request to send: Signals control the data channel transmit function of the DCE. The ON condition causes the DCE to assume the data channel transmit mode. The OFF condition causes the DCE to assume the data channel nontransmit mode when all data transferred on circuit 103 have been transmitted.

Circuit 106—Ready for sending: Signals indicate whether the DCE is prepared to accept signals for transmission on the channel; signals also indicate maintenance tests under control of the DTE. The ON condition indicates the DCE is prepared to accept data signals from the DTE. The OFF condition indicates the DCE is not prepared to accept data signals from the DTE.

Circuit 107—Data set ready: Signals indicate whether the DCE is ready to operate. The ON condition (where circuit 142 is OFF or is not implemented) indicates the equipment is connected to the line and the DCE is ready to exchange data signals with the DTE for test purposes. The OFF condition indicates that the DCE is not ready to operate.

Circuit 108/1—Connect data set to line: Signals control switching of the signal-conversion or similar equipment to or from the line. The ON condition causes the DCE to connect the signal-conversion or similar equipment to the line. The OFF condition causes the DCE to remove the signal-conversion or similar equipment from the line, after the transmission of all data previously transferred on circuit 103 and/or circuit 118 has been completed.

Circuit 108/2—Data terminal ready: Signals control switching of the signal-conversion or similar equipment to or from the line. The ON condition prepares the DCE to connect the signal-conversion or similar equipment to the line and maintains this connection after it has been established by supplementary means. The DTE can preset the ON condition on circuit 108/2 when it is ready to transmit or receive data. The OFF condition causes the DCE to remove the signal-conversion or similar equipment from the line, after the transmission of all data previously transferred on circuit 103 and/or circuit 118 has been completed.

Circuit 109—Data channel received line signal detector: Signals indicate whether the received data channel line signal is within appropriate limits. The ON condition indicates that the received signal is within appropriate limits. The OFF condition indicates that the received signal is not within appropriate limits.

Circuit 110—Data signal quality detector: Signals indicate if there is a reasonable probability of an error in the data received. The ON condition indicates a probability of an uncorrupted transmission. The OFF condition indicates a reasonable probability of an error.

Circuit 111—Data signaling rate selector (DTE source): Signals are used to select one of two data signaling rates of a dual rate synchronous or asynchronous DCE. The ON condition selects the higher rate or range of rates. The OFF condition selects the lower rate or range of rates.

Circuit 112-Data signaling rate selector (DCE source): Signals are used to select one of the two data signaling rates in the DTE to coincide with the data signaling rate in use in a dual rate synchronous or asynchronous DCE. The ON condition selects the higher rate. The OFF condition selects the lower rate.

Circuit 113—Transmitter signal element timing (DTE source): Signals provide the DCE with signal element timing information. The condition on this circuit shall be ON and OFF for equal periods, and the transition from ON to OFF condition indicates the center of each signal on circuit 103.

Circuit 114—Transmitter signal element timing (DCE source): Signals provide the DTE with signal element timing information. The condition on this circuit shall be ON and OFF for equal periods. The DTE presents a signal on circuit 103 in which the transitions between signal elements occur at the time of the transitions from OFF to ON condition of circuit 114.

Circuit 115—Receiver signal element timing (DCE source): Signals provide the DTE with signal element timing information. The condition of this circuit is ON and OFF for equal periods, and a transition from ON and OFF condition indicates the center of each signal element on circuit 104.

Circuit 116—Select standby: Signals are used to select the normal or standby facilities, such as signal converters and data channels. The ON condition selects the standby mode of operation, causing the DCE to replace predetermined facilities by their reserves. The OFF condition causes the DCE to replace the standby facilities with others. The OFF condition is maintained whenever the standby facilities are not used.

Circuit 117—Standby indicator: Signals indicate whether the DCE is conditioned to operate in standby mode with the primary facilities replaced by standbys. The ON conditions indicates that the DCE can operate in its standby mode. The OFF condition indicates that the DCE can operate in its normal mode.

Circuit 118—Transmitted backward channel data: This circuit is equivalent to circuit 103, for backward (reverse) channel transmission.

Circuit 119—Received backward channel data: This circuit is equivalent to circuit 104 for backward (reverse) channel transmission.

Circuit 120—Transmit backward channel line signal: This circuit is equivalent to circuit 105 for backward (reverse) transmit function of the DCE. The ON condition causes the DCE to assume the backward channel transmit mode. The OFF condition causes the DCE to assume the backward channel nontransmit mode, after all data transferred on circuit 118 have been transmitted to line.

Circuit 121—Backward channel ready: This circuit is equivalent to circuit 106 for backward (reverse) channel transmission. The ON condition indicates that the DCE can transmit data on the backward channel. The OFF condition indicates that the DCE cannot transmit data on the backward channel.

Circuit 122—Backward channel received line signal detector: This circuit is equivalent to circuit 109, except that it is used to indicate whether the received backward channel line signal is within appropriate limits.

Circuit 123—Backward channel signal quality detector: This circuit is equivalent to circuit 110, except that it is used to indicate the signal quality of the received backward channel line signal.

Circuit 124—Select frequency groups: Signals are used to select the desired frequency groups available in the DCE. The ON condition causes the DCE to use all frequency groups to represent data signals. The OFF condition causes the DCE to use a specified reduced number of frequency groups to represent data signals.

Circuit 125—Calling indicator: Signals indicate whether a calling signal is being received by the DCE. The ON condition indicates that a calling signal is being received. The OFF condition indicates no calling signal is being received.

Circuit 126—Select transmit frequency: Signals are used to select the required transmit frequency of the DCE. The ON condition selects the higher transmit frequency. The OFF condition selects the lower transmit frequency.

Circuit 127—Select receive frequency: Signals are used to select the required receive frequency of the DCE. The ON condition selects the lower receive frequency. The OFF condition selects the higher receive frequency.

Circuit 128—Receiver signal element timing (DTE source): Signals provide DCE with signal element timing information. The condition of this circuit is ON and OFF for equal periods. The DCE presents a data signal on circuit 104 in which the transitions between signal elements occur at the time of the transition from OFF to ON condition of the signal on circuit 128.

Circuit 129—Request to receive: Signals are used to control the receive function of the DCE. The ON condition causes the DCE to assume the receive mode. The OFF condition causes the DCE to assume the nonreceive mode.

Circuit 130—Transmit backward tone: Signals control the transmission of a backward channel tone. The ON condition causes the DCE to transmit a backward channel tone. The OFF condition causes the DCE to stop the transmission of a backward channel tone.

Circuit 131—Received character timing: Signals provide the DTE with character timing information. The specific V series recommendation should be checked.

Circuit 132—Return to nondata mode: Signals are used to restore the nondata mode provided with the DCE, without releasing the line connection to the remote station. The ON condition causes the DCE to restore the nondata mode. When the nondata mode has been established, this circuit is turned OFF.

Circuit 133—Ready for receiving: Signals control the transfer of data on circuit 104, indicating whether the DTE is capable of accepting a given amount of data as specified in the recommendation for intermediate equipment. The ON condition is maintained whenever the DTE is capable of accepting data and causes the intermediate equipment to transfer the received data to the DTE. The OFF condition indicates that the DTE is not able to accept data and causes the intermediate equipment to retain the data.

Circuit 134—Received data present: Signals are used to separate information messages from supervisory messages transferred on circuit 104. The ON condition indicates the data that represent information messages. The OFF condition shall be maintained at all other times.

Circuit 136—New signal: Signals are used to control the response times of the DCE receiver. The ON condition instructs the DCE receiver to prepare itself to detect rapidly the disappearance of the line signal (by disabling the response time circuitry associated with circuit 109). After the received line signal falls below the threshold of the received line signal detector, the DCE will turn OFF circuit 109 and prepare itself to detect rapidly the appearance of a new line signal.

Circuit 140—Loopback/maintenance test: Signals are used to initiate and release loopback or other maintenance test conditions in DCEs. The ON condition causes initiation of the maintenance test condition. The OFF conditions cause release of the maintenance test condition.

Circuit 141—Local loopback: Signals are used to control the loop 3 test condition in the local DCE. The ON condition of circuit 141 causes the establishment of the loop 3 test condition in the local DCE. The OFF condition of circuit 141 causes the release of the loop 3 test condition of the local DCE.

Circuit 142—Test indicator: Signals indicate whether a maintenance condition exists. The ON condition indicates that a maintenance condition exists in the DCE, precluding reception of transmission of data signals from or to a remote DTE. The OFF condition indicates that the DCE is not in a maintenance test condition.

Circuit 191—Transmitted voice answer: Signals generated by a voice answer unit in the DTE are transferred on this circuit to the DCE.

Circuit 192—Received voice answer: Received voice signals, generated by a voice answering unit at the remote DTE, are transferred on this circuit to the DTE.

200 Series

Circuit 201—Signal ground or common return: This conductor establishes the signal common reference potential for all 200-series interchange circuits.

Circuit 202—Call request: Signals are used to condition the automatic calling equipment to originate a call and to switch the automatic calling equipment to or from the line. The ON condition causes the DCE to condition the automatic calling equipment to originate a call and to connect this equipment to the line. The OFF condition causes the automatic calling equipment to be removed from the line and indicates that the DTE has released the automatic calling equipment.

Circuit 203—Data line occupied: Signals indicate if the associated line is in use (e.g., for automatic calling, data transmission, voice communication, or test procedures). The ON condition indicates that the line is in use. The OFF condition indicates that the line is not in use, and that the DTE may originate a call.

Circuit 204—Distant station connected: Signals indicate if a connection has been established to a remote station. The ON condition indicates the receipt of a signal from a remote DCE signaling that a connection to that equipment has been established. The OFF condition shall be maintained at all other times.

Circuit 205—Abandon call: Signals indicate whether a preset time has elapsed between successive events in the calling procedure. The ON condition indicates that the call should be abandoned. The OFF condition indicates that the call origination can proceed.

Digital signal circuits: On circuits 206 (digital signal (2^0)), 207 (digital signal (2^1)), 208 (digital signal (2^2)), 209 (digital signal (2^3)), the DTE presents the code combinations for the binary dialing digits.

Circuit 210—Present next digit: Signals indicate whether the automatic calling equipment is ready to accept the next code combination. The ON condition indicates that the automatic calling equipment is ready to accept the next code combination. The OFF condition indicates that the automatic calling equipment is not ready to accept signals on the digit signal circuits.

Circuit 211—Digit present: Signals control the reading of the code combination presented on the digit signal circuits. The ON condition causes the automatic calling equipment to read the code combination presented on the digit signal circuits. The OFF condition on this circuit prevents the automatic calling equipment from reading a code combination on the digit signal circuits.

Circuit 213—Power indication: Signals indicate whether power is available within the automatic calling equipment. The ON condition indicates that power is available within the automatic calling equipment. The OFF condition indicates that power is not available within the automatic calling equipment.

V.25: Automatic Answering Equipment and/or Parallel Automatic Calling Equipment on the General Switched Telephone Network Including Procedures for Disabling of Echo Control Devices for Both Manually and Automatically Established Calls

This specification is widely used in several parts of the world. It describes the conventions for automatic calling and answering. However, be aware that vendors may vary in their use and interpretation of V.25. A careful review of their specifications is necessary to determine compatibility of equipment. (Many North American vendors consider the V.25 command set too complex and cumbersome to use).

As with other V series interfaces, the V.24 circuits are used. It also makes use of the 200-series interchange circuits of V.24. It includes procedures for disabling echo control devices. This recommendation is applied to the V series modems that have automatic dial and answer capabilities.

The V.24 100 and 200 series circuits are defined for the following functions:

CT 104	=	Circuit 104 — Received Data
CT 105	=	Circuit 105 — Request to Send
CT 106	=	Circuit 106 — Ready for Sending
CT 107	=	Circuit 107 — Data Set Ready
CT 108/1	=	Circuit 108/1 — Connect Data Set to Line
CT 108/2	=	Circuit 108/2 — Data Terminal Ready
CT 109	=	Circuit 109 — Data Channel Received Line Signal Detector
CT 119	=	Circuit 119 — Received Backward Channel Data
CT 120	=	Circuit 120 — Transmit Backward Channel Line Signal
CT 121	=	Circuit 121 — Backward Channel Ready
CT 122	=	Circuit 122 — Backward Channel Received Line Signal Detector
CT 125	=	Circuit 125 — Calling Indicator
CT 201	=	Circuit 201 — Signal Ground or Common Return
CT 202	=	Circuit 202 — Call Request
CT 203	=	Circuit 203 — Data Line Occupied
CT 204	=	Circuit 204 — Distant Station Connected
CT 205	=	Circuit 205 — Abandon Call
CT 206	=	Circuit 206 — Digit Signal (2^0)
CT 207	=	Circuit 207 — Digit Signal (2^1)
CT 208	=	Circuit 208 — Digit Signal (2^2)
CT 209	=	Circuit 209 — Digit Signal (2^3)
CT 210	=	Circuit 210 — Present Next Digit
CT 211	=	Circuit 211 — Digit Present
CT 213	=	Circuit 213 — Power Indication
DCE	=	Data Circuit-Terminating Equipment
DTE	=	Data Terminal Equipment
EON	=	End-of-Number Control Character
SEP	=	Separation Control Character

As indicated in the introduction, the 2100 Hz tone disables any echo suppressors on the line.

The DTE is responsible for:

- ensuring that the DCE is available
- providing the telephone number
- abandoning the call if necessary
- establishing proper identification
- exchanging traffic
- initiating a disconnect

The procedures for the calling and answering station are established by V.25 as shown in Box 2.

Stations operating in a manual mode are handled by a procedure quite similar to the automatic sequences, but no tone is transmitted from the calling station. The person who dials the number, on hearing the 2100 Hz signal from the called station, presses the "data" button to connect the DCE to the telephone line. Then, CT 107 comes ON.

V.25 bis: Automatic Calling and/or Answering Equiment on the General Switched Telephone Network (GTSN) Using the 100-Series Interchange Circuits

This recommendation uses the same concepts as V.25, except V.25 bis uses serial transmission. Unlike V.25, the bis version uses only one circuit (V.24 circuit 103) to present a dialed digit. This is a common interface for workstations and personal computers. The V.24 circuits used by V.25 bis are shown in Table 9.

V.25 bis provides for three types of calls:

- serial automatic calling data station to automatic answering data station
- manual calling data station to automatic answering data station
- serial automatic calling data station to manual answering data station

The DTE is responsible for:

- ensuring that the DCE is available
- providing the telephone number or selecting a telephone number stored at the DCE
- deciding to abandon the call
- controlling data transfer
- initiating disconnect at calling or answering data stations

V.25 bis provides for several commands and indications by which the DTE instructs the DCE to enter into a specific state (operation). These commands are accompanied by instructional parameters shown in Table 10.

V.25 bis permits the commands and indications to be transmitted in one of three ways:

- asynchronous
- synchronous character oriented
- synchronous bit oriented

Box 2: Automatic Dial and Answer

Calling Station:

Event

1   DTE checks if CT 213 ON, and the following circuits OFF: CT 202, CT 210, CT 205, CT 204, CT 203.
2   DTE turns CT 202 ON.
3   DTE turns CT 108/2 ON.
4   For half-duplex modems, DTE puts CT 105 ON if the calling end wishes to transmit first.
5   Line goes off hook; same effect as picking up your telephone.
6   DCE turns CT 203 ON.
7   Telephone office or PBX puts dial tone on line.
8   DCE turns CT 210 ON.
9   DTE presents the appropriate telephone number digit on CT 206, CT 207, CT 208 and CT 209. (Four circuits are needed to represent a base 10 number of 0-9 in binary base 2).
10 DTE turns CT 211 ON after digit signals have been presented.
11 DCE dials first digit; then turns CT 210 OFF.
12 DTE turns CT 211 OFF.
13 Events 8 to 12 are repeated (which may be interrupted by SEP) until the last digit signal is presented and transferred. Event 8 is then repeated but event 14 follows.
14 DTE present EON on CT 206, CT 207, CT 208 and CT 209; it then turns CT 211 ON.
15 DCE turns CT 210 OFF.
16 DTE turns CT 211 OFF and turns CT 108/2 ON, if not previously ON.
17 A calling tone is transmitted from calling DCE.
18 When calling DCE recognizes an answer has occurred, it stops the calling tone and transfers control of the line from CT 202 to CT 108/2.

Called Station:

Event

1   A ring signal is detected on line. DCE turns ON CT 125.
2   If CT 108/2 is ON, then DCE goes off hook. However, if CT 108/1 or CT 108/2 is OFF then DCE waits for one of them to come ON. Otherwise, the call is not answered.
3   The DCE, upon going off hook, does nothing for a period of 1.8 to 2.5 seconds.
4   DCE transmits a 2100 Hz ($\pm$ 15 Hz) answer tone. This tone can disable echo suppressors by performing 180° phase reversals of the tone at 425 to 475 millisecond intervals.
5   The 2100 Hz tone is discontinued upon the calling station responding for 100 milliseconds. (This specification can be relaxed for "slower" devices like acoustic modems).
6   After a 75 millisecond ($\pm$ 20 ms), the DCE turns on CT 107.

PHYSICAL LEVEL INTERFACES AND PROTOCOLS

Table 9: V.25 bis Interchange Circuits for Automatic Calling/Answering

Interchange Circuit		Direction	
No.	Name	From DCE	To DCE
103	Transmitted Data and Commands		X
104	Received Data and Indications	X	
106	Ready for Sending	X	
107	Data Set Ready	X	
108/2	Data Terminal Ready		X
125	Calling Indicator	X	

Table 10: V.25 bis Commands and Indications

Command or Indication	DTE to DCE (Command)	DCE to DTE (Indication)	Parameters
Call Request	X		• Number To Be Dialed • Memory Address of the Number To Be Dialed • Double Dial-up Request • Identification Number
Program	X		• Number to Be Dialed • Memory Address for the Number To Be Dialed • Identification Number
List Request	X		• Under Study
Disregard Incoming Call	X		• None
Connect Incoming Call	X		• None
Call Failure		X	• Engaged Tone • Number Not Stored • Local DCE Busy • Ring Tone (Time Out) • Abort Call (Time Out) • V.25 Answer Tone Not Tested • Forbidden Call
Delayed Call		X	• Time To Permissible Call Request (Minute)
Incoming Call		X	• None
Valid		X	• None
Invalid		X	• Under Study
List		X	• Memory Address Number To Be Dialed • Status Identification

The commands/indications are coded into these three formats as part of the message or information (I) field (see Figure 25).

V.28: Electrical Characteristics for Unbalanced Double-Current Interchange Circuits

V.28 is usually applied to all interchange circuits operating below the limit of 20,000 bit/s. The data stream (binary 1s and 0s) are represented as described here.

The recommendation provides specifications for other electrical characteristics as well. The reader should consult the CCITT specifications for these details, if they are needed. On a more general level, the signals must conform to these characteristics (see Table 11).

For data interchange circuits, the signal shall be considered in the binary 1 condition when the voltage (V_1) on the interchange circuit measured at the interchange point is more negative than -3 volts. The signal shall be considered in the binary 0 condition when the voltage (V_1) is more positive than +3 volts.

For control and timing interchange circuits, the circuit shall be considered ON when the voltage (V_1) on the interchange circuit is more positive than +3 volts and shall be considered OFF when the voltage (V_1) is more negative than -3 volts.

Asynchronous:

I	CR	LF

Synchronous, Character-Oriented:

SYN	SYN	STX	I	ETX

Synchronous, Bit-Oriented

F	A	C	I	FCS	F

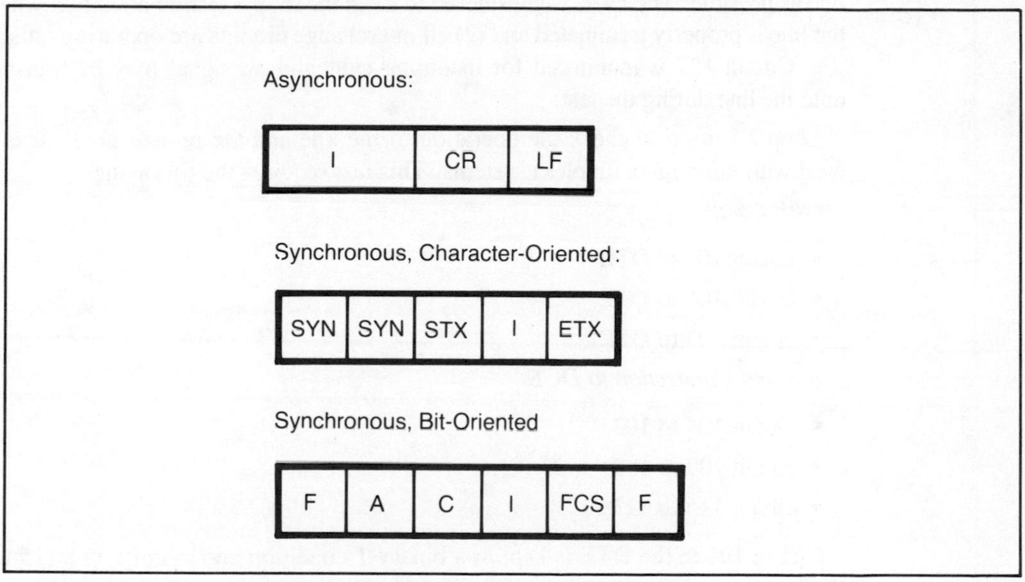

I:	Information Field; Connection Management Information
CR:	Carriage Return
LF:	Line Feed
SYN:	Synchronization Characters
STX:	Start of Text
ETX	End of Text
F:	Flag
A:	Address
C:	Control
FCS:	Frame Check Sequence (Error Detection)

Figure 25: V.25 bis Formats

Table 11: V.28 Significant Levels

V1 < − 3 Volts	V1 > + 3 Volts
1	0
OFF	ON

V.54: Loop Test Devices for Modems

Loopback testing is often used to isolate a problem on a data communications line. Section 1 provides a brief tutorial on the subject, and describes the many terms (often conflicting) used by the vendors to describe their products. V.54 defines four loopback tests (loop). They are numbered 1 through 4.

Loop 1 is used to test the DTE by returning the DTE's signals back to it. The transmitted data circuit (103) is connected to the received data circuit (104) within the DTE. V.54 requires (1) circuit 108/1 or 108/2 be in the same condition as before the test, (2) circuit 105 must be in the OFF condition, (3) circuit 125 should be monitored by the DTE to give precedence to an incoming call.

Loop 3 is an analog signal to check the local DCE. It is performed as close to the line as possible. The DCE is considered to be in the loop 3 testing condition when (1) the line is properly terminated and (2) all interchange circuits are operating satisfactorily. Circuit 125 is monitored for incoming calls and no signal may be transmitted onto the line during the test.

Loop 2 is used to check the operation of the line and the remote DCE. It is only used with full duplex (duplex) systems. This test requires the following:

OFF Condition

- circuit 109 to DTE
- circuit 106 to DTE
- circuit 107 to DTE

Internal Connection to DCE

- circuit 104 to 103
- circuit 109 to 105
- circuit 115 to 113

Circuit 104 in the DTE is kept in a binary 1 condition and circuits 114/115 to the DTE, if used, must continue to function.

Loop 4 is used to test the line and is used only for four-wire circuits. The two pair cable are disconnected from the DCE for the testing. Generally, this test is performed by the telephone company.

PHYSICAL LEVEL INTERFACES AND PROTOCOLS

**Section 4:
The EIA Standards**

Section 4: The EIA Standards

EIA-232-D

The Electronics Industries Association (EIA) (see Section I for a description of EIA) has replaced the prefix RS (recommended standard) with EIA. The change represents no technical alterations to the standard, but was made to allow a user to identify the source of the standard.

The EIA sponsors the EIA-232-D standard. It is used extensively in North America, as well as other parts of the world. Table 12 defines the interchange circuits of EIA-232-D. (This section uses the terms pins, circuits, and interchange circuits to convey the same meaning).

EIA-232-D applies to the following data communications systems:

- serial communications
- synchronous and asynchronous
- dedicated leased or private lines
- switched service
- two-wire or four-wire
- point-to-point or multipoint

Be aware that EIA-232-D provides for the automatic answering of switched calls but does not designate the interchange circuits for call origination. This procedure is covered in EIA-366-A *Interface between Data Terminal Equipment and Automatic Calling Equipment for Data Communications*.

Modifications to RS-232-C

Prior to January 1987, this EIA standard was named RS-232-C. The D version brings the specification in line with CCITT V.24, V.28, and ISO 2110. The revision also includes the addition of the local loopback, remote loopback, and test mode interchange circuits. Protective ground has been redefined and a shield has been added. Also, the term DCE is changed from data communications equipment (and data set) to data circuit-terminating equipment. The terms driver and termination are changed to generator and receiver, respectively.

The EIA-232-D circuit performs one of four functions:

- data transfer across the interface
- control of signals across the interface
- clocking signals to synchronize data flow and regulate the bit rate
- electrical ground

Characteristics of Mechanical Interface

The interface between the DTE and DCE is a 25-position pluggable connector (see Figures 26 and 27). All interchange circuits use the connector. The female connector is associated with the DCE. The interface cable with a male connector is provided as part of the DTE. The DCE has a male shell (receptacle connector). EIA-232-D specifies no arrangement for fastening the connectors together.

Table 12: EIA-232-D Interchange Circuits

Interchange Circuit	CCITT Equivalent	Description	Ground	Data		Control		Timing	
				From DCE	To DCE	From DCE	To DCE	From DCE	To DCE
AB(7)	102	Signal Ground/Common Return	X						
BA(2)	103	Transmitted Data			X				
BB(3)	104	Received Data		X					
CA(4)	105	Request to Send					X		
CB(5)	106	Clear to Send				X			
CC(6)	107	DCE Ready				X			
CD(20)	108.2	DTE Ready					X		
CE(22)	125	Ring Indicator				X			
CF(8)	109	Received Line Signal Detector				X			
CG(21)	110	Signal Quality Detector				X			
CH(23)	111	Data Signal Rate Selector (DTE)					X		
CI(23)	112	Data Signal Rate Selector (DCE)				X			
DA(24)	113	Transmitter Signal Element Timing (DTE)							X
DB(15)	114	Transmitter Signal Element Timing (DCE)						X	
DD(17)	115	Receiver Signal Element Timing (DCE)						X	
SBA(14)	118	Secondary Transmitted Data			X				
SBB(16)	119	Secondary Received Data		X					
SCA(19)	120	Secondary Request to Send					X		
SCB(13)	121	Secondary Clear to Send				X			
SCF(12)	122	Secondary Received Line Signal Detector				X			
RL(21)	140	Remote Loopback					X		
LL(18)	141	Local Loopback					X		
TM(25)	142	Test Mode				X			

Note 1—The numbers in parentheses under the column labeled "Interchange Circuit" are the EIA-232-D pin designations.

Note 2—For new designs with circuit SCF, circuits CH and CI are assigned to pin 23. If SCF is not used, CI is assigned to pin 12.

Functions of Interchange Circuits

The functional descriptions of the circuits are summarized below. Each vendor's offering should be examined carefully, since several options exist on how to use the recommended standard. The EIA-232-D document provides more specific descriptions of each circuit. Our explanation explains each circuit, followed by guidelines for their use. For ease of reading, the circuit designation is followed by the EIA-232-D

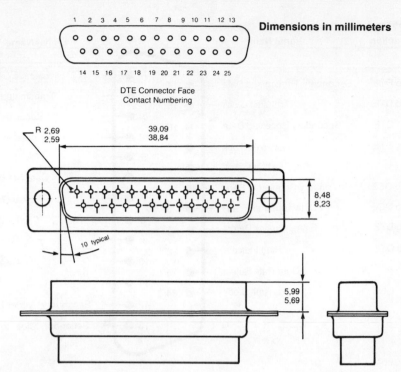

Dimensions in millimeters

(a) EIA-232-D DTE Connector

Dimensions in millimeters

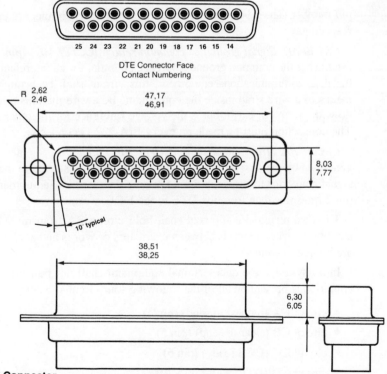

(b) EIA-232-D DCE Connector

Figure 26: EIA-232-D and ISO Connectors

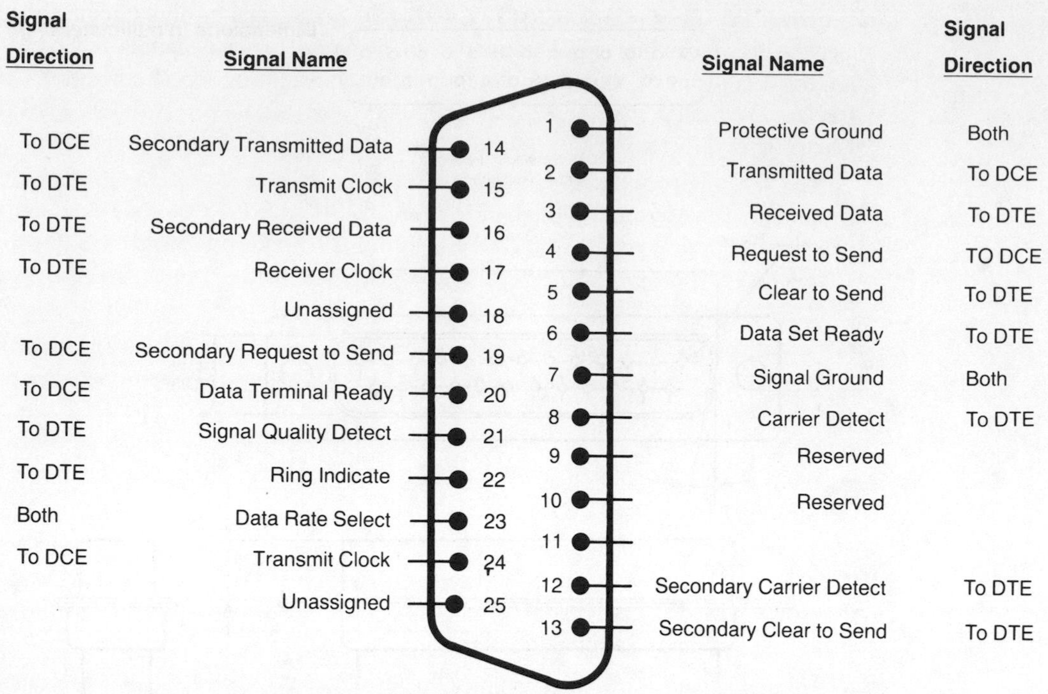

Signal Direction	Signal Name			Signal Name	Signal Direction
			1	Protective Ground	Both
To DCE	Secondary Transmitted Data	14	2	Transmitted Data	To DCE
To DTE	Transmit Clock	15	3	Received Data	To DTE
To DTE	Secondary Received Data	16	4	Request to Send	TO DCE
To DTE	Receiver Clock	17	5	Clear to Send	To DTE
	Unassigned	18	6	Data Set Ready	To DTE
To DCE	Secondary Request to Send	19	7	Signal Ground	Both
To DCE	Data Terminal Ready	20	8	Carrier Detect	To DTE
To DTE	Signal Quality Detect	21	9	Reserved	
To DTE	Ring Indicate	22	10	Reserved	
Both	Data Rate Select	23	11		
To DCE	Transmit Clock	24	12	Secondary Carrier Detect	To DTE
	Unassigned	25	13	Secondary Clear to Send	To DTE

Figure 27: EIA-232-D Connector and Pin Assignments

pin number. The EIA terms ON and OFF mean the circuits are enabled or disabled respectively.

Circuit AB: Signal ground or common return (CCITT 102) (pin 7): This conductor establishes the common ground reference potential for all interchange circuits. Within the data communications equipment, this circuit shall be brought to one point by means of a wire strap inside the equipment. Be aware that this circuit has nothing to do with ground or earth, but is the voltage reference for the other interface circuitry. The connection must be made on every EIA-232-D connector.

Circuit BA: Transmitted data (CCITT 103) (pin 2): Signals on this circuit are generated by the data terminal equipment and are transferred to the local transmitting signal converter for transmission to remote data terminal equipment. In other words, pin 2 transmits data from the DTE to the DCE.

The data terminal equipment shall hold circuit BA (transmitted data) in marking condition during intervals between characters or words and at all times when no data are being transmitted.

In all systems, the data terminal equipment shall not transmit data unless an ON condition is present on all of the following four circuits, where implemented.

- circuit CA (request to send) (pin 4)
- circuit CB (clear to send) (pin 5)
- circuit CC (DCE ready) (pin 6)
- circuit CD (DTE ready) (pin 20)

Circuit BB: Received data (CCITT 104) (pin 3): Signals on this circuit are generated by the receiving signal converter in response to data signals received from remote data terminal equipment via the remote transmitting signal converter. Circuit BB (received data) shall be held in the binary one (marking) condition at all times when circuit CF (received line signal detector, pin 8) is in the OFF condition.

On a half duplex channel, circuit BB shall be held in the binary one (marking) condition when circuit CA (request to send, pin 4) is in the ON condition and for a brief interval following the ON to OFF transition of circuit CA (pin 4) to allow for the completion of transmission (see circuit BA, transmitted data, pin 2), and the decay of line reflections.

Since this book is intended as both a tutorial and a reference guide, it is appropriate to pause briefly and ensure the reader is cognizant of the relationships between pins 2 and 3. The DTE transmits on pin 2 and receives on pin 3. The DCE does the opposite: It receives on pin 2 and transmits on pin 3. As we shall see later, this convention must be altered when two like devices (DTE-to-DTE or DCE-to-DCE) are connected to each other.

Circuit CA: Request to send (CCITT 105) (pin 4): This circuit (also abbreviated to RTS) is used to condition the local data communications equipment for data transmission and, on a half duplex channel, to control the direction of data transmission of the local data communications equipment.

On one-way only channels or duplex channels, the ON condition maintains the data communications equipment in the transmit mode. The OFF condition maintains the data communications equipment in a nontransmit mode.

On a half duplex channel, the ON condition maintains the data communications equipment in the transmit mode and inhibits the receive mode. The OFF condition maintains the data communications equipment in the receive mode.

EIA-232-D establishes several rules for the use of pin 4:

1. A transition from OFF to ON instructs the DCE to enter a transmit mode.
2. The DCE takes necessary actions and turns on circuit CB (clear to send, pin 5).
3. A transition from ON to OFF instructs the DCE to complete transmission of all data that was sent across circuit BA (transmit data, pin 2).
4. The DCE turns off circuit CB (clear to send, pin 5) in response.
5. Circuit CA (pin 4) cannot be turned on again until circuit CB (pin 5) is turned off by the DCE.

Circuit CB: Clear to send (CCITT 106) (pin 5): Signals on this circuit (also abbreviated to CTS) are generated by the data communications equipment to indicate if the device is ready to transmit data.

The ON condition, together with the ON condition on interchange circuits CA (request to send, pin 4), CC (data set ready, pin 6) and, where implemented, CD (data terminal ready, pin 20), is an indication to the data terminal equipment that signals presented on circuit BA (transmitted data, pin 2) will be transmitted to the communications channel.

The OFF condition is an indication to the data terminal equipment that it should not transfer data across the interface on interchange circuit BA (pin 2).

The clear to send signal is used in different ways by the modem, multiplexer, and DSU manufacturers. With full duplex DCE that is configured with clear to send/

carrier detect common (or CB/CF common), the CF is connected directly to the carrier detection (CF, pin 8) circuitry. The CB ON signal usually indicates if an acceptable carrier is on the channel.

A full duplex DCE may use a CB/CF separate option, and half duplex modems use the clear to send as a delayed response to the request to send signal. On receiving the request to send from the DTE, the DCE waits a specific time and then turns on clear to send to the DTE. The reader should carefully check the DCE specifications for the following options:

- use of CB/CF common
- use of CB/CF separate
- clear to send controlled by carrier detect (CF, pin 8)
- clear to send controlled by a specific timing delay within DCE
- proper timing coordination between DTE and DCE with the RTS and CTS delay interval

Circuit CC: DCE ready (CCITT 107) (pin 6): Signals on this circuit are used to indicate the status of the local DCE (data set). The ON condition on this circuit indicates

1. The local data communications equipment is connected to a communications channel (off hook in switched service).
2. The local data communications equipment is not in test (local or remote), talk (alternate voice), or dial mode.
3. The local data communications equipment has completed any timing functions required by the switching system and the transmission of any discrete answer tone.

This circuit shall be used only to indicate the status of the DCE. The ON condition shall not be interpreted as either an indication that a communications channel has been established to a remote data station or the status of any remote station equipment.

The OFF condition on this circuit indicates

1. It is not ready to operate.
2. It has detected a problem.
3. For switched operations, it has detected a disconnect indication.

The OFF condition is used differently for switched and dedicated service:

1. *Switched service*: When OFF occurs during the progress of a call before CD (DTE ready, pin 20) is turned OFF, the DTE interprets this event as a lost connection and terminates the call.
2. *Dedicated service*: When OFF occurs, the DTE interprets this event as a hard failure and must set BA (transmitted data, pin 2) to MARK and terminate any communications sessions in progress.

The OFF condition shall appear at all other times and shall be an indication that the data terminal equipment is to disregard signals appearing on any other interchange circuit with the exception of circuit CE (ring indicator, pin 22).

Circuit CD: DTE ready (CCITT 108.2) (pin 20): Signals on this circuit are used to control switching of the data communications equipment to the communications channel. The ON condition prepares the data communications equipment to be connected to the communications channel and maintains the connection established by external means (manual calling, manual answering, or automatic calling).

When the station is equipped for automatic answering of received calls and is in the automatic answering mode, connection to the line occurs only in response to a combination of a ringing signal and the ON condition of circuit CD (data terminal ready). However, the data terminal equipment is normally permitted to present the ON condition on circuit CD whenever it is ready to transmit or receive data. However, with switched lines, circuit CD shall not be turned on again until circuit CC (DCE ready, pin 6) is turned off by DCE.

It is possible for data terminal ready (pin 20) to be left on to answer calls (along with other circuits, described shortly). While this approach works well enough for answering the calls, it creates a problem for call termination. Some vendors use a line signal (polarity reversal) to indicate the called party has terminated the call.

Also, some modems use the CCITT V.24 circuit 108.1: connect data set to line (see Table 6). When this circuit is used, the DTE I/O driver asserts circuit 108.1 only upon receiving an incoming call indication. The use of the DTE ready (pin 20 for EIA and CCITT 108.2) and connect data set to line (CCITT 108.2) varies among vendors. The reader should check the specifications carefully. This point is especially important for international communications because different countries use different approaches with these circuits.

Circuit CE: Ring indicator (CCITT 125) (pin 22): The ON condition of this circuit indicates that a ringing signal is being received on the communications channel. The ON condition shall appear approximately coincident with the ON segment of the ringing cycle (during rings) on the communications channel.

The OFF condition shall be maintained during the OFF segment of the ringing cycle (between "rings") and at all other times when ringing is not being received. The operation of this circuit shall not be disabled by the OFF condition on circuit CD (data terminal ready, pin 20).

The ring indicator is used to direct the receiving I/O driver to activate data terminal ready (if it is OFF) or activate connect data set to line (CCITT 108.1). One of its other important functions is to alert the I/O driver to check for the calling modem's carrier (with the received line signal detector, discussed next).

It is possible for a temporary loss of carrier to occur during the communications process. Once the carrier has returned, the receiver recognizes the on-going transmission because the ring indicator has not signaled a new call. To guard against an undetected call coming into the user DTE, the I/O driver and/or user application program should initiate the following actions:

1. Terminate application operations when a new call indication signal is detected.
2. Terminate application operations when the carrier is lost for more than a specified period (usually 500 milliseconds).

Circuit CF: Received line signal detector (CCITT 109) (pin 8): The ON condition on this circuit is presented when the data communications equipment is receiving a signal that meets its suitability criteria, which are established by the data communications equipment manufacturer.

The OFF condition indicates that no signal is being received or that the received signal is unsuitable for demodulation.

The OFF condition of circuit CF (received line signal detector) shall cause circuit BB (received data, pin 3) to be clamped to the binary one (MARK) condition.

On half duplex channels, circuit CF is held in the OFF condition whenever circuit CA (request to send, pin 4) is in the ON condition and for a brief interval following the ON to OFF transition of circuit CA (request to send).

Circuit CF (pin 8) is more commonly called "carrier detect." Its use varies with half duplex and full duplex operations:

1. *Half duplex:* A carrier is on the line and the local interface's request to send is OFF.

2. *Full duplex:* A carrier is on the line and the remote interface's request to send is ON.

However, exceptions to the use of CF and RTS do exist, and the reader should consult with the individual vendor for the specific characteristics of the carrier detect circuit.

The carrier detect lead will not go OFF if the carrier is lost for a short time. For example, carrier losses of up to 30 milliseconds usually do not affect the CD lead.

Many communications systems stipulate the "behavior" of the physical level circuits. For example, the X.25 packet network interface specification permits the carrier detect (CCITT 109) to enter the OFF condition because of temporary failures to modem retraining. Higher level protocols detemine when the interface is considered out of order.

If the reader reviews the material on the three circuits just described, it should be evident that these circuits are required for a switched (dial-up) connection. In some systems, the DCE ready (EIA-232-D CC, pin 6 or CCITT 107) is also required. To summarize, the three circuits are

EIA-232-D Designation	Pin Number	Function	CCITT Equivalent
CD	20	DTE Ready	108.2 (maybe 108.1)
CE	22	Ring Indicator	125
CF	8	Received Line Signal Detect	8

Circuit CG: Signal quality detector (CCITT 110) (pin 21): Signals on this circuit are used to indicate whether or not there is a high probability of an error in the received data. An ON condition is maintained whenever there is no reason to believe that an error has occurred. This circuit is not recommended for new designs.

An OFF condition indicates that there is a high probability of an error. It may, in some instances, be used to call automatically for the retransmission of the previously transmitted data signal. Preferably, the response of this circuit shall be such as to permit identification of individual questionable signal elements on circuit BB (received data, pin 3).

Circuit CH: Data signal rate selector (DTE source) (CCITT 111) (pin 23): Signals on this circuit are used to select between the two data signaling rates in the case of dual rate synchronous DCEs or the two ranges of data signaling rates in the case of dual range nonsynchronous DCEs. An ON condition shall select the higher data signaling rate or range of rates.

The rate of timing signals, if included in the interface, shall be controlled by this circuit as appropriate.

Circuit CI: Data signal rate selector (DCE source) (CCITT 112) (pin 23): Signals on this circuit are used to select between the two data signaling rates in the case of dual rate synchronous DCEs or the two ranges of data signaling rates in the case of dual range nonsynchronous DCEs. An ON condition shall select the higher data signaling rate or range of rates.

The rate of timing signals, if included in the interface, shall be controlled by this circuit as appropriate.

EIA-232-D provides three timing circuits. They are first explained, and then some examples are provided as on their use.

Circuit DA: Transmitter signal element timing (DTE source) (CCITT 113) (pin 24): Signals on this circuit are used to provide the transmitting signal converter with signal element timing information.

The ON to OFF transition shall nominally indicate the center of each signal element on circuit BA (transmitted data, pin 2). When circuit DA is implemented in the DTE, the DTE shall normally provide timing information on this circuit whenever the DTE is in a power ON condition.

Circuit DB: Transmitter signal element timing (DCE source) (CCITT 114) (pin 15): Signals on this circuit are used to provide the data terminal equipment with signal element timing information. The data terminal equipment shall provide a data signal on circuit BA (transmitted data, pin 2) in which the transitions between signal elements normally occur at the time of the transitions from OFF to ON condition of the signal on circuit DB. When circuit DB is implemented in the DCE, the DCE shall normally provide timing information on this circuit whenever the DCE is in a power ON condition.

Circuit DD: Receiver signal element timing (DCE source) (CCITT 115) (pin 17): Signals on this circuit are used to provide the data terminal equipment with received signal element timing information. The transition from ON to OFF condition shall nominally indicate the center of each signal element on circuit BB (received data). Timing information on circuit DD shall be provided at all times when circuit CF (received line signal detector) is in the ON condition.

The timing pins are often a source of confusion. Pins 15 (DB), 17 (DD), and 24 (DA) can be used to provide timing signals between the DTE and DCE. These timing signals are not required for asynchronous systems but are necessary for synchronous devices because synchronous data streams do not have the start/stop timing bits. Figure 28 shows various timing options.

If the transmitting DTE provides the timing signals, then pin 24 (DA) is used. At the remote end, the receiving DCE (B) uses pin 17 (DD) to time the signals to its receiving DTE (B) (see Figure 28a). Pin 15 (DB) is used if the transmitting (DCE A) provides the timing to the transmitting DTE (Figure 28b). If this is the case, the transmitting DTE (DTE A) is set for external timing.

What happens if DTE B transmits? It can use pin 24 (DA) to provide the timing or DCE B can provide transmit timing on pin 15 (DB). It is preferable to have as few timing sources as possible, so one option for synchronous systems is to use the receive timing lead (17/DD) to control DTE B's transmission. This entails looping the timing from pin 17 (DD) to pin 15 (DB). So, pin 15 (DB) is slaved from pin 17 (DD) (see Figure 28c).

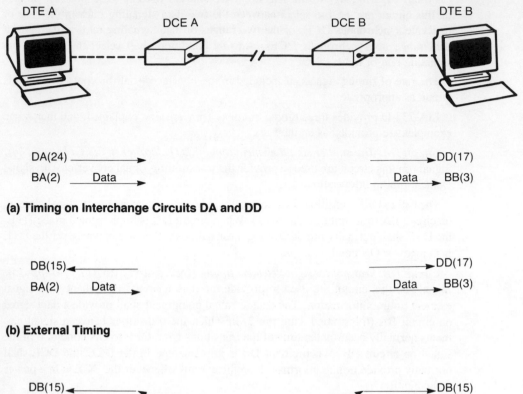

(a) Timing on Interchange Circuits DA and DD

(b) External Timing

(c) Derived Timing (Slaved Timing)

Figure 28: Timing Options on DTE/DCE Interchange

In summary, the timing pins are used as follows:

Pin	Name	Source
15	Transmit Timing	Transmitting DCE
17	Receive Timing	Receiving DCE
24	Transmit Timing	Transmitting DTE

EIA-232-D provides five secondary channels. They function in the same manner as their primary channel counterparts. They are used in conjunction with the split stream/backward channel (discussed in the introduction) or other control-type operations:

EIA-232-D Designation	Pin Number	Secondary Channel Function	CCITT Equivalent
SBA	14	Transmitted Data	118
SBB	16	Received Data	119
SCA	19	Request to Send	120
SCB	13	Clear to Send	121
SCF	12	Carrier Detect	122

Circuit SBA: Secondary transmitted data (CCITT 118) (pin 14): This circuit is equivalent to circuit BA (transmitted data, pin 2) except that it is used to transmit data via the secondary (i.e., reverse or backward) channel.

Signals on this circuit are generated by the data terminal equipment and are connected to the local secondary channel transmitting signal converter for transmission of data to remote data terminal equipment.

The data terminal equipment shall hold circuit SBA (secondary transmitted data) in marking condition during intervals between characters or words and at all times when no data are being transmitted.

Although not stated in EIA-232-D, the data terminal equipment does not usually transmit data on the secondary channel unless an ON condition is present on all of the following four circuits, where implemented:

- circuit SCA (secondary request to send)
- circuit SCB (secondary clear to send)
- circuit CC (DCE ready)
- circuit CD (DTE ready)

Circuit SBB: Secondary received data (CCITT 119) (pin 16): This circuit is equivalent to circuit BB (received data, pin 3) except that it is used to receive data on the secondary (i.e., reverse or backward) channel.

Circuit SCA: Secondary request to send (CCITT 120) (pin 19): This circuit is equivalent to circuit CA (request to send, pin 4) except that it requests the establishment of the secondary channel instead of requesting the establishment of the primary data channel.

Although not stated in EIA-232-D, when the secondary channel is used as a backward channel, the ON condition of circuit CA (request to send, pin 4) usually disables circuit SCA and it is not possible to condition the secondary channel transmitting signal converter to transmit during any time interval when the primary channel transmitting signal converter is so conditioned. Where system considerations dictate that one or the other of the two channels be in transmit mode at all times but never both simultaneously, this can be accomplished by permanently applying an ON condition to circuit SCA (secondary request to send) and controlling both the primary and secondary channels, in complementary fashion, by means of circuit CA (request to send, pin 4). Alternatively, in this case, circuit SCB need not be implemented in the interface.

Also, although not stated in EIA-32-D, when the secondary channel is usable only for circuit assurance or to interrupt the flow of data in the primary data channel, circuit SCA can serve to turn ON the secondary channel unmodulated carrier. The OFF condition of circuit SCA can turn OFF the secondary channel carrier and thereby signal an interrupt condition at the remote end of the communications channel.

Circuit SCB: Secondary clear to send (CCITT 121) (pin 13): This circuit is equivalent to circuit CB (clear to send, pin 5) except that it indicates the availability of the secondary channel instead of indicating the availability of the primary channel. This circuit is not provided where the secondary channel is usable only as a circuit assurance or an interrupt channel.

Circuit SCF: Secondary received line signal detector (CCITT 122) (pin 12): This circuit is equivalent to circuit CF (received line signal detector, pin 8) except that it indicates the proper reception of the secondary channel line signal instead of indicating the proper reception of a primary channel received-line signal.

Although not stated in EIA-232-D, where the secondary channel is usable only as a circuit assurance or an interrupt channel (see circuit SCA, secondary request to send), circuit SCF can be used to indicate the circuit assurance status or to signal the interrupt. The ON condition can indicate circuit assurance or a noninterrupt condition. The OFF condition can indicate circuit failure (no assurance) or the interrupt condition.

Circuit LL: Local loopback (CCITT 141) (pin 18): This circuit is used to control the local loopback (LL) test condition in the local DCE. With LL in an ON condition, the DCE sends its output of its transmitting signal converter from the channel to its receiving signal converter. It then turns on circuit TM (test mode, pin 25). After TM is ON, the DTE can operate in duplex mode and exercise all the circuits in the interface.

Circuit RL: Remote loopback (CCITT 140) (pin 21): This circuit is used to control the RL test condition in the remote DCE. With RL in an ON condition, the local DCE signals to the remote DCE the establishment of the RL condition. With RL ON and after detecting an ON on circuit TM (test mode, pin 25), the local DTE can operate in duplex mode and exercise all the circuitry of the local and remote DCE.

The RL condition places the system out of service to the DTE that is attached to the DCE containing the RL loopback. Note that this circuit uses the same pin as the signal quality detector circuit (EIA-232-D CG and CCITT 110).

Circuit TM: Test mode (CCITT 142) (pin 25): This circuit indicates if the local DCE is in a test condition. The ON condition is in response to an ON in either LL (local loopback) or RL (remote loopback).

An EIA-232-D Data Flow

Figure 29 depicts a typical communications process across the interface. The events are labeled with notes 1-6. The notes depict the following communications activities:

1. Signal reference connections are made.
2. DTEs turn on pins 20 to indicate readiness and DCEs turn on pins 6.
3. DTE A requests a transmission with pin 4 turned on. DCE A sends out a carrier signal to DCE B and turns on pin 5 to DTE A. DCE B detects the carrier signal and turns on pin 8 to DTE B.
4. DTE A begins transmitting application data over pin 2 to DCE A. Pin 24 synchronizes DTE A and DCE A. Data are modulated and transmitted to DCE B, which demodulates it and transmits it to DTE B using pin 3. DCE B sends the

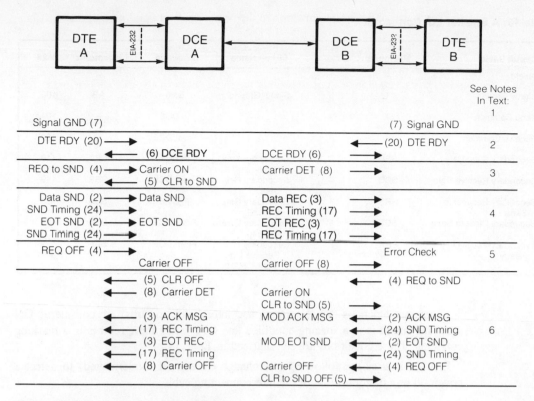

Figure 29: EIA-232-D Communications

proper timing signals to DTE B on pin 17.

5. The end of transmission (EOT) procedures causes DTE A to turn off pin 4, which instructs DCE A to turn off its carrier signal. DCE B detects the carrier being turned off and turns off pin 8 to B.

6. DTE B responds to the DTE A data by transmitting its own data by using the same process as in events 1 through 5.

Notes on EIA-232-D

Many devices have adapted a smaller connector, with fewer pins. For example, personal computers use only a few of the EIA-232/449 circuits. So the nine-pin connector is often used on the PCs. Table 13 describes this interface; more detail is available in EIA-449.

The U.S. Military Standard (MIL) is compatible with RS-232-C except for the voltage levels (plus or minus 6 volts) and the bit sense is reversed.

Electrical Characteristics of EIA-232-D

Figure 30 depicts the EIA-232-D interchange circuit. The signal on an interchange circuit is in a marking condition when the voltage (V_1) is more negative than -3 volts with respect to circuit AB (signal ground). The signal is considered to be in a spacing condition when the voltage (V_1) is more positive than 3 volts with respect to AB. The region between +3 and -3 volts is a transition region. The marking condition is used to represent a binary 1 and the spacing condition is used to represent a binary 0.

Table 13: A Smaller EIA Connector

Circuit Name	Mnemonic	Pin No.	RS-232C Circuit Name	Circuit Direction	Mnemonic	V.24
Shield	–	1	–	–	–	–
Signal Ground	SG	5	Signal Ground	Both	AB	102
Send Common	SC	9	–	To DCE	–	102A
Receive Common	RC	6	–	From DCE	–	102B
Secondary Send Data	SSD	3	Secondary Xmit Data	To DCE	SBA	118
Secondary Receive Data	SRD	4	Secondary Rec. Data	From DCE	SBB	119
Secondary Request to Send	SRS	7	Secondary Req. to Send	To DCE	SCA	120
Secondary Clear to Send	SCS	8	Secondary Clear to Send	From DCE	SCB	121
Secondary Receiver Ready	SRR	2	Secondary Receive Line Signal Detect	From DCE	SCF	122

The circuit functions (for the timing and interchange circuits) are considered ON when the circuit is in a spacing condition and OFF when the circuit is in a marking condition. These conditions are summarized in Table 14.

EIA-232-D uses the following interchange circuits (if implemented) to detect a power off or a disconnection of the interconnecting cable:

- circuit CA: request to send
- circuit CC: DCE ready
- circuit CD: DTE ready
- circuit SCA: secondary request to send

The open-circuit generator voltage (V_0) in relation to signal ground (AB) on any circuit is not allowed to exceed 25 volts in magnitude. When the receiver open circuit voltage (EL) is zero, the potential (V_1) shall range between 5 and 15 volts.

The signals transmitted across the interface point must adhere to the following conventions:

1. Signals entering the transition region shall proceed through it to the opposite signal state.

2. No reversal of voltage is permitted while the signal is in the transition region.

3. The time to pass through the transition region (for control interchange circuits) shall not exceed one millisecond.

4. The data and timing interchange circuits have the transition time requirements shown in Table 15.

Protective ground (frame ground) is achieved by an electrical bounding to the equipment frame or through the third wire in a power cord.

EIA-449 (EIA-422-A and EIA-423-A)

The EIA also sponsors EIA-449. It was developed to overcome some of the limitations of EIA-232-D. The EIA-232-D standard utilizes several specifications that limit its effectiveness. For instance, it is limited to a 20 Kbit/s and a few hundred feet

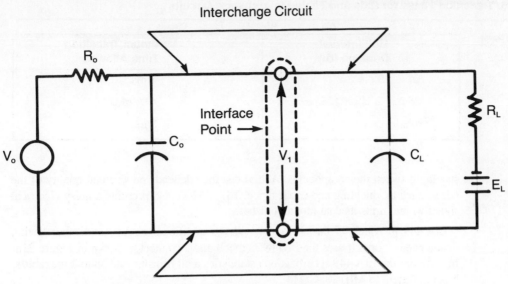

Interchange Circuit

Interface Point →

Circuit AB, Signal Ground

V_o: The open-circuit generator voltage.

R_o: The generator internal dc resistance.

C_o: The total effective capacitance associated with the generator, measured at the interface point and including any cable to the interface point.

V_1: The voltage at the interface point.

C_L: The total effective capacitance associated with the receiver measured at the interface point and including anyu cable to the interface point.

R_L: The receiver load dc resistance.

E_L: The open circuit receiver voltage (bias).

Figure 30: EIA-232-D Interchange Equivalent Circuit

Table 14: EIA Signal Conditions

Designation	V1 Voltage	
	Negative	Positive
Binary State	1	0
Signal Condition	Marking	Spacing
Function	OFF	ON

Table 15: Transition Times for Data and Timing Interchange Circuits

Unit Interval Duration (UI)	Maximum Transition Time Allowed
UI ≥ 25 ms	1 ms
25 ms ≥ UI ≥ 125 μs	4 % of UI
125 μs > UI	5 μs

spacing between the components. Actual distance depends on size and quality of the wires, such as shielding and capacitance. EIA-232-D also presents a noisy electrical signal which limits its data rate and distance.

EIA-449 provides 37 basic circuits with 10 additional circuits and other testing maintenance loops. It uses the ISO 4902 mechanical connector shown in Figure 31a. In addition, the EIA-449 specification establishes a bit transfer rate up to 2 megabit/s. It is equivalent to MIL 188C/114.

EIA-449 can be used with two other specifications: EIA-422-A and EIA-423-A. The electrical interface EIA-422-A is a balanced electrical interface (refer to Figure 20). It is less noise sensitive and can transmit over a greater distance at a faster data rate than EIA-423-A, which is an unbalanced electrical interface. The basic difference is the balanced interface uses equipment that allows half the signal to be transmitted on each wire of the pair that is used. This type of interface is much less noise sensitive because the receiver can use the noise on each wire to cancel each other out. The unbalanced circuit provides for the transmission of the signal on one wire, with a common return for all wires (like EIA-232-D). A summary of EIA-422-A and EIA-423-A follows (also refer to Figure 32).

EIA-422-A

- balanced generator
- dedicated return path for category 1 circuits
- differential receiver: 2 to 6 volts differential signal
- 100 Kbit/s at 1 km to 10 Mbit/s at 10 m
- equivalent to CCITT V.11, Federal Standard 1020 and MIL 188C/114

EIA-423-A

- unbalanced generator
- common return for each direction
- bi-polar voltage, where:
  +4 to +6 volts = 0, ON
  -4 to -6 volts = 1, OFF
- 1 Kbit/s at 1 km to 100 Mbit/s at 10 m
- equivalent to CCITT V.10, Federal Standard 1030 and MIL 188C/114
- works with both EIA-232-D/V.24 and EIA-422/V.11

To summarize the various recommended standards, several comparisons are provided in Table 16. The EIA-449 circuits are described in Table 17.

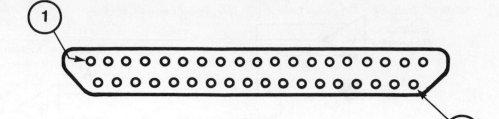

(a) RS-449/ISO 4902

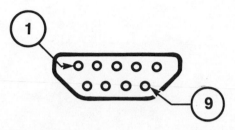

(b) EIA-232-D PC Variation

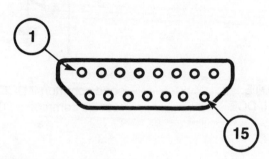

(c) X.21/ISO 4903

Figure 31: Mechanical Connectors

Additional Interchange Circuits

The recommendation uses the following additional circuits:

Circuit SC send common: Connected to DTE to serve as a reference voltage for unbalanced receivers.

Circuit RC receive common: Connected to DCE to serve as a reference voltage at DTE for unbalanced receivers.

Circuit IS terminal in service: Signal to indicate if DTE is available. This prevents an incoming call from being connected to the DCE when DTE is busy. If DTE is out

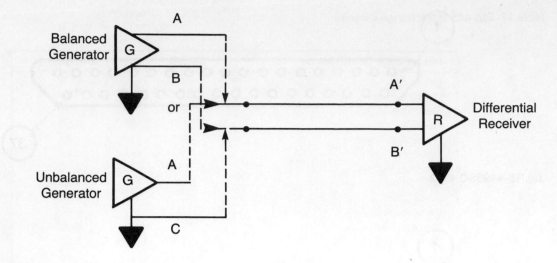

(a) Category I Circuit

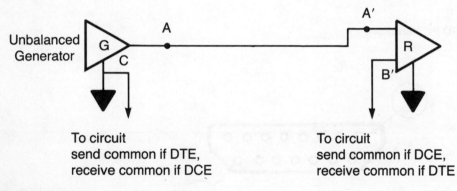

To circuit
send common if DTE,
receive common if DCE

To circuit
send common if DCE,
receive common if DTE

(b) Category II Circuit

Figure 32: Category I and II Circuits

Table 16: EIA and U.S. Federal Interfaces

EIA	U.S. Federal	CCITT Recommendations (Electrical/ Functional)	ISO (Mechanical)
EIA-423-A	1030A	V.10	–
EIA-422-A	1020A	V.11	–
EIA-449	1031	V.24/V.10/V.11	4092
EIA-232-D	None	V.24/V.28	2110

Table 17: EIA-449 Interchange Circuits

Interchange Circuit Name	Circuit	Pin No.
Shield	–	1
Signal Ground	SG	19
Send Common	SC	37
Receive Common	RC	20
Terminal in Service	IS	28
Incoming Call	IC	15
Terminal Ready	TR	12,30
Data Mode	DM	11,29
Send Data	SD	4,22
Receive Data	RD	6,24
Terminal Timing	TT	17,35
Send Timing	ST	5,23
Receive Timing	RT	8,26
Request to Send	RS	7,25
Clear to Send	CS	9,27
Receiver Ready	RR	13,31
Signal Quality	SQ	33
New Signal	NS	34
Select Frequency	SF	16
Signal Rate Selector	SR	16
Signal Rate Indication	SI	2
Local Loopback	LL	10
Remote Loopback	RL	14
Test Mode	TM	18
Select Standby	SS	32
Standby Indicator	SB	36
Spares	–	3,21

of service, this signal can make a port busy during a rotary hunt to that machine. (A rotary is a device that rotates (selects) a "free" telephone number within a group of numbers: a hunt group).

Circuit NS new signal: Signal to alert master stations in a multipoint network when a new signal from DTE to DCE is about to begin. Used to improve response time in multipoint polling networks.

Circuit SF select frequency: Signal used to select the transmit and receive frequencies of the DCE. Used in a multipoint circuit where the stations have equal status.

Circuit LL local loopback: Signal to check the local DTE/DCE interface. The signal also checks the transmit and receive circuitry of the local DCE.

Circuit RC remote loopback: Signal to check both directions through the common carrier path and through the remote DCE up to the remote DCE/DTE interface.

Circuit TM test mode: Signal from DCE to DTE that DCE is in test condition (conditions LL or RC).

Circuit SI standby indicator: This signal indicates whether DCE is set up to operate with the SC (select standby) circuit.

Comparison of Physical Level Interfaces

The performance characteristics of EIA-422-A, EIA-423-A, and EIA-232-D are compared in Figure 33, which shows EIA-232-D, EIA-423-A unbalanced, and EIA-422-A balanced connections.

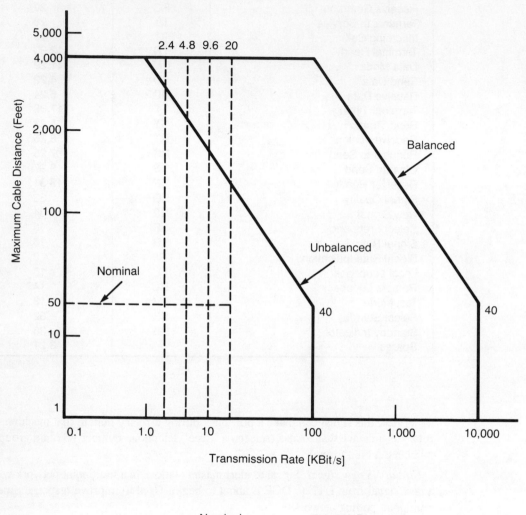

Nominal:	EIA-232-D
	V.24/V.28
Unbalanced:	RS-423-A
	V.10[X.26]
Balanced:	RS-422-A
	V.11[X.27]

Figure 33: Performance Comparisons of EIA-232, EIA-422-A, and EIA-423-A

Table 18 compares the EIA-232-D and EIA-449 interfaces, while Table 19 compares other physical level connectors, and Table 20 provides additional comparisons of the various interface standards and characteristics. (The CCITT X standards are explained later.) Finally, Table 21 is provided to compare RS-232-C to EIA-232-D.

The EIA-422-A specification provides a balanced configuration with differential signaling over both wires. EIA-423-A uses a balanced differential receiver with a common return connected to signal ground only at the generator end. Both EIA-422-A and EIA-423-A specify a balanced differential receiver even though they use different types of generators.

EIA-232-D uses a single-ended receiver with signal ground providing a common return. EIA-232-D also requires a very sharp rise time of the binary signal (less than 3 percent of the bit duration). As a consequence, considerable noise is created. EIA-423-A allows the rise time to be 30 percent slower and is not as noisy.

EIA-530: High Speed 25-Position Interface

The EIA also publishes EIA-530. This standard is intended to gradually replace EIA-449 for protocols that require higher data rates than 20,000 bit/s. It has been developed to serve as a complement to EIA-232-D and uses the EIA-232-D mechanical connector.

The standard can be used for data rates from 20 Kbit/s to 2 Mbit/s and is applicable to the following systems:

- asynchronous or synchronous
- switched, nonswitched, dedicated, leased, or private lines
- two-wire or four-wire circuits
- point-to-point or multipoint operations

The interchange circuits for EIA-530 are shown in Tables 22 and 23. As with EIA-232-D, the circuits are classified as (1) ground or common return, (2) data, (3) control, and (4) timing.

EIA-530 Mechanical Interface

The mechanical interface between the DTE and DCE is a pluggable connector between the equipments. The demarcation point must be less than 10 feet (3 meters) from the DCE. The conventional 25 position is specified for all interchange circuits. The DCE provides the male shell and the female contacts. The DTE has the male contacts and the female shell. The total length of the DTE cable is not to exceed 200 feet (60 meters).

Definitions of Interchange Circuits

The definitions of the interchange circuits are quite similar to those in EIA-232-D. They are summarized in this section.

Circuit AB: Signal ground: This conductor connects the DTE circuit ground (circuit common) to the DCE circuit ground (circuit common).

Circuit CC: DCE ready: The circuit is used to indicate the status of the local DCE. It does not indicate any status of the communications channel or the remote equipment. The OFF condition on this circuit indicates the DTE is to disregard signals on all other interchange circuits except circuit TM (test mode).

Table 18: Comparisons of EIA-449 and EIA-232-D

EIA-449 Circuit Name	EIA-449 Mnemonic	EIA-449 Pin No.	EIA-232-D Circuit Name	Circuit Direction	EIA-232-D Mnemonic	V.24(6)
None	–	–	None	–	–	101
Shield	–	1	–	–	–	–
Signal Ground	SG	19	Signal Ground	Both	AB	102
Send Common (Note 1)	SC	37	–	To DCE	–	102a
Receive Common (Note 1)	RC	20	–	From DCE	–	102b
Terminal in Service (Note 1)	IS	28	–	To DCE	–	
Incoming Call	IC	15	Ring Indication	From DCE	CE	125
Terminal Ready	TR	12,30	Data Terminal Ready	To DCE	CD	108.2
Data Mode	DM	11,29	DCE Ready	From DCE	CC	107
Send Data	SD	4,22 Note 2	Transmit Data	To DCE	BA	103
Receive Data	RD	6,24 Note 2	Receive Data	From DCE	BB	104
Terminal Timing	TT	17,35	Transmit Sig. Elem. Timing	To DCE	DA	113
Send Timing	ST	5,23	Transmit Sig. Elem. Timing	From DCE	DB	114
Receive Timing	RT	8,26	Receive Sig. Elem. Timing	From DCE	DD	115
Request to Send	RS	7,25 Note 2	Request to Send	To DCE	CA	105
Clear to Send	CS	9.27 Note 2	Clear to Send	From DCE	CB	106
Receiver Ready	RR	13,31 Note 2	Received Line Detector	From DCE	CF	109
Signal Quality	SQ	33	Quality Detector Signal	From DCE	CG	110 Note 3
New Signal (Note 1)	NS	34	–	To DCE	–	136
Select Frequency (Note 1)	SF	16	–	To DCE	–	126
Signal Rate Selector	SR	16	Data Signal Rate Select	To DCE	CH	111 Note 4
Signal Rate Indication	SI	2	Data Signal Rate Select / Sec. Rec. Line Detect	From DCE / From DCE	CI / SCF	112 Note 4 / 122 Note 5
Local Loopback	LL	10	Local Loopback	To DCE	LL	141
Remote Loopback	RL	14	Remote Loopback	To DCE	RL	140 Note 3
Test Mode	TM	18	Test Mode	From DCE	TM	142
Select Standby (Note 1)	SS	32	–	To DCE	–	116
Standby Indicator (Note 1)	SB	36	–	From DCE	–	117
Spares	–	3,21	–	–	–	–

Note 1—Circuits not in EIA-232-D.

Note 2—Second pin is equivalent to EIA-232-D secondary circuits (see Table 12).

Note 3—Both circuits use pin 21, but CG no longer recommended.

Note 4—CH/CI assigned to pin 23; if SCF not used on pin 12, CI uses pin 12.

Note 5—SCF and CI may be assigned to this circuit, see Note 4.

Note 6—The secondary circuits used by EIA-232-D are not shown in this table (118,119,120,121; see Table 12).

Table 19: Comparisons of EIA-232-D, V.35, EIA-449 Interfaces

EIA-232-D/CCITT V.24 25-Pin	CCITT V.35 37 or 34-Pin	EIA-449 37 Pin	EIA-232-D or EIA-449 9 Pin
1-Shield		1-Shield 37-Send Common	1-Shield 9-Send Common
2-Transmitted Data	Transmit Data	4-Send Data (A)	
3-Received Data	r-Received Data (a)	6-Receive Data (A) 24-Receive Data (B)	
4-Request to Send	Request to Send	7-Request to Send (A) 25-Request to Send (B)	
5-Clear to Send	Clear to Send	9-Clear to Send (A) 27-Clear to Send (B)	
6-DCE Ready	Ready for Sending	11-Data Mode (A) 29-Data Mode (B)	
7-Signal Ground	Signal Ground	19-Signal Ground	5-Signal Ground (C)
8-Signal Detect	Receive Line Signal Detect	13-Receiver Ready (A) 31-Receiver Ready (B)	
9-Reserved for Testing			
		20-Receive Common	6-Receive Common
10-Reserved for Testing		10-Local Loop (A) 14-Remote Loop (A)	
11-Unassigned		3-Spare 21-Spare	
12-Sec. Carrier Detect		32-Select Standby	2-Sec. Receiver Ready
13-Sec. Clear to Send			8-Sec Clear to Send
14-Sec. Transmitted Data			3-Sec. Send Data
15-Transmit Signal Element Timing	TX Signal Element Timing	5-Send Timing(A) CE Source 23-Send Timing (B) DCE Source	
16-Sec. Received Data			4-Sec. Received Data
17-Receive Signal Element Timing	RX Signal Element Timing	8-Receive Timing (A) 26-Receive Timing (B)	
18-Local Loopback		18-Test Mode(A) 28-Term in Service (A) 34-New Signal	
19-Sec. Request to Send			7-Sec. Request to Send
20-Data Terminal Ready		12-Terminal Ready (A) 30-Terminal Ready (B)	
21-Signal Quality Detector/ Remote Loopback		33-Signal Quality (A)	
22-Ring Indicator		15-Incoming Call (A)	
23-Data Signal Rate Selector		2-Signaling Rate Indicator (A) 16-Signaling Rate Selector (A)	
24-Transmit Signal Element Timing		17-Terminal Timing(A) 35-Terminal Timing (B)	
25-Test Mode		36-Stand by indicator	

Table 20: Comparisons of EIA, MIL, and X Series Interfaces

Common Name	Mechanical	Electrical	Functional	Maximum Speed
EIA–232–D	ISO 2110	V.28	V.24	20 Kbit/s
MIL–188C	ISO 2110	V.28	V.24	20 Kbit/s
EIA–422-A	ISO 4902	V.11 (X.27)	V.24	10 Mbit/s
EIA–423-A	ISO 4902	V.10 (X.26)	V.24	100 Kbit/s
X.20	ISO 4902	Note 1	X.24	Note 1
X.20 bis	ISO 2110	V.28	V.24	20 Kbit/s
X.21	ISO 4903	Note 2	X.24	Notes 1 & 2
X.21 bis	Note 3	Note 3	V.24	48 Kbit/s

Note 1—The electrical characteristics at the DCE side will comply with X.26. At the DTE side X.26, X.28, or V.28 may be used.

Note 2—With 9600 bit/s and below, the DCE side of the interface should comply with X.27. The DTE side should comply with X.26 or X.27 (see standards for more details). With data rates of 9600 bit/s and above, both sides of the interface will comply with X.27.

Note 3—The electrical characteristics of the interchange circuits at both the DCE side and the DTE side of the interface may comply either with recommendation V.28 using the 25-pin connector and ISO 2110 or with recommendation X.26 using the 37-pin connector and ISO 4902. Where interworking occurs between V.28 equipment on one side of the interface and X.26 equipment on the other side of the interface, refer to recommendation X.26 and ISO 4902.

For applications of the data signaling rate of 48 Kbit/s,the connector and electrical characteristics at both the DCE side and the DTE side of the interface are the ISO standard for the 34-pin interface connector ISO 2595 and in recommendation V.35, respectively. Alternatively, for the data signaling rate of 48 Kbit/s, the connector and electrical characteristics at both the DCE side and the DTE side of the interface may use ISO 4902 and recommendation X.26/X.27, respectively, as applied for recommendation V.36. This alternative configuration will not interwork with the ISO 2593 and recommendation V.35 configuration.

Circuit BA: Transmitted data: This circuit is used to transmit data signals to the DCE. The DCE is to disregard signals on BA if an OFF condition is present on any of these circuits:

- CA (request to send)
- CB (clear to send)
- CC (DCE ready)
- CD (DTE ready)

Circuit BB: Received data: This circuit is used to transmit data signals from the DCE to the DTE.

Circuit DA: Transmit signal element timing (DTE source): This circuit is used to provide the DCE with transmit timing information. The OFF and ON signal transitions indicate the center of each signal element on the transmit data circuit BA.

Circuit DB: Transmit signal element timing (DCE source): This circuit is used to provide the DTE with transmit signal element timing information.

Table 21: Comparisons of RS-232-C and EIA-232-D

Pin No.	CCITT Name	EIA-232-C Name	Direction	Name	Pin No.	CCITT Name	EIA-232-D Name	Direction	Name	
1	101	AA	Both	Protective Ground	1			GND	Shield	
7	102	AB	Both	Signal Ground	7	102	AB	GND	Signal Ground/Common Return	
2	103	BA	To-DCE	Transmit Data	2	103	BA	To-DCE	Transmit Data	
3	104	BB	To-DTE	Receive Data	3	104	BB	To-DTE	Receive Data	
4	105	CA	To-DCE	Request to Send	4	105	CA	To-DCE	Request to Send	
5	106	CB	To-DTE	Clear to Send	5	106	CB	To-DTE	Clear to Send	
6	107	CC	To-DTE	Modem Ready	6	107	CC	To-DTE	DCE Ready	
20	108.2	CD	To-DCE	Terminal Ready	20	108.2	CD	To-DCE	DTE Ready	
22	125	CE	To-DTE	Ring Indicator	22	125	CE	To-DTE	Ring Indicator	
8	109	CF	To-DTE	Rcv Line Signal Detect (Carrier) Detect)	8	109	CF	To-DTE	RCV Line Signal Detect (Carrier) Detect)	
21	110	CG	To-DTE	Signal Quality Detector	21	140/110	RL/CG	To-DTE	Remote Loopback/Signal Quality Detector	CG Not Recommended on New Systems Used
23	111/112	CH/CI	Either	Data Signaling Rate Selector/Indicator	23	111/112	CH/CI	Either	Data Signaling Rate Selector/Indicator	
24	113	DA	To-DCE	Transmit Clock-DTE Source	24	113	DA	To-DCE	Transmit Clock-DTE Source	
15	114	DB	To-DTE	Transmit Clock-DCE Source	15	114	DB	To-DTE	Transmit Clock-DCE Source	
17	115	DB	To-DTE	Rec Clock-DCE Source	17	115	DD	To-DTE	Rec Clock-DCE Source	
14	118	SBA	To-DCE	Secondary Transmit Data	14	118	SBA	To-DCE	Secondary Transmit Data	
16	119	SBB	To-DTE	Secondary Receive Data	16	119	SBB	To-DTE	Secondary Receive Data	
19	120	SCA	To-DCE	Secondary Req to Send	19	120	SCA	To-DCE	Secondary Req to Send	
13	121	SCB	To-DTE	Secondary Clear to Send	13	121	SCB	To-DTE	Secondary Clear to Send	

Table 21: Comparisons of RS-232-C and EIA-232-D (Continued)

Pin No.	CCITT Name	EIA-232-C Name	Direction	Name	Pin No.	CCITT Name	EIA-232-D Name	Direction	Name
12	122	SCF	To-DTE	Secondary Carrier Det	12	122/112	SCF/CI	To-DTE	Secondary Carrier Det	If SCF Not Used, Then CI Is Used on Pin 12
					9	–	–	–	Reserved for Testing
					10	–	–	–	Reserved for Testing
					11	–	–	–	Unassigned
					18	141	LL	To-DCE	Local Loopback
					25	142	TM	To-DTE	Test Mode

Table 22: Comparisons of EIA-449 and EIA-530

Signal Name	EIA-449 EIA Name	CCITT Name	Pin Number	Pin Number	CCITT Name	EIA-530 EIA Name	Signal Name
Shield	–	–	1	1	–	–	Shield
Send Data	SD(A) SD(B)	103	4 22	2 14	103	BA(A) BA(B)	Transmitted Data
Receive Data	RD(A) RD(B)	104	6 24	3 16	104	BB(A) BB(B)	Received Data
Request to Send	RS(A) RS(B)	105	7 25	4 19	105	CA(A) CA(B)	Request to Send
Clear to Send	CS(A) CS(B)	106	9 27	5 13	106	CB(A) CB(B)	Clear to Send
Data Mode	DM(A) DM(B)	107	11 29	6 22	107	CC(A) CC(B)	DCE Ready
Terminal Ready	TR(A) TR(B)	108	12 30	20 23	108	CD(A) CD(B)	DTE Ready
Signal Ground	SG	102	19	7	102	AB	Signal Ground
Receiver Ready	RR(A) RR(B)	109	13 31	8 10	109	CF(A) CF(B)	Received Line Signal Detect (Carrier Detect)
Send Timing	ST(A) ST(B)	114	5 23	15 12	114	DB(A) DB(B)	Transmit Signal Element Timing-DCE Source
Receive Timing	RT(A) RT(B)	115	8 26	17 9	115	DD(A) DD(B)	Receiver Signal Element Timing-DCE Source

Table 22: Comparisons of EIA-449 and EIA-530 (Continued)

Local Loopback	LL	141	10	18	141	LL	Local Loopback
Remote Loopback	RL	140	14	21	140	RL	Remote Loopback
Terminal Timing	TT(A) TT(B)	113	17 35	24 11	113	DA(A) DA(B)	Transmit-Signal Element Timing-DTE Source
Test Mode	TM	142	18	25	142	TM	Test Mode
Send Common	SC	102A	37				Not Used
Receive Common	RC	102B	20				Not Used
Terminal in Service	IS	135	28				Not Used
Incoming Call	IC	125	15				Not Used
Signal Quality	SQ	110	33				Not Used
New Signal	NS	136	34				Not Used
Signaling Rate Indicator	SI	112	2				Not Used
Select Freq/Sig Rate Selector	SF/SR	126/111	16				Not Used
Select Standby	SS	116	32				Not Used
Standby Indicator	SB	117	36				Not Used
Spares			3,21				Not Used

Table 23: EIA-530 High-Speed Interface

Circuit Mnemonic	Circuit Name	Circuit Direction	Circuit Type
AB	Signal Ground	–	–
BA	Transmitted Data	To DCE	Data
BB	Received Data	From DCE	
DA	Transmit Signal Element Timing (DTE Source)	To DCE	Timing
DB	Transmit Signal Element Timing (DCE Source)	From DCE	
DD	Receiver Signal Element Timing (DCE Source)	From DCE	
CA	Request to Send	To DCE	Control
CB	Clear to Send	From DCE	
CF	Received Line Signal Detector	From DCE	
CC	DCE Ready	From DCE	
CD	DTE Ready	To DCE	
LL	Local Loopback	To DCE	Control
RL	Remote Loopback	To DCE	
TM	Test Mode	From DCE	

Circuit DD: Receiver signal element timing (DCE source): This circuit is used to provide the DTE with receive signal element timing information.

Circuit CB: Clear to send: This circuit is used to indicate if the DCE is ready to transmit data. This circuit, circuit CA (request to send), and circuit CC (DCE ready) are used to indicate to the DTE that signals on circuit BA (transmitted data) will be sent.

Circuit CF: Received line signal detector: This circuit is used to indicate if the receiving DCE is receiving a signal that is of sufficient quality to receive data signals from the communications channel.

Circuit CD: DTE ready: This circuit is used to prepare the DCE to connect to the communications channel.

Circuit LL: Local loopback: This circuit is used to control the LL test condition in the local DCE. The ON condition causes the DCE to send its output to the receiving signal converter at the same DCE.

Circuit RL: Remote loopback: This circuit is used to control the RL test condition in the remote DCE. The ON condition causes the local DCE to signal the RL test condition to the remote DCE. After this signal is ON and after an ON condition is detected on circuit TM (test mode), the local DTE operates in a duplex mode to test the circuitry of both DCEs.

Circuit TM: Test mode: This signal is used to indicate whether the local DCE is in a test condition. The ON condition indicates to the DTE that the DCE is in a test condition. The circuit goes ON in response to an ON condition in circuit LC or circuit RL. It can also be activated by other tests if the vendor and telephone administration so chooses.

EIA-485: Standard for Electrical Characteristics of Generator and Receivers for Use in Balanced Digital Multipoint Systems

The EIA standards summarized thus far in this section deal with point-to-point interfaces. For multipoint circuits, RS-485 is available. It specifies the electrical characteristics for the generators and receivers. The specification is similar to RS-422-A, which allows the generators and receivers to operate by using either standard. However, RS-485 does not specify other characteristics normally in the EIA standards such as pin assignments, timing, or signal quality characteristics. The intent of RS-485 is that it be used with other specifications which specify these characteristics for the complete equipment interfacing.

RS-485 includes one or more generators connected by a balanced cable to one or more receivers. The specification defines the current, voltage, and resistence values at the receiver and generator interconnection points. It applies only to the receiver and generator components that use binary signals and have a DC component. The specification includes interconnections for data rates up to 10 Mbit/s. It also permits any device to operate with a common mode voltage in the range of plus or minus 7 volts.

Although RS-485 does not specify the particular type of cable, it does define the characteristics for the following parameters of cable characteristics:

- signaling rate (and therefore the unit interval)
- minimum voltage signal transmitted to the receiver
- maximum acceptable distortion
- cable length requirement

EIA-366-A: Dial and Answer Systems

AT&T/Bell uses the EIA-366 specification to define the interface for an automatic call unit (ACU), a modem, and a DTE. The DTE and the ACU perform four major functions:

- ensure that the DCE is operable
- provide the telephone number (from the DTE)
- manage call abandonment
- monitor the call continuously to determine when to disconnect

Table 24 lists the EIA pins used for automatic dial and answer systems. A brief description of these pins follows.

Figure 34 is provided to assist the reader in understanding the following process.

The power indication (PWI) signal is used to determine if the ACU is powered up. The data line occupied circuit (DLO) is used to determine if the communications line is in use. With another communications session, the call request circuit (CRQ) must be activated to initiate control of the communications line. To provide this service, the DTE checks if the ACU has power on and if the line is free. If these conditions are met, DTE turns on CRQ to the ACU. A common scenario is the data terminal ready (DTR) signal is presented to the interface of the modem. If this is the case, the communications line is in an off-hook condition (placed by the ACU). The telephone system would then return a dial tone to the ACU.

Table 24: EIA-336-A Pins for Dial and Answer

Pin No.	Circuit	Direction	Description
1	FGD	Both	Frame Ground
2	DPR	To ACU	Digit Present
3	ACR	To Terminal	Abandon Call & Retry
4	CRQ	To ACU	Call Request
5	PND	To Terminal	Present Next Digit
6	PWI	To Terminal	Power Indication
7	SGD	Both	Signal Ground
8			Unassigned
9			Unassigned
10			Unassigned
11			Unassigned
12			Unassigned
13	DSS	To Terminal	Data Set Status
14	NB1	To ACU	Digit Lead
15	NB2	To ACU	Digit Lead
16	NB4	To ACU	Digit Lead
17	NB8	To ACU	Digit Lead
18			Unassigned
19			Unassigned
20			Unassigned
21			Unassigned
22	DLO	To Terminal	Data Line Occupied
23			Unassigned
24			Unassigned
25			Unassigned

On recognizing the dial tone, the ACU activates its present next digit circuit (PND) to the DTE. This informs the DTE the ACU is ready to accept the dialed numbers. In turn, the DTE presents the telephone numbers across four circuits labeled NB1, NB2, NB4, and NB8. (This is one of the few examples in this book of a parallel communications processing.) At the same time the data lines are activated, a signal is provided on the digit present circuit (DPR). If the ACU accepts the telephone number, it so indicates it by turning off the PND circuit.

The PND circuit is turned on when the ACU has completed dialing the digit. This indicates that a new digit can be presented to the ACU. The process continues until the last number is dialed. Then the DTE places a end of number (EON) code on the digit lead. This informs the ACU that no more numbers are to be dialed and it can disconnect itself from the call set-up process.

This process is accomplished by the ACU's turning on a timer upon receiving the EON code. If the call is answered by the receiving DTE, a tone is sent back to the ACU and the timer is turned off. However, if the call is not answered, or if a problem occurs, the ACU will time-out and turn on the abandoned call (ACR) circuit to the DTE. This informs the DTE that it is to disconnect itself from the line. The DTE performs this function by turning off the circuit CRQ.

Later discussions will focus on another popular dial and answer specification used with Hayes modems.

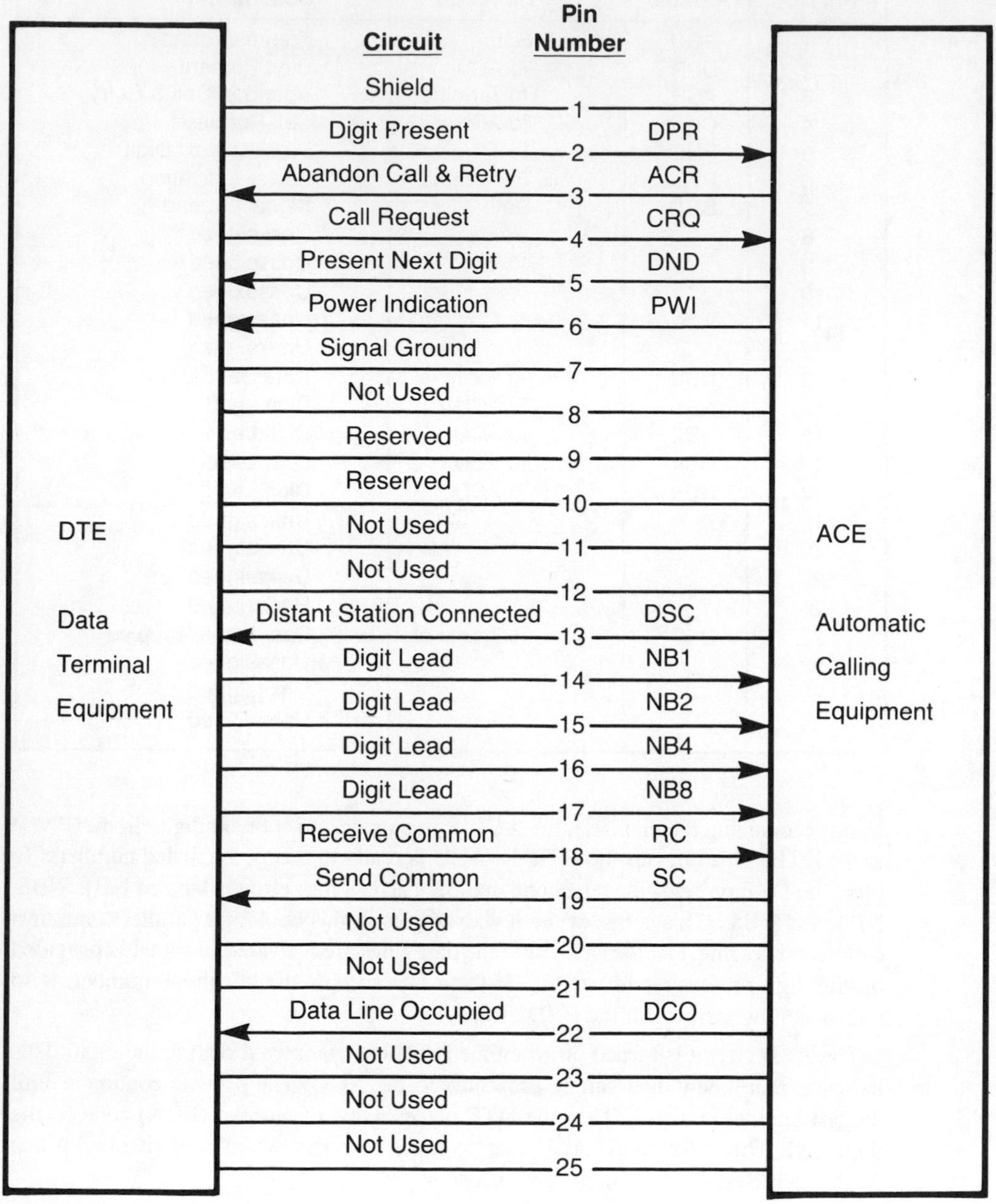

Figure 34: EIA-366-A Automatic Dial and Answer

Other Pertinent EIA Interfaces

Appendix A contains the address of the Electronics Industries Association and other organizations. For additional detail, the reader should obtain the relevant EIA standards. In addition, the following EIA documents are quite useful for the person tasked with installing and maintaining physical level systems (several of these recommendations are described in this book):

EIA-422-A:	Electrical Characteristics of Balanced Voltage Digital Interface Circuits
EIA-423-A:	Electrical Characteristics of Unbalanced Voltage Digital Interface Circuits
EIA-449 and EIA-449-1:	General Purpose 37-Position and 9-Position Interface for Data Terminal Equipment and Data Circuit-Terminating Equipment Employing Serial Binary Data Interchange
EIA-496:	Interface between Data Circuit-Terminating Equipment (DCE) and the Public Switched Telephone Network (PSTN)
EIA-366-A:	Interface between Data Terminal Equipment and Automatic Calling Equipment for Data Communications
EIA-232-D:	Interface between Data Terminal Equipment and Data Circuit-Terminating Equipment Employing Serial Binary Data Interchange
EIA-491:	Interface between a Numerical Control Unit and Peripheral Equipment Employing Asynchronous Data Interchange over Circuits Having EIA-423-A Characteristics
EIA-334-A:	Signal Quality at Interface between Data Processing Terminal Equipment and Synchronous Data Communications Equipment for Serial Data Transmission
EIA-339-A-1:	Application of Signal Quality Requirements to EIA-449
EIA-485:	Standard for Electrical Characteristics of Generators and Receivers for Use in Balanced Digital Multipoint Systems
EIA-363:	Standard for Specifying Signal Quality for Transmitting and Receiving Data Processing Terminal Equipments Using Serial Data Transmission at the Interface with Nonsynchronous Data Communications Equipment
EIA-410:	Standard for the Electrical Characteristics of Class A Closure Interchange Circuits
EIA-404-A and EIA-404-1	Standard for Start-Stop Signal Quality for Nonsynchronous Data Terminal Equipment
EIA-408:	Interface between Numerical Control Equipment and Data Terminal Equipment Employing Parallel Binary Data Interchange

PHYSICAL LEVEL INTERFACES AND PROTOCOLS

Section 5:
The V Series Modems

Section 5: The V Series Modems

This section is intended to provide a reference guide for readers who need knowledge on the specific types of "CCITT-specified" modems. Most of these modems use the "foundation" V specifications explained earlier. Each V series modem is described in relation to the material in Table 4. Unless otherwise noted, the V.24 circuit tables all use the following information for Note 1:

All essential interchange circuits and any others that are provided shall comply with the functional and operational requirements of recommendation V.24. All interchange circuits indicated by X shall be properly terminated in the data equipment and in the data circuit terminating equipment in accordance with the appropriate recommendation.

For more detail, refer to the CCITT Red Book: *Data Communications over the Telephone Network: Recommendation of the V Series; Volume VIII, Fascicle VIII.1.* Addresses are provided in Appendix A.

V.19: Modems for Parallel Data Transmission Using Telephone Signaling Frequencies

Frequencies on this type of modem are used to transmit the character sets in Table 25. This recommendation allows the push-button telephone to be used for sending data. For example, a user could key in a bank account number through a telephone by using the telephone push buttons.

V.20: Parallel Data Transmission Modems Standard for Use in the General Switched Telephone Network

The frequencies in Table 26 are recommended for systems where a large number of sending stations transmit to a central station. The table shows that one frequency from each group can be transmitted simultaneously.

Table 25: V.19 Frequency Pairs

	$B_1 = 1209$ Hz	$B_2 = 1336$ Hz	$B_3 = 1447$ Hz	$B_4 = 1633$ Hz
$A_1 = 697$ Hz	1	2	3	A
$A_2 = 770$ Hz	4	5	6	B
$A_3 = 852$ Hz	7	8	9	C
$A_4 = 941$ Hz	*	0	#	D

Table 26: V.20 Frequency Allocations and Designations

Channel / Group	1	2	3	4
A	920 Hz	1000 Hz	1080 Hz	1160 Hz
B	1320 Hz	1400 Hz	1480 Hz	1560 Hz
C	1720 Hz	1800 Hz	1880 Hz	1960 Hz

V.21: 300 Bit/s Duplex Modem Standardized for Use in the General Switched Telephone Network

The V.21 recommendation is used on slow-speed systems. Some vendors offer speeds of 50-300 bit/s. V.21 is offered by some vendors as a small inexpensive modem that fits under a standard telephone.

This recommendation uses frequency shift modulation. The modulation rate equals the bit rate. The mean frequency for channel 1 is 1080 Hz; for channel 2 it is 1750 Hz. Both synchronous or asynchronous procedures are allowed. The nominal characteristic frequencies are shown below. Each channel uses one of two frequencies to represent binary data:

Channel 1	Channel 2
$F_A = 1180$ Hz (0)	$F_A = 1850$ Hz (0)
$F_Z = 980$ Hz (1)	$F_Z = 1650$ Hz (1)

V.21 uses the V.24 circuits as described in Table 27.

Table 27: V.21 Interchange Circuits

Interchange Circuit		General Switched Telephone Network Including Terminals Equipped for Manual Calling, Manual Answering, Automatic Calling, Automatic Answering (Note 1)	Nonswitched Leased Telephone Circuit (Note 1)	
Number	Designation		Point-to-Point	Multi-Point
102	Signal Ground or Common Return	X	X	X
103	Transmitted Data	X	X	X
104	Received Data	X	X	X
105	Request to Send	–	X (Note 2)	X
106	Ready for Sending	X	X	X
107	Data Set Ready	X	X	X
108/1	Connect Data Set to Line	X (Note 3)	X	X
108/2	Data Terminal Ready	X (Note 3)	X (Note 4)	–
109	Data Channel Received Line Signal Detector	X	X	X
125	Calling Indicator	X	–	–
126	Select Transmit Frequency	–	–	X

Note 1—All essential interchange circuits and any others that are provided shall comply with the requirements of recommendation V.24. All interchange circuits indicated by X shall be properly terminated in the data equipment and in the data circuit-terminating equipment in accordance with the appropriate recommendation.

Note 2—Circuit 105 is not required when alternate voice/data service is used on nonswitched leased point-to-point circuits.

Note 3—This circuit shall be capable of operation as circuit 108/1 or circuit 108/2 depending on its use.

Note 4—In the leased point-to-point case, where alternate voice/data service is to be provided, circuit 108/2 may be used optionally.

V.22: 1200 Bit/s Duplex Modem Standardized for Use in the General Switched Telephone Network and on Point-to-Point, Two-Wire Leased Telephone-Type Circuits

The V.22 recommendation, which serves as the foundation for many 1200 bit/s modems, is similar to the Bell modem 212A and is used by some of the Hayes modems (Bell and Hayes modems are discussed in other sections).

With this modem, channels are separated by frequency division and each channel is phase shift modulated. A 600 baud signal carries two bits per baud (dibits) using the encoding scheme shown in Table 28. It uses the V.24 circuits as described in Table 29.

Several implementations of V.22 allow the data rate to be selected from the DCE front panel, and many vendors offer automatic standby switching. If a private line failure occurs (no activity on the V.24 circuit 103 (transmitted data) for a specified period), the outstation modem will automatically respond by switching incoming calls to a standby line.

The V.22 implementations typically use V.25 dial and answer and V.54 loop testing procedures.

Carrier frequencies are 1200 Hz for the low channel and 2400 Hz for the high channel. V.22 permits several options in mixing 1200/600/300 bit/s and synchronous/asynchronous transmission. It also supports several start/stop formats:

Alternative A

>   1200 bit/s synchronous
>   600 bit/s synchronous (optional)

Alternative B

>   1200 bit/s synchronous (as in alternative A)
>   600 bit/s synchronous (optional)
>   1200 bit/s start-stop
>   600 bit/s start-stop (optional)

Alternative C

>   1200 bit/s synchronous
>   600 bit/s synchronous (optional)
>   1200 bit/s start-stop (as in Alternative B)
>   600 bit/s start-stop (optional)

An asynchronous mode having the capability of handling 1200 bit/s start-stop and an alternative capability of 300 bit/s. The carrier frequencies are 1200 plus or minus 0.5 Hz for the low channel and 2400 plus or minus 0.5 Hz for the high channel.

V.22 bis: 2400 Bit/s Duplex Modem Using the Frequency Division Technique Standardized for Use on the General Switched Telephone Network and on Point-to-Point, Two-Wire Leased Telephone-Type Circuits

The V.22 bis recommendation is implemented in many modems. The personal

Table 28: V.22 Encoding

Dibit Values (1200 Bit/s)	Bit Values (600 Bit/s)	Phase Change (Modes i,ii,iii iv)	Phase Change (Mode v)
00	0	+90°	+270°
01	–	0°	+180°
11	1	+270°	+90°
10	–	+180°	0°

Table 29: V.22 Interchange Circuits

	Interchange Circuit (Note 1)		Notes
No.		Description	
102		Signal Ground or Common Return	
103		Transmitted Data	
104		Received Data	
105		Request to Send	2
106		Ready for Sending	
107		Data Set Ready	
108/1		Connect Data Set to Line	3
108/2		Data Terminal Ready	3
109		Data Channel Received Line Signal Detector	
111		Data Signalling Rate Selector (DTE Source)	4
113		Transmitter Signal Element Timing (DTE Source)	5
114		Transmitter Signal Element Timing (DCE Source)	6
115		Receiver Signal Element Timing (DCE Source)	6
125		Calling Indicator	7
140		Loopback/Maintenance Test	
141		Local Loopback	
142		Test Indicator	

Note 1—All essential interchange circuits and any others that are provided shall comply with the requirements of recommendation V.24. All interchange circuits indicated by X shall be properly terminated in the data equipment and in the data circuit-terminating equipment in accordance with the appropriate recommendation.

Note 2—Certain automatic calling equipment emit a calling tone to the line by turning ON circuit 105 to the calling modem. The general switched telephone network (GSTN) constant carrier handshake is such that no calling tone will be emitted by the V.22 modem when used with this equipment.

Note 3—This circuit shall be capable of operation as circuit 108/1 or 108/2.

Note 4—This circuit is optional if only the 1200 bit/s speed is provided in the modem. If the 600 bit/s speed is also provided, this circuit is essential.

Note 5—When the modem is not operating in a synchronous mode any signals on this circuit shall be disregarded.

Note 6—When the modem is not operating in a synchronous mode, this circuit shall be clamped to the OFF condition and the data terminal equipment may not terminate the circuit.

Note 7—This circuit is for use with the general switched telephone network only.

BLACK

computer (PC) industry uses V.22 bis for medium speed, dial-up systems. The newer Hayes modems offer V.22 bis as one option.

Most V.22 bis products include unattended switching to a standby line, automatic dial and answer, adaptive equalization, and extensive diagnostics. Be aware that some vendors use different originate and answer frequencies. For example, the V.22 bis recommendation uses an answer tone of 2100 Hz, and many European DCEs do not accept the Bell tone of 2225 Hz. Therefore, a handshake with those two types of modems may not occur successfully. The vendors' specifications sheet should be checked carefully.

These modems separate the channels by frequency division. Then each channel is quadrature amplitude modulated (QAM). A 600 baud signal carries four bits per baud (quadbits) with the coding scheme in Table 30. The constellation pattern is depicted in Figure 35, and the V.24 circuits are described in Table 31.

Carrier frequencies are 1200 Hz for the the low channel and 2400 Hz for the high channel. Both synchronous and start/stop transmissions are supported.

The modem can be configured for the following modes of operation:

- mode 1: 2400 bit/s plus or minus 0.01 % synchronous
- mode 2: 2400 bit/s start-stop 8, 9, 10, or 11 bits per character
- mode 3: 1200 bit/s + 0.01% synchronous
- mode 4: 1200 bit/s start-stop 8, 9, 10, or 11 bits per character

Also, the basic signaling rates supported by V.22 bis are

- 303.0 characters per second for 8-bit characters
- 269.3 characters per second for 9-bit characters
- 242.4 characters per second for 10-bit characters
- 220.4 characters per second for 11-bit characters

When the character rate is

- from 300.0 to 303.0 characters per second for 8-bit characters
- from 266.7 to 269.3 characters per second for 9-bit characters
- from 240.0 to 242.2 characters per second for 10-bit characters
- from 218.2 to 220.4 characters per second for 11-bit characters

When the character rate provided by the DTE on circuit 103 is less than

- 300.0 characters per second for 8-bit characters
- 266.7 characters per second for 9-bit characters
- 240.0 characters per second for 10-bit characters
- 218.2 characters per second for 11-bit characters

The calling modem receives signals on the high channel and transmits signals on the low channel. The answering modem transmits signals on the high channel and receives signals on the low channel. Both modems must adhere to several timing conventions in the synchronization process before data can be exchanged.

Table 30: V.22 bis Encoding

First Two Bits in Quadbit (2400 Bit/s) or Dibit Values (1200 Bit/s)	Phase Quadrant Change	
	From – To	
00	1 2 2 3 3 4 4 1	90°
01	1 1 2 2 3 3 4 4	0°
11	1 4 2 1 3 2 4 3	270°
10	1 3 2 4 3 1 4 2	180°

V.23: 600/1200 Baud Modem Standardized for Use in the General Switched Telephone Network

The V.23 modem has not been implemented extensively in North America but is supported by many European vendors and telephone administrations. This modem frequency modulates channels in the following manner:

	F0	FZ	FA
		(symbol 1, MARK)	(symbol 0, SPACE)
Mode 1: up to 600 baud	1500 Hz	1300 Hz	1700 Hz
Mode 2: up to 1200 baud	1700 Hz	1300 Hz	2100 Hz

V.23 is often implemented as a dual-rate modem with a 600/1200 bit/s half duplex set up. Several vendors provide the backward channel option of 75 bit/s transmit and 600/1200 bit/s receive. The majority of V.23 modems also use the V.25 dial and answer specification and selected test loops of V.54.

V.23 permits both synchronous or asynchronous modes of operation although many vendors offer only the asynchronous version. V.23 uses the V.24 circuits as described in Table 32 for a switched line and Table 33 for a nonswitched leased line.

V.26: 2400 Bit/s Modem Standardized for Use on Four-Wire Leased Telephone-Type Lines

The V.26 recommendation is not used very much today. Many vendors now offer V.26 bis or V.26 ter.

This type of modem uses four-phase modulation with a synchronous mode of operation and may also include a backward channel of up to 75 baud.

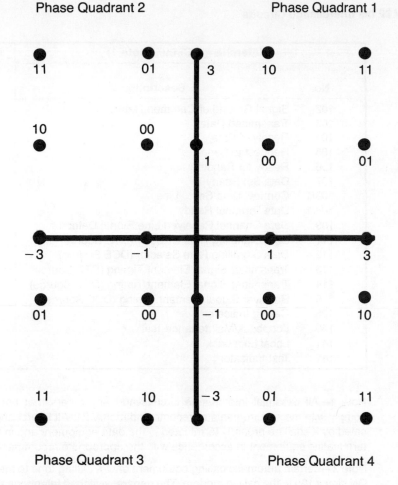

Figure 35: V.22 bis Constellation Pattern

Figure 35: V.22 bis Constellation Pattern

The recommendation operates with a carrier frequency at 1800 Hz and with a modulation rate of 1200 baud. Data are encoded into pairs of bits (dibits); each dibit is encoded as a phase change relative to the immediately preceding signal. Two alternatives exist on how the coding is performed. These alternatives are shown in Table 34, whereas V.24 circuits are used as described in Table 35.

V.26 bis: 2400/1200 Bit/s Modem Standardized for Use in the General Switched Telephone Network

V.26 bis is implemented by some vendors on dial-up lines. Its use in Europe is more extensive than in North America.

This recommended standard uses carrier frequency, modulation, and coding according to V.26, alternative B. It also includes provisions for a reduced rate at 1200 bit/s, as well as a backward channel of up to 75 baud.

The recommendation operates with a carrier frequency of 1800 Hz. Refer to V.26 for information on the coding and modulation pattern. For operation at 1200 bit/s, the

Table 31: V.22 bis Interchange Circuits

Interchange Circuit (Note 1)		Notes
No.	**Description**	
102	Signal Ground or Common Return	
103	Transmitted Data	
104	Received Data	
105	Request to Send	2
106	Ready for Sending	
107	Data Set Ready	
108/1	Connect Data Set to Line	3
108/2	Data Terminal Ready	3
109	Data Channel Received Line Signal Detector	
111	Data Signaling Rate Selector (DTE Source)	4
112	Data Signaling Rate Selector (DCE Source)	
113	Transmitter Signal Element Timing (DTE Source)	5
114	Transmitter Signal Element Timing (DCE Source)	6
115	Receiver Signal Element Timing (DCE Source)	6
125	Calling Indicator	7
140	Loopback/Maintenance Test	
141	Local Loopback	
142	Test Indicator	

Note 1—All essential interchange circuits and any others that are provided shall comply with the requirements of recommendation V.24. All interchange circuits indicated by X shall be properly terminated in the data equipment and in the data circuit-terminating equipment in accordance with the appropriate recommendation.

Note 2—Certain automatic calling equipment emit a calling tone to the line by turning ON circuit 105 to the calling modem. The general switched telephone network (GSTN) constant carrier handshake is such that no calling tone will be emitted by the V.22 bis modem when used with this equipment.

Note 3—This circuit shall be capable of operation as circuit 108/1 or 108/2.

Note 4—This circuit is optional.

Note 5—When the modem is not operating in a synchronous mode at the interface, any signals on this circuit shall be disregarded and the data terminal equipment may not have a generator connected.

Note 6—When the modem is not operating in a synchronous mode at the interface, this circuit shall be clamped to the OFF condition and the data terminal equipment may not terminate the circuit.

Note 7—This circuit is for use with the general switched telephone network only.

Table 32: V.23 Interchange Circuits for Dial-Up Lines

No.	Designation	Forward (Data) Channel One Way System (Note 1)				Forward (Data) Channel Either Way System (Note 1)	
		Without Backward Channel		With Backward Channel		Without Backward Channel	With Backward Channel
		Transmit End	Receive End	Transmit End	Receive End		
102	Signal Ground or Common Return	X	X	X	X	X	X
103	Transmitted Data	X	–	X	–	X	
104	Received Data	–	X	–	X	X	X
105	Request to Send	–	–	–	–	X	X
106	Ready for Sending	X	–	X	–	X	X
107	Data Set Ready	X	X	X	X	X	X
108/1 or 108/2 (Note 2)	Connect Data Set to Line Data Terminal Ready	X	X	X	X	X	X
109	Data Channel Received Line Signal Detector	–	X	–	X	X	X
111	Data Signaling Rate Selector (DTE)	X	X	X	X	X	X
114 (Note 3)	Transmitter Signal Element Timing (DCE)	X	–	X	–	X	X
115 (Note 3)	Receiver Signal Element Timing (DCE)	–	X	–	X	X	X
118	Transmitted Backward Channel Data	–	–	–	X	–	X
119	Received Backward Channel Data	–	–	X	–	–	X
120	Transmit Backward Channel Line Signal	–	–	–	–	–	X
121	Backward Channel Ready	–	–	–	X	–	X
122	Backward Channel Received Line Signal Detector	–	–	X	–	–	X
125	Calling Indicator	X	X	X	X	X	X

Note 1—All essential interchange circuits and any others that are provided shall comply with the requirements of recommendation V.24. All interchange circuits indicated by X shall be properly terminated in the data equipment and in the data circuit-terminating equipment in accordance with the appropriate recommendation.

Note 2—This circuit shall be capable of operation as circuit 108/1 or circuit 108/2.

Note 3—These circuits are required when the clock is in the modem.

Table 33: V.23 Interchange Circuits for Leased Lines

No.	Designation	Forward (Data) Channel One Way System (Note 1)				Forward (Data) Channel Either Way System (Note 1)	
		Without Backward Channel		With Backward Channel		Without Backward Channel	With Backward Channel
		Transmit End	Receive End	Transmit End	Receive End		
102	Signal Ground or Common Return	X	X	X	X	X	X
103	Transmitted Data	X	–	X	–	X	X
104	Received Data	–	X	–	X	X	X
105	Request to Send	X	–	X	–	X	X
106	Ready for Sending	X	–	X	–	X	X
107	Data Set Ready	X	X	X	X	X	X
108/1	Connect Data Set to Line	X	X	X	X	X	X
109	Data Channel Received Line Signal Detector	–	X	–	X	X	X
111	Data Signaling Rate Selector (DTE)	X	X	X	X	X	X
114 (Note 2)	Transmitter Signal Element Timing (DCE)	X	–	X	–	X	X
115 (Note 2)	Receiver Signal Element Timing (DCE)	–	X	–	X	X	X
118	Transmitted Backward Channel Data	–	–	–	X	–	X
119	Received Backward Channel Data	–	–	X	–	–	X
120	Transmit Backward Channel Line Signal	–	–	–	X	–	X
121	Backward Channel Ready	–	–	–	X	–	X
122	Backward Channel Received Line Signal Detector	–	–	X	–	–	X

Note 1—All essential interchange circuits and any others that are provided shall comply with the requirements of recommendation V.24. All interchange circuits indicated by X shall be properly terminated in the data equipment and in the data circuit-terminating equipment in accordance with the appropriate recommendation.

Note 2—These circuits are required when the clock is in the modem.

Table 34: V.26 Encoding

Dibit	Phase Change (Note 1)	
	Alternative A	Alternative B
00	0°	+45°
01	+90°	+135°
11	+180°	+225°
10	+270°	+315°

Note 1—The phase change is the phase shift in the transition region from the center of one signaling element to the center of the following signaling element.

Table 35: V.26 Interchange Circuits

Interchange Circuit		Forward (Data) Channel Half Duplex or Full Duplex (Note 1)	
No.	Designation	Without Backward Channel	With Backward Channel
102	Signal Ground or Common Return	X	X
103	Transmitted Data	X	X
104	Received Data	X	X
105	Request to Send	X	X
106	Ready for Sending	X	X
107	Data Set Ready	X	X
108/1	Connect Data Set to Line	X	X
109	Data Channel Received Line Signal Detector	X	X
113	Transmitter Signal Element Timing (DTE Source)	X	X
114	Transmitter Signal Element Timing (DCE Source)	X	X
115	Receiver Signal Element Timing (DCE Source)	X	X
118	Transmitted Backward Channel Data	–	X
119	Received Backward Channel Data	–	X
120	Transmit Backward Channel Line Signal	–	X
121	Backward Channel Ready	–	X
122	Backward Channel Received Line Signal Detector	–	X

Note 1—All essential interchange circuits and any others that are provided shall comply with the requirements of recommendation V.24. All interchange circuits indicated by X shall be properly terminated in the data equipment and in the data circuit-terminating equipment in accordance with the appropriate recommendation.

modem uses a two phase shift with 0 for 90° and 1 for 270°. In this option, the modulation rate is still 1200 baud. The V.24 circuits are used as described in Table 36.

Table 36: V.26 bis Interchange Circuits

Interchange Circuit		Forward (Data) Channel One Way System (Note 1)				Forward (Data) Channel Either Way System (Note 1)	
		Without Backward Channel		With Backward Channel		Without Backward Channel	With Backward Channel
No.	Designation	Transmit End	Receive End	Transmit End	Receive End		
102	Signal Ground or Common Return	X	X	X	X	X	X
103	Transmitted Data	X	–	X	–	X	X
104	Received Data	–	X	–	X	X	X
105	Request to Send	X	–	X	–	X	X
106	Ready for Sending	X	–	X	–	X	X
107	Data Set Ready	X	X	X	X	X	X
108/1 or 108/2 Note 2	Connect Data Set to Line Data Terminal Ready	X	X	X	X	X	X
109	Data Channel Received Line Signal Detector	–	X	–	X	X	X
111	Data Signaling Rate Selector (DTE Source)	X	X	X	X	X	X
113	Transmitter Signal Element Timing (DTE Source)	X	–	X	–	X	X
114	Transmitter Signal Element Timing (DCE Source)	X	–	X	–	X	X
115	Receiver Signal Element Timing (DCE Source)	–	X	–	X	X	X
118	Transmitted Backward Channel Data				X		X
119	Received Backward Channel Data	–	–	X	–	–	X
120	Transmit Backward Channel Line Signal	–	–	–	–	–	X
121	Backward Channel Ready	–	–	–	X	–	X
122	Backward Channel Received Line Signal Detector	–	–	X	–	–	X
125	Calling Indicator	X	X	X	X	X	X

Note 1—All essential interchange circuits and any others that are provided shall comply with requirements of recommendation V.24. All interchange circuits indicated by X shall be properly terminated in the data equipment and in the data circuit-terminating equipment in accordance with the appropriate recommendation.

Note 2—This circuit shall be capable of operation as circuit 108/1 or circuit 108/2.

BLACK

V.26 ter: 2400 Bit/s Duplex Modem Using the Echo Cancelation Technique Standardized for Use on the General Switched Telephone Network and on Point-to-Point, Two-Wire Leased Telephone-Type Circuits

V.26 ter is a relative newcomer to the industry and has not yet seen extensive use. The principal characteristics of this modem are

1. Duplex (FDX) mode of operation is possible on switched and point-to-point leased circuits

2. Half duplex (HDX) mode of operation is optional on switched and point-to-point leased circuits

3. Channel separation is done by echo cancelation

4. Differential phase-shift modulation is performed for each channel with synchronous line transmission at 1200 baud

5. Inclusion of a scrambler

6. Inclusion of an equalizer

7. Inclusion of test facilities

8. Operation with data terminal equipment (DTE) is available in the following modes: 2400 bit/s synchronous, 1200 bit/s synchronous (fall-back rate), 2400 bit/s start stop (optional), and 1200 bit/s start stop (optional) (fall-back rate)

9. Inclusion of an operating sequence intended to allow interworking with two-wire duplex 4800 bit/s modem

The carrier frequency operates at 1800 Hz, power levels conform to V.2, and the signaling rate is 1200 baud with the 2400 and 1200 bit/s rate coded as shown in Tables 37 and 38.

Table 37: V.26 ter Encoding at 2400 Bit/s

Dibit Values	Phase Change (Note 1)
00	0°
01	90°
11	180°
10	270°

Note 1—The phase change is the phase shift in the transition region from the center of one signaling element to the center of the next signaling element.

Table 38: V.26 ter Encoding at 1200 Bit/s

Bit Values	Phase Change (Note 1)
0	0°
1	180°

Note 1—The phase change is the phase shift in the transition region from the center of one signaling element to the center of the next signaling element.

Synchronization signals are provided by two segments. The first segment is comprised of continuous phase reversals for 32 symbol intervals. The second segment is derived by scrambling the data stream and by using phase changes (see Table 39). The V.24 circuits are used as described in Table 40.

Table 39: V.26 ter Synchronizing Signal Patterns

Data Signaling Rate (Bit/s)	Scrambler	Segment 2 Phase Changes (Degrees)
2400	GPC	0,180,180,180,180,0,0,0,0,180,180,270,90,180 0,0,90,180,0
2400	GPA	0,180,180,180,180,0,0,0,0,180,180,270,90,180 0,180,180,270,0
1200	GPC	0,0,180,180,180,180,180,180,180,180,0,0,0,0, 0,0,0,0,180,180,180,180,180,0,0,180,180,180 0,0,0,0,0,180,180,180
1200	GPA	0,0,180,180,180,180,180,180,180,180,0,0,0,0, 0,0,0,0,180,180,180,180,180,0,0,180,180,180, 0,0,180,180,180,0,180,0

V.27: 4800 Bit/s Modem with Manual Equalizer Standardized for Use on Leased Telephone-Type Circuits

Most of the V.27 implementations now use the V.27 bis or V.27 ter recommendations. The principal characteristics of this modem are:

1. It is capable of operating in a full duplex (FDX) mode or half duplex (HDX) mode.

2. It uses differential 8-phase modulation with synchronous mode of operation.

3. It can provide a backward (supervisory) channel at modulation rates up to 75 baud in each direction of transmission, the use of these channels being optional.

4. It includes a manually adjustable equalizer.

Modulation occurs with an 1800 Hz carrier, the power levels conform to V.2, the data stream is divided into three consecutive bits (tribits). Each tribit is encoded as a phase change relative to the phase of the immediately preceding signal elements. Modulation rate is 1600 baud. The tribit values are coded into the phase changes described in Table 41. The V.24 circuits are used as described in Table 42.

V.27 bis: 4800/2400 Bit/s Modem with Automatic Equalizer Standardized for Use on Leased Telephone-Type Circuits

The characteristics of V.27 bis are very similar to V.27, except this recommendation uses different equalization techniques and provides for 4800 or 2400 bit/s speeds. This use is more prevalent in Europe than in North America. Its principal characteristics are:

1. It operates in a full duplex or half duplex mode over four-wire leased circuits or in a half duplex over two-wire leased circuits.

2. At 4800 bit/s operation, modulation is eight-phase differentially encoded as described in recommendation V.27.

3. At a reduced rate capability at 2400 bit/s, it uses four-phase differentially encoded modulation as described in recommendation V.26, alternative A.

4. It may include a backward (supervisory) channel at modulation rates up to 75 bauds in each direction of transmission.

5. It includes an automatic adaptive equalizer.

Table 40: V.26 ter Interchange Circuits

	Interchange Circuit (Note 1)	
No.	Designaton	Notes
102	Signal Ground or Common Return	
103	Transmitted Data	
104	Received Data	
105	Request to Send	
106	Ready for Sending	
107	Data Set Ready	
108/1 or	Connect Data Set to Line	2
108/2	Data Terminal Ready	2
109	Data Channel Received Line Signal Detector	
111	Data Signaling Rate Selector (DTE Source)	
112	Data Signaling Rate Selector (DCE Source)	3
113	Transmitter Signal Element Timing (DTE Source)	4
114	Transmitter Signal Element Timing (DCE Source)	5
115	Receiver Signal Element Timing (DCE Source)	5
125	Calling Indicator	6
140	Loopback/Maintenance Test	
141	Local Loopback	
142	Test Indicator	

Note 1—All essential interchange circuits and any others that are provided shall comply with the requirements of recommendation V.24. All Interchange circuits indicated by X shall be properly teminated in the data equipment and in the data circuit-terminating equipment in accordance with the appropriate recommendation.

Note 2—This circuit shall be capable of operation as circuit 108/1 or circuit 108/2.

Note 3—This circuit is optional.

Note 4—When the modem is not operating in a synchronous mode at the interface, any signals on circuit 113 shall be disregarded and the DTE may not have a generator connected.

Note 5—When the modem is not operating in a synchronous mode, this circuit shall be clamped to the OFF condition and the DTE may not terminate the circuit.

Note 6—This circuit is for use with the general switched telephone network only.

Table 41: V.27 Encoding

Tribit Values			Phase Change (Note 1)
0	0	1	0°
0	0	0	45°
0	1	0	90°
0	1	1	135°
1	1	1	180°
1	1	0	225°
1	0	0	270°
1	0	1	315°

Note 1—The phase change is the shift in the transition region from the center of one signaling element to the center of the next signaling element.

Most vendors include features such as adaptive equalization, automatic retraining, scrambling, and extensive tests and diagnostics.

Modulation occurs with an 1800 Hz carrier; the power levels conform to V.2, modulation at 4800 bit/s with 1600 baud and 2400 bit/s with 1200 baud. The encoding schemes for these two techniques are described in Tables 43 and 44. The V.24 circuits are used as shown in Table 45.

V.27 ter: 4800/2400 Bit/s Modem Standardized for Use in the General Switched Telephone Network

The majority of European PTTs (postal and telegraph) administrations support either V.27 bis or V.27 ter. These interfaces are not used much in North America. The principal characteristics of this modem are:

1. It uses data signaling rate of 4800 bit/s with eight phase differentially encoded modulation as described in recommendation V.27.

2. It operates at a reduced rate capability at 2400 bit/s with four phase differentially encoded modulation as described in recommendation V.26, alternative A.

3. It may include a backward channel at modulation rates up to 75 baud.

4. It includes an automatic adaptive equalizer.

Modulation occurs at 1800 Hz power levels conform to V.2, modulation patterns and codes are identical to the V.27 recommendation. The reduced rate uses V.26, alternative A. Refer to V.27 and V.26 for these descriptions. The V.24 circuits are used as shown in Table 46.

V.29: 9600 Bit/s Modem Standardized for Use on Point-to-Point, Four-Wire Leased Telephone-Type Circuits

V.29 is a widely used recommendation, which is found in many North American and European products. The Bell V.29 modem is based on CCITT V.29.

This high-speed modem operates in duplex (FDX) or half duplex (HDX) mode, using amplitude and phase modulation with synchronous transmission. It also provides for fall back data rates of 7200 and 4800 bit/s. The carrier frequency is 1700 Hz.

This recommendation uses a modulation rate of 2400 baud and provides for three types of bit encoding for the three available speeds. At 9600 bit/s the bits are divided into groups of four (quadbits). The first bit is used to represent amplitude and the other three bits provide for eight possible phase shifts as shown in Table 47.

Table 42: V.27 Interchange Circuits

Interchange Circuit		Forward (Data) Channel Half Duplex or Full Duplex (Note 1)	
No.	Designation	Without Backward Channel	With Backward Channel
102	Signal Ground or Common Return	X	X
103	Transmitted Data	X	X
104	Received Data	X	X
105 (Note 2)	Request to Send	X	X
106	Ready for Sending	X	X
107	Data Set Ready	X	X
108/1	Connect Data Set to Line	X	X
109	Data Channel Received Line Signal Detector	X	X
113	Transmitter Signal Element Timing (DTE Source)	X	X
114	Transmitter Signal Element Timing (DCE Source)	X	X
115	Receiver Signal Element Timing (DCE Source)	X	X
118	Transmitted Backward Channel Data		X
119	Received Backward Channel Data		X
120	Transmit Backward Channel Line Signal		X
121	Backward Channel Ready		X
122	Backward Channel Received Line Signal Detector		

Note 1—All essential interchange circuits and any others that are provided shall comply with the requirements of recommendation V.24. All interchange circuits indicated by an X shall be properly terminated in the data equipment and in the data circuit-terminating equipment in accordance with the appropriate recommendation.

Note 2— Not essential for four-wire full duplex continuous carrier operation.

Table 43: V.27 bis Encoding at 4800 Bit/s

Tribit Values			Phase Change (Note 1)
0	0	1	0°
0	0	0	45°
0	1	0	90°
0	1	1	135°
1	1	1	180°
1	1	0	225°
1	0	0	270°
1	0	1	315°

Note 1—The phase change is the shift in the transition region from the center of one signaling element to the center of the next signaling element.

Table 44: V.27 bis Encoding at 2400 Bit/s

Dibit Values	Phase Change (Note 1)
00	0°
01	90°
11	180°
10	270°

Note 1—The phase change is the shift in the transition region from the center of one signaling element to the center of the next signaling element.

At a fall back rate of 7200 bit/s, the same phase shifts are used, but the "amplitude bit" is not used. At a fall back rate of 4800 bit/s, the phase changes are identical to V.26 (alternative A) (0°, 90°, 180°, 270° shifts). The V.24 circuits are used as described in Table 48.

V.32: A Family of Two-Wire Duplex Modems Operating at Data Signaling Rates of up to 9600 Bit/s for Use on the General Switched Telephone Network and on Leased Telephone-Type Circuits

Those modems are relatively new to the industry and have created considerable interest because they can operate at rates up to 9600 bit/s at full duplex on a dial-up, two-wire telephone network. Several manufacturers offer a V.32 product. The principal characteristics of the modem are

1. It provides duplex mode of operation on switched and two-wire, point-to-point leased circuits;

2. Channel separation is by echo cancelation techniques;

3. Quadrature amplitude modulation (QAM) is used for each channel with synchronous line transmission at 2400 bauds;

4. Any combination of the following data signaling rates may be implemented in the modems: 9600 bit/s synchronous, 4800 bit/s synchronous, and 2400 bit/s synchronous (for further study);

5. At 9600 bit/s, two alternative modulation schemes, one using 16 carrier states and one using trellis coding with 32 carrier states, are provided for in this recommendation. However, modems providing the 9600 bit/s data signaling rate shall be capable of interworking using the 16-state alternative;

6. Exchange of rate sequences during start-up to establish the data rate, coding, and any other special facilities;

7. Asynchronous mode of operation is for further study (see note 2).

Table 45: V.27 bis Interchange Circuits

Interchange Circuit		Forward (Data) Channel Half Duplex or Full Duplex (Note 1)	
No.	Designation	Without Backward Channel	With Backward Channel
102	Signal Ground or Common Return	X	X
103	Transmitted Data	X	X
104	Received Data	X	X
105	Request to Send	X	X
106	Ready for Sending	X	X
107	Data Set Ready	X	X
108/1	Connect Data Set to Line	X	X
109	Data Channel Received Line Signal Detector	X	X
111	Data Signal Rate Selector (DTE Source)	X	X
113	Transmitter Signal Element Timing (DTE Source)	X	X
114	Transmitter Signal Element Timing (DCE Source)	X	X
115	Receiver Signal Element Timing (DCE Source)	X	X
118	Transmitted Backward Channel Data		X
119	Received Backward Channel Data		X
120	Transmit Backward Channel Line Signal		X
121	Backward Channel Ready		X
122	Backward Channel Received Line Signal Detector		X

Note 1—All essential interchange circuits and any others that are provided shall comply with the requirements of recommendation V.24. All interchange circuits indicated by X shall be properly terminated in the data equipment and in the data circuit-terminating equipment in accordance with the appropriate recommendation.

Table 46: V.27 ter Interchange Circuits

Interchange Circuit		Forward (Data) Channel One Way System (Note 1)				Forward (Data) Channel Either Way System (Note 1)	
No.	Designation	Without Backward Channel		With Backward Channel		Without Backward Channel	With Backward Channel
		Transmit End	Receive End	Transmit End	Receive End		
102	Signal Ground or Common Return	X	X	X	X	X	X
103	Transmitted Data	X		X		X	X
104	Received Data		X		X	X	X
105	Request to Send	X		X		X	X
106	Ready for Sending	X		X		X	X
107	Data Set Ready	X	X	X	X	X	X
108/1 or 108/2 (Note 2)	Connect Data Set to Line / Data Terminal Ready	X	X	X	X	X	X
109	Data Channel Received Line Signal Detector		X		X	X	X
111	Data Signaling Rate Selector (DTE Source)	X	X	X	X	X	X
113	Transmitter Signal Element Timing (DTE Source)	X		X		X	X
114	Transmitter Signal Element Timing (DCE Source)	X		X		X	X
115	Receiver Signal Element Timing (DCE Source)		X		X	X	X
118	Transmitted Backward Channel Data				X		X
119	Received Backward Channel Data			X			X
120	Transmit Backward Channel Line Signal						X
121	Backward Channel Ready				X		X
122	Backward Channel Received Line Signal Detector			X		-	X
125	Calling Indicator	X	X	X	X	X	X

Note 1—All essential interchange circuits and any others that are provided shall comply with the requirements of recommendation V.24. All interchange circuits indicated by X shall be properly terminated in the data equipment and in the data circuit-terminating equipment in accordance with the appropriate recommendation.

Note 2—This circuit shall be capable of operation as circuit 108/1 or circuit 108/2.

Table 47: V.29 Encoding

Q2	Q3	Q4	Phase Change (Note 1)
0	0	1	0°
0	0	0	45°
0	1	0	90°
0	1	1	135°
1	1	1	180°
1	1	0	225°
1	0	0	270°
1	0	1	315°

Note 1—The phase change is the phase shift in the transition region from the center of one signaling element to the center of the next signaling element.

Table 48: V.29 Interchange Circuits

Interchange Circuit (Note 1)	
No.	**Designation**
102	Signal Ground or Common Return
103	Transmitted Data
104	Received Data
105 (Note 2)	Request to Send
106	Ready for Sending
107	Data Set Ready
109	Data Channel Received Line Signal Detect
111 (Note 3)	Data Signaling Rate Selector (DTE Source)
113	Transmitter Signal Element Timing (DTE Source)
114	Transmitter Signal Element Timing (DCE Source)
115	Receiver Signal Element Timing (DCE Source)
140 (Note 4)	Loopback/Maintenance Test
141 (Note 4)	Local Loopback
142	Test Indicator

Note 1—All essential interchange circuits and any others that are provided shall comply with the requirements of recommendation V.24. All interchange circuits indicated by X shall be properly terminated in the data equipment and in the data circuit-terminating equipment in accordance with the appropriate recommendation.

Note 2—Not essential for continuous carrier operation.

Note 3—A manual selector shall be implemented that determines the two data signaling rates selected by circuit 111. The manual selector positions shall be designated 9600/7200, 9600/4800 and 7200/4800. The ON condition of circuit 111 selects the higher data signaling rate, and the OFF condition of circuit 111 selects the lower data signaling rate.

Note 4—Interchange circuits 140 and 141 are optional.

Note 1—On certain international switched connections, it may be necessary to use a greater degree of equalization within the modem than would be required for use on most national general switched telephone network connections.

Note 2—Protocol of asynchronous to synchronous conversion will be derived from one already used in recommendations V.22, V.22 bis, and V.26 ter.

The frequency carrier operates at 1800 Hz, transmitted power levels conform to V.2, and the modulation rate is 2400 baud. V.32 provides two alternative coding schemes for 9600 bit/s and one scheme for 4800 bit/s. The 9600 bit/s alternative uses either the nonredundant coding scheme or trellis coding.

Nonredundant coding divides the data stream into four consecutive data bits (quadbits). The user data bits are designated $Q1_n$, $Q2_n$, $Q3_n$, and $Q4_n$ respectively. The first two bits in time $Q1_n$ and $Q2_n$ are coded into output bit values $Y1_n$ and $Y2_n$ and used with $Q3_n$ and $Q4_n$ according to Table 49. Notice the values of $Y1_n$ and $Y2_n$ are dependent on $Q1_n$ and $Q2_n$ and the previous output values of $Y1_n$ and $Y2_n$. Also note that the encoding table (Table 49) also shows the encoding scheme for the 4800 bit/s rate. However, with this speed, the $Y1_n$ and $Y2_n$ bits only are used to represent any combination of the input stream of $Q1_n$ and $Q2_n$. That is, the 4800 bit/s scheme uses dibit encoding. The nonredundant modulation constellation is depicted in Figure 36. For 9600 bit/s, the 16 possible states are shown. For the 4800 bit/s rate, the constellation pattern is labeled subsets A, B, C, and D to depict the output bits $Y1_n$ and $Y2_n$:

$$00 = A$$
$$01 = B$$
$$11 = C$$
$$10 = D$$

Table 49: V.32 Encoding for 4800 and 9600 Bit/s

Inputs		Previous Outputs		Phase Quadrant Change	Outputs		Signal State for 4800 Bit/s
$Q1_n$	$Q2_n$	$Y1_{n-1}$	$Y2_{n-1}$		$Y1_n$	$Y2_n$	
0	0	0	0	+ 90°	0	1	B
0	0	0	1		1	1	C
0	0	1	0		0	0	A
0	0	1	1		1	0	D
0	1	0	0	0°	0	0	A
0	1	0	1		0	1	B
0	1	1	0		1	0	D
0	1	1	1		1	1	C
1	0	0	0	+ 180°	1	1	C
1	0	0	1		1	0	D
1	0	1	0		0	1	B
1	0	1	1		0	0	A
1	1	0	0	+ 270°	1	0	D
1	1	0	1		0	0	A
1	1	1	0		1	1	C
1	1	1	1		0	1	B

The concepts of trellis coded modulation (TCM) are explained in Section 1; it may be usful to review the section titled "Trellis Coded Modulation" before reading the next section.

The V.32 TCM modem creates an additional bit for every four bits. As was previously discussed, the data bits are encoded based on previous user data input.

Trellis coding also uses the quadbit approach like that of nonredundant coding. However, bits $Q1_n$ and $Q2_n$ are first coded into bit values $Y1_n$ and $Y2_n$ according to Table 50. These two bits are then input into an encoder that produces a fifth bit, $Y0_n$. This redundant bit is based on various combinations of bits $Y1_n$ and $Y2_n$.

Since previous bit patterns (states) determine the values of current bit patterns (states), the receiving modem compares previous states to the current states. If the current state is logically inconsistent, the decoder logic searches for the nearest logically consistent state in the constellation pattern. This point is selected, and the modem decodes the point back to the (one hopes) original four bit data stream. In this manner, the V.32 TCM modem performs forward error correction.

The trellis coding modulation pattern is depicted in Figure 37. It has a 32-point signal structure since five bits are used to convey the information ($2^5 = 32$). The 4800 bit/s modem's A, B, C, and D states are coded in the same manner as in the nonredundant coding scheme. These states are also depicted in the constellation pattern in Figure 37.

Finally, Table 51 shows the two alternative signal-state mappings, and Table 52 shows the use of the V.24 circuits.

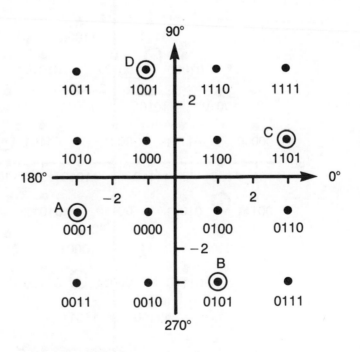

Figure 36: 16-Point V.32 Constellation Pattern

Table 50: V.32 Trellis Encoding

Inputs		Previous Outputs		Outputs	
Q1$_n$	Q2$_n$	Y1$_{n-1}$	Y2$_{n-1}$	Y1$_n$	Y2$_n$
0	0	0	0	0	0
0	0	0	1	0	1
0	0	1	0	1	0
0	0	1	1	1	1
0	1	0	0	0	1
0	1	0	1	0	0
0	1	1	0	1	1
0	1	1	1	1	0
1	0	0	0	1	0
1	0	0	1	1	1
1	0	1	0	0	1
1	0	1	1	0	0
1	1	0	0	1	1
1	1	0	1	1	0
1	1	1	0	0	0
1	1	1	1	0	1

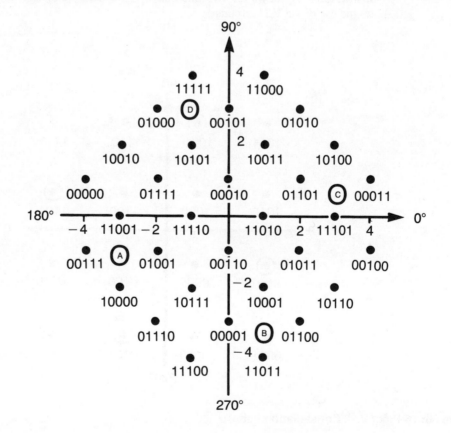

Figure 37: 32-Point V.32 Trellis Coded Modulation (TCM)

Table 51: Alternative Signal-State Mappings for 9600 Bit/s

Coded Inputs					Nonredundant Coding		Trellis Coding	
(Y0)	Y1	Y2	Q3	Q4	Re	Im	Re	Im
0	0	0	0	0	-1	-1	-4	1
	0	0	0	1	-3	-1	0	-3
	0	0	1	0	-1	-3	0	1
	0	0	1	1	-3	-3	4	1
	0	1	0	0	1	-1	4	-1
	0	1	0	1	1	-3	0	3
	0	1	1	0	3	-1	0	-1
	0	1	1	1	3	-3	-4	-1
	1	0	0	0	-1	1	-2	3
	1	0	0	1	-1	3	-2	-1
	1	0	1	0	-3	1	2	3
	1	0	1	1	-3	3	2	-1
	1	1	0	0	1	1	2	-3
	1	1	0	1	3	1	2	1
	1	1	1	0	1	3	-2	-3
	1	1	1	1	3	3	-2	1
1	0	0	0	0			-3	-2
	0	0	0	1			1	-2
	0	0	1	0			-3	2
	0	0	1	1			1	2
	0	1	0	0			3	2
	0	1	0	1			-1	2
	0	1	1	0			3	-2
	0	1	1	1			-1	-2
	1	0	0	0			1	4
	1	0	0	1			-3	0
	1	0	1	0			1	0
	1	0	1	1			1	-4
	1	1	0	0			-1	-4
	1	1	0	1			3	0
	1	1	1	0			-1	0
	1	1	1	1			-1	4

Wideband Modems

The CCITT also publishes a number of recommended standards on wideband modems. These devices operate with high-frequency carrier signals and achieve a high data rate.

V.35: Data Transmission at 48 Kbit/s Using 60-108 KHz Group Band Circuits

This modem operates at 48 Kbit/s. The data signal is translated to the 60-108 kHz

Table 52: V.32 Interchange Circuits

	Interchange Circuit (Note 1)	
No.	**Designation**	**Notes**
102	Signal Ground or Common Return	
103	Transmitted Data	
104	Received Data	
105	Request to Send	
106	Ready for Sending	
107	Data Set Ready	
108/1 or	Connect Data Set to Line	2
108/2	Data Terminal Ready	2
109	Data Channel Received Line Signal Detector	
111	Data Signaling Rate Selector (DTE Source)	3
112	Data Signaling Rate Selector (DCE Source)	3
113	Transmitter Signal Element Timing (DTE Source)	
114	Transmitter Signal Element Timing (DCE Source)	
115	Receiver Signal Element Timing (DCE Source)	
125	Calling Indicator	4
140	Loopback/Maintenance Test	
141	Local Loopback	
142	Test Indicator	

Note 1—All essential interchange circuits and any others that are provided shall comply with the requirements of recommendation V.24. All interchange circuits indicated by X shall be properly terminated in the data equipment and in the data circuit-terminating equipment in accordance with the appropriate recommendation.

Note 2—This circuit shall be capable of operation as circuit 108/1 or circuit 108/2 depending on its use. Operation of circuits 107 and 108/1 shall be in accordance with recommendation V.24.

Note 3—This circuit is not essential when only one data signaling rate is implemented in modem.

Note 4—This circuit is for use with the general switched telephone network only. V.32 also uses the V.25 recommendation for automatic dial and answer.

band as a sideband suppressed carrier AM signal. The carrier frequency operates at 100kHz. The interface cable is a balanced twisted pair.

It is commonly (and erroneously) assumed that V.35 is specified as a 56 Kbit/s interface. The actual CCITT specification stipulates 48 Kbit/s. However, many systems operate the V.35 at 56 Kbit/s with the DDS (digital data system) offering originally established by AT&T. DDS is explained later in this book.

It should also be noted that V.35 uses both the V.28 unbalanced interface as well as balanced pair (see Table 53). V.35 makes use of the V.24 circuits, this is also shown in Table 53.

Table 53: V.35 Interchange Circuits

No.	Function
102 (1)	Signal Ground or Common Return
103	Transmitted Data
104	Received Data
105 (1)	Request to Send
106 (1)	Ready for Sending
107 (1)	Data Set Ready
109 (1)	Data Channel Receive Line Signal Detector
114	Transmitter Signal Element Timing
115	Receiver Signal Element Timing

Note 1—Circuits conform to V.28. The other circuits are a balanced pair.

V.36 Modems for Synchronous Data Transmission Using 60-108 kHz Group Band Circuits

This modem type is used on leased circuits as well as several other kinds of facilities. V.36 actually stipulates six applications.

1. Transmission of data between customers on leased circuits;

2. Transmission of a multiplex aggregate bit stream for public data networks;

3. Extension of a PCM channel at 64 Kbit/s over analog facilities;

4. Transmission of a common channel signaling system for telephony and/or public data networks;

5. Extension of a single-channel-per-carrier (SCPC) circuit from a satellite earth station;

6. Transmission of a multiplex aggregate bit stream for telegraph and data signals.

Application 1: The recommended data signaling rate for international use is 48 Kbit/s. For certain national applications or with bilateral agreement, the following data signaling rates are applicable: 56, 64, and 72 Kbit/s.

Applications 2, 3, and 4: For these applications, the recommended data signaling rate is synchronous at 64 Kbit/s. For those synchronous networks requiring the end-to-end transmission of both the 8 and 64 kHz timing together with the data at 64 Kbit/s, a data signaling rate of 72 Kbit/s on the line is suggested.

Application 5: The recommended data signaling rate for international use is synchronous at 48 Kbit/s. For certain national applications or with bilateral agreement, the data signaling rate of 56 Kbit/s is applicable.

Application 6: The recommended data signaling rate is synchronous at 64 Kbit/s. V.36 uses the V.24 circuits as described in Table 54.

V.37 Synchronous Data Transmission at a Data Signaling Rate Higher than 72 Kbit/s Using 60–108 kHz Group Band Circuits

This modem is also used on leased circuits. The only group reference pilot fre-

Table 54: V.36 Interchange Circuits

No.	Interchange Circuit (Note 1)	Note
102	Signal Ground or Common Return	2
102a	DTE Common Return	3
102b	DCE Common Return	3
103	Transmitted Data	
104	Received Data	
105	Request to Send	
106	Ready for Sending	
107	Data Set Ready	
109	Data Channel Received Line Signal Detector	
113	Transmitter Signal Element Timing (DTE Source)	
114	Transmitter Signal Element Timing (DCE Source)	
115	Receiver Signal Element Timing (DCE Source)	
140	Loopback/Maintenance Test	2
141	Local Loopback	2
142	Test Indicator	2

Note 1—When the modem is installed at the repeater station, this interface should appear at the customer's premises without restrictions regarding the data signaling rate and the provision of the voice channel. The method to achieve this is subject to national regulations.

Note 2—Equipment may be in service that does not implement these circuits.

Note 3—Interchange circuits 102a and 102b are required where the electrical characteristics defined in recommendation V.10 are used.

quency which can be used in conjunction with this modem is 104.08 kHz. Its principal characteristics:

1. Transmission of any type of high-speed synchronous data in duplex constant carrier mode on four-wire (60–108 kHz) group band circuits;

2. Primary data signaling rates up to 144 Kbit/s;

3. Inclusion of an automatic adaptive equalizer;

4. Partial response pulse amplitude single sideband signaling and modulation;

5. Optional inclusion of an overhead-free multiplexer combining existing data signaling rates;

6. Optional voice channel.

V.37 uses the V.24 circuits as described in Table 55.

Table 55: V.37 Interchange Circuits

No.	Interchange Circuit (Note 1)	Note
102	Signal Ground or Common Return	2
102a	DTE Common Return	3
102b	DCE Common Return	3
103	Transmitted Data	
104	Received Data	
105	Request to Send	4
106	Ready for Sending	4,5
107	Data Set Ready	
109	Data Channel Received Line Signal Detector	
113	Transmitter Signal Element Timing (DTE Source)	4
114	Transmitter Signal Element Timing (DCE Source)	
115	Receiver Signal Element Timing (DCE Source)	
128	Receiver Signal Element Timing (DTE Source)	
140	Loopback/Maintenance Test	
141	Local Loopback	4
142	Test Indicator	6

Note 1—When the modem is installed at the repeater station, this interface should appear at the customer's premises without restrictions regarding the data signaling rate and the provision of the voice channel. The method to achieve this is subject to national regulations.

Note 2—The provision of this conductor is optional.

Note 3—Interchange circuits 102a and 102b are required where the electrical characteristics defined in recommendation V.10 are used.

Note 4—Not essential in subchannel.

Note 5—During the synchronization process of the main modem, the OFF condition of circuit 106 is signaled at all port interfaces.

Note 6—Circuit 142 is present on all ports of the multiplexer, but may be activated on an individual port basis for individual port tests. All are activated simultaneously for entire modem tests.

PHYSICAL LEVEL INTERFACES AND PROTOCOLS

Section 6:
The X Series Interfaces

BLACK

This section covers some of the more prevalent physical level X series interfaces. The X series is titled "Data Communication Networks Interfaces." Higher level X series interfaces, such as the X.25 packet network interface, are not explained here.

These interfaces are used in a variety of ways. For example, X.21 bis is best known as the physical level interface for the X.25 network level protocol, whereas X.21 is implemented as both a physical level interface and a network level protocol with circuit-switching capabilities. These attributes are explained further in this section.

X.24: List of Definitions for Interchange Circuits between Data Terminal Equipment (DTE) and Data Circuit-Terminating Equipment (DCE) on Public Data Networks

The X.24 recommendation (like V.24 for the V series) defines the interchange circuits used with some of the other X series interfaces. Table 56 summarizes these circuits. The X.24 circuits perform the following functions:

Circuit G—Signal ground or common return—This conductor establishes the signal common reference potential for unbalanced double-current interchange circuits with the electrical characteristics of recommendation V.28. With interchange circuits of recommendations V.10 and V.11, it interconnects the zero volt reference points of a generator and a receiver to reduce signal interference.

Table 56: X.24 Interchange Circuits

Interchange Circuit Designation	Interchange Circuit Name	Data		Control		Timing	
		From DCE	To DCE	From DCE	To DCE	From DCE	To DCE
G	Signal Ground or Common Return						
Ga	DTE Common Return				X		
Gb	DCE Common Return			X			
T	Transmit		X		X		
R	Receive	X		X			
C	Control				X		
I	Indication			X			
S	Signal Element Timing					X	
B	Byte Timing					X	
F	Frame Start Indentification					X	
X	DTE Signal Element Timing						X

For unbalanced interchange circuits with the electrical characteristics of V.10, two common-return conductors are required, one for each direction of signaling. Where used, they are defined as follows:

Circuit Ga—DTE common return—This conductor is connected to the DTE circuit common and is used as the reference for the unbalanced X.26 type circuits within the DCE.

*Circuit Gb—DCE common return—*This conductor is connected to the DCE circuit common and is used as the reference for the unbalanced X.26 type circuits within the DTE.

Circuit T—Transmit—Direction: To DCE: The binary signals originated by the DTE to be transmitted during the data transfer phase on the circuit to one or more remote DTEs are transferred on this circuit to the DCE. This circuit also transfers the call control signals originated by the DTE, in the call establishment and other call control phases.

Circuit R—Receive—Direction: From DCE: The binary signals sent by the DCE during the data transfer phase from a remote DTE are transferred on this circuit to the DTE. This circuit also transfers the call control signals during the call establishment and other call control phases as specified by the relevant recommendations for the procedural characteristics of the interface.

Circuit C—Control—Direction: To DCE: Signals on this circuit control the DCE for a particular signaling process. Representation of a control signal requires additional coding of circuit T-Transmit as stated in the relevant recommendation. During the data phase, this circuit shall remain ON.

Circuit I—Indication—Direction: From DCE: Signals on this circuit indicate to the DTE the state of the call. Representation of a control signal requires additional coding of circuit R-Receive, as specified in a relevant recommendation. The ON condition signifies that signals on circuit R contain information from the remote DTE. The OFF condition signifies control signaling condition, which is defined by the signal on circuit R.

Circuit S—Signal element timing—Direction: From DCE: Signals on this circuit provide the DTE with timing information. The condition of the circuit shall be ON and OFF for nominally equal periods of time.

Circuit B—Byte timing—Direction: From DCE: Signals on this circuit provide the DTE with 8-bit byte timing information. The condition of this circuit shall be OFF for the period of the ON condition of circuit S-Signal element timing, which indicates the last bit of an 8-bit byte. It shall be ON at all other times within the period of the 8-bit byte.

Circuit F—Frame start identification—Direction: From DCE: Signals on this circuit provide the DTE with a multiplex frame start indication when connected to a multiplexed interface.

Circuit X—DTE transmit signal element timing—Direction: To DCE: Signals on this circuit provide timing information for the transmit direction in cases where circuit S only provides timing for the receive direction.

A Summary of the X Series

X.21: Interface between Data Terminal Equipment (DTE) and Data Circuit-Terminating Equipment (DCE) for Synchronous Operation on Public Data Networks.

X.21 is yet another interface standard that has received considerable attention in the industry and is used in several European countries and Japan. It has not seen as extensive implementation as EIA-232-D and the V series. The standard was first published in 1972 and was amended in 1976, 1980, and 1984. Unlike EIA-232-D and most of the V series, X.21 uses a 15-pin connector (see Figure 31). The circuits are defined in ISO document 4903.

The X.24 T and R circuits transmit and receive signals across the interface. Unlike EIA-232-D and the V series, X.21 uses the T and R circuits for user data and control. The C circuits provide an OFF/ON signal to the DCE and the I circuit provides the OFF/ON to the DTE. These two circuits serve to activate and deactivate the DCE-DTE interface session. The S and B circuits provide for signals to synchronize the signals between the DTE and DCE. The G circuit acts as a signal ground or a common return.

X.21 is designed around the concepts of states and state diagrams. By the use of state protocol logic, X.21 can be used in a simple manner similar to the EIA-232/V.24 interchange circuits or in a more elaborate manner, such as circuit-switched call management. An examination of the X.21 states shows these properties:

State Number	State Name
1	Ready
2	Call Request
3	Proceed to Select
4	Selection Signals
5	DTE Waiting
6A	DCE Waiting
6B	DCE Waiting
7	DCE Provided Information (Call Progress Signals)
8	Incoming Call
9	Call Accepted
10A	DCE Provided Information (Called DTE Line Identification)
10B	DCE Provided Information (Calling DTE Line Identification)
11	Connection in Progress
12	Ready for Data
13	Data Transfer
13S	Send Data
13R	Receive Data
14	DTE Controlled Not Ready, DCE Ready
15	Call Collision
16	DTE Clear Request
17	DCE Clear Confirmation
18	DTE Ready, DCE Not Ready
19	DCE Clear Indication
20	DTE Clear Confirmation
21	DCE Ready
22	DTE Uncontrolled Not Ready, DCE Not Ready
23	DTE Controlled Not Ready, DCE Not Ready
24	DTE Uncontrolled Not Ready, DCE Ready

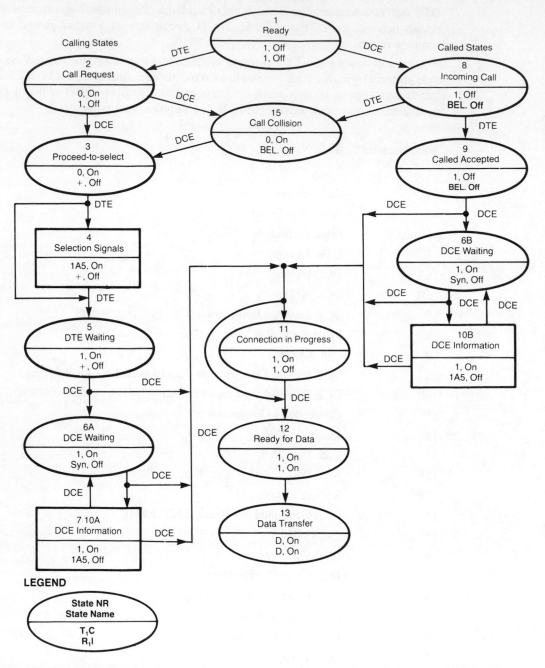

Figure 38: X.21 State Diagram

Call establishment is accomplished by the user DTE and network DCE both signaling READY (state 1) (see Figure 38). From this state the DTE enters the call-request state (state 2), which the DCE acknowledges by entering the proceed-to-select state (state 3). At the other end, the remote DCE signals its DTE by entering the incoming-call state (state 8) and the DTE responds with a call-accepted state (state 9).

Hereafter, the components pass through several optional states. The DTE and DCE can wait for the calls (states 5, 6A, and 6B). An additional state, connection in progress (state 11) is available to allow additional network delay. The DCEs now enter the ready for data state (state 12), then data transfer begins (state 13).

Figure 38 is a state diagram for X.21 calls. The designations in the ellipses identify the state number and name (top half of ellipse) and the values on the T, C, R, and I interchange circuits (bottom half of ellipse). It is obvious that X.21 provides some powerful data network management features. However, its use in many parts of the world is minimal.

X.22: DTE/DCE Multiplex Interface

Recommendation X.22 defines a synchronous DTE/DCE interface for a data network. The most common use of X.22 is the multiplexing of 8-bit bytes from the DTEs across the X.24 transmit (T) and receive (R) interchange circuits. X.22 also uses other X.24 interchange circuits (see Table 56).

X.22 complies with X.27 at both the DCE and DTE side of the interface. It uses the 15-pin connector of ISO 4903.

X.22 permits an aggregate data rate of 48 Kbit/s in several combinations of user (DTE) multiplexed channels:

Number of User Channels	Data Rate of Each Channel
5	9600 Kbit/s
10	4800 Kbit/s
20	2400 Kbit/s
80	600 Kbit/s

The transmit (T) and receive (R) circuits convey the 8 bits of user data, with the user data streams multiplexed together. The control (C) and indication (I) signals are used in accordance with X.21. The channel signals are in the same time slots as respective data (T, R) circuits. The frame start identification circuit (F) indicates the start of a frame.

Figure 39 shows the X.22 frame format. Its examination will permit us to expand the earlier discussions on physical level timing and synchronization. The DTE and DCE (multiplexer) establish character alignment by exchanging two or more contiguous control characters (ASCII "SYN" characters).

The X.21 control (C) and indication (I) circuits provide the physical level synchronization. The C circuit undergoes an OFF to ON transition of the S circuit at the beginning of each 8-bit character. The C circuit then remains steady for the entire character. The I circuit undergoes the OFF to ON transition of circuit S at the beginning of each 8-bit character. The F circuit (frame start identification) indicates

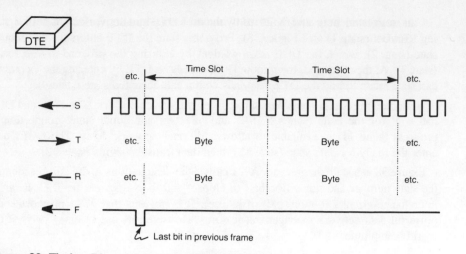

Figure 39: Timing Diagram for a Multiplex Interface

the start of the multiplex frame (also called a multiplex block or multiplex message). The circuit goes to an OFF condition in the last position of each frame to signal the beginning of a new frame. The S circuit operates to provide timing information for each bit. The reader may recall from earlier discussions that this technique allows the devices to achieve synchronization with each other.

A Survey of the Other X Series

Here is a list of the other major series that are used as physical level interfaces:

- *X.20:* Interface between data terminal equipment (DTE) and data circuit-terminating equipment (DCE) for start-stop transmission services on public data networks

- *X.20 bis:* Use on public data networks of data terminal equipment (DTE) which is designed for interfacing to asynchronous duplex V series modems

- *X.21 bis:* Use on public data networks of data terminal equipment (DTE) which is designed for interfacing to synchronous V series modems

- *X.21 bis:* Deserves special mention. It is often used as an interface in to an X.25 packet network. While X.25 is beyond the scope of this book, a few comments about the interface should be helpful to the reader.

- *X.21 bis:* Uses the V.24 circuits. It also has several options of how the ISO connectors and the other V and X interfaces are used. The electrical characteristics of the interchange circuits at both the DCE side and the DTE side of the interface may comply either with recommendation V.28 by using the 25-pin connector and ISO 2110 or with recommendation X.26 by using the 37-pin connector and ISO 4902.

   For applications of the data signaling rate of 48 Kbit/s, the connector and electrical characteristics at both the DCE side and the DTE side of the interface are given in the 34-pin interface connector (ISO 2593) and in recommendation V.35.
   A DTE could use X.21 bis to establish a call with a DCE (packet exchange) in the following manner (although X.21 bis does not show as complete a dialogue

as suggested here and X.25 uses higher level signaling to accomplish a call connection):

Local DTE and DCE	Meaning	Remote DTE and DCE
1. V.24 108 ON	Call Request	
2.	Incoming Call	V.24 125 ON
3.	Call Accepted	V.24 108 ON
4. V.24 125 ON	Call Connected	

- *X.26:* Electrical characteristics for unbalanced double-current interchange circuits for general use with integrated circuit equipment in the field of data communications
- *X.27:* Electrical characteristics for balanced double-current interchange circuits for general use with integrated circuit equipment in the field of data communications

  X.26 and X.27 are functionally equivalent to V.10 and V.11, respectively.

PHYSICAL LEVEL INTERFACES AND PROTOCOLS

Section 7:
The "Bell" Modems

Section 7: The "Bell" Modems

Bell modems (data sets) are widely used throughout the U.S. and other parts of the world. Table 57 summarizes the Bell modems and their interface type. The Bell technical reference numbers are also listed for readers who wish more detail. This section describes the more widely used Bell modems.

Table 57: Bell DCEs (Modems and DSUs)

Code	Technical Reference (Pub. No.)	Interface
	Voiceband Data Sets	
103J	41106	EIA RS-232C
108F	41215	EIA RS-232C
108G	41215	EIA RS-232C
113C	41106	EIA RS-232C
113D	41106	EIA RS-232C
201C	41216	EIA RS-232C
202S	41212	EIA RS-232C
202T	41212	EIA RS-232C
208A	41209	EIA RS-232C
208B	41211	EIA RS-232C
209A	41213	EIA RS-232C
212A	41214	EIA RS-232C
407C	41409	EIA RS-232C
2024A	41910	EIA RS-449
2048A	41910	EIA RS-449
2048C	41910	EIA RS-449
2096A	41910	EIA RS-449
2096C	41910	EIA RS-449
	Wideband Data Sets	
303	41302	Coaxial Cable
306	41304	CCITT V.35
	DSUs	
500B	41450	EIA RS-232C
500B	41450	CCITT V.35

The physical level interfaces in North America have been largely dictated by the Bell system specifications. For example, the vast majority of vendors base their automatic dial and answer DCEs on the Bell 103/212A specifications, and the 103, 113, 201C, 208 A/B, and 212A specifications are used by many vendors as a basis for their DCE designs.

The term "Bell modem" has been associated with those modems produced by AT&T/Bell/Western Electric before divestiture. For convenience, the term is still widely used. The newer CCITT V series modem specifications are increasingly used in North America. As noted in this section, the Bell modems and the supposed CCITT counter-parts are not always compatible.

Generally speaking, the Bell modems use the EIA-232 recommendation as it is defined by the EIA. However, exceptions exist. For example, the Bell 212A DCE defines pin 12 differently than does the EIA. As stated several times, a careful review of the vendors' specifications is quite important.

The first Bell modem was introduced in 1957; it used a frequency shift keying (FSK) modulation technique and transmitted data at 1 Kbit/s. From that initial endeavor, Bell/AT&T developed an extensive line of modems, which today are called DATAPHONE datasets. The more recent Bell modems are designated as Dataphone II and use microprocessor-based synchronous protocols. These systems also provide adaptive equalizers and extensive diagnostic capabilities. The modems continuously monitor themselves and analyze the quality of the received signal. If necessary, they identify problems and report these problems to diagnostic control devices. Generally, the trouble reporting is provided over the reverse channel discussed in earlier parts of this book.

As with most modems today, the Bell modems provide the user with test menus and command menus, which allow them to isolate and diagnose problems. Several of these modems are obsolete. For example, the Bell 201 is seldom used today.

103/113 Series Modems

The 103 and 113 modems transmit and receive data at rates from 0 to 300 bit/s asynchronously using FSK modulation. These modems operate full duplex on two-wire systems using two distinct frequency bands. This is the split channel modem concept discussed in the Introduction:

Transmit:	SPACE	1070 Hz
(Originate)	MARK	1270 Hz
Receive:	SPACE	2025 Hz
(Answer)	MARK	2225 Hz

Note that a similar V series modem, V.21, uses different frequencies.

The 103 can either originate or answer calls and can be used with a direct connection or by acoustic coupler. The 103 modem is automatically switched to the originate mode when a call is originated and to answer mode when the call is answered. The 113 is a variant on the 103.

The 103/113 modems are available with a variety of call and answer options:

- automatic answer: 103A, 103J, 113B, 113D
- manual originate/answer: 103A, 103J
- manual answer: 113D
- manual originate: 113A, 113C

108 Series Modems

The 108 series is a successor to the 103F. They use the line in the following manner:

Originate:	1070 Hz = 0 (SPACE)
(Send)	1270 Hz = 1 (MARK)
Answer:	2025 Hz = 0 (SPACE)
(Receive)	2225 Hz = 1 (MARK)

201 Series Modems

The 201 series of modems transmit and receive at 2000 and 2400 bit/s. The 201A operates at 2000 bit/s and the 201B or 201C operates at 2400 bit/s. The modem functions synchronously with PSK (four-level) modulation. The carrier is changed to 45°, 135°, 225°, or 315° shifts. Two bits (dibit) are used to encode four specific phase shifts. The 201 series operates half duplex on two-wire systems or full duplex on four-wire systems. The 201C will operate over unconditioned lines.

The 201 modems use the V.26 (alternative B) phase encoding methods, refer to Table 34.

202 Series Modems

The 202 series of modems transmit and receive data at rates of 1800 bit/s on conditioned leased lines or 0 to 1200 BPS on the dial-up network. Like the 103, this modem functions asynchronously utilizing FSK modulation. It uses a tone of 2200 Hz to represent a SPACE and a tone of 1200 Hz to represent a MARK.

The 202 modem operates half duplex on two-wire systems, or in a leased-line version on four-wire systems. On two-wire systems, a reverse channel is commonly used to return low bit rate information such as ACK-NAK to the transmit modem. The reverse channel accomplishes this by ON/OFF keying a 387 Hz carrier. The 202 also uses the soft carrier turn off frequency. Both transmitters are strapped ON continuously, no line turn-arounds are involved. The 202S supports manual originate/ answer or automatic answer.

Note that the 202 series use similar techniques to the V.23 modem but both use different carrier frequencies and closer frequency spacing. Also, the V.23 modem uses FSK instead of ON/OFF keying (390 Hz = MARK; 450 Hz = SPACE).

208 Series Modems

The 208 series of modems transmit and receive data at 4800 bit/s. The 208A is a private line modem and the 208B is a dial network modem. The modem functions synchronously utilizing PSK (eight level) modulation. Three bits of information (tribits) are used to encode one of eight phase shifts. The 208 series of modems operates half duplex on two-wire systems or full duplex on four-wire systems. It will operate at 4800 bit/s on unconditioned lines. The 208A supports point-to-point or multipoint configurations. The training time is selectable at 50 or 150 milliseconds.

The 208 series modems use the V.27 phase encoding methods (refer to Table 41).

212A Series Modems

As electronic components decreased in price, the more advanced modulation techniques (phase modulation) were placed into asynchronous modems. The Bell 212 was introduced in the late 1970s with phase modulation capabilities.

The 212A modem transmits and receives data at 1200 bit/s or 300 bit/s. This modem functions asynchronously utilizing PSK modulation for 1200 bit/s mode of operation and FSK techniques for 300 bit/s mode of operation. The modem can also function as a synchronous device in the 1200 bit range. When the 212A functions in the 300 bit/s mode, it can communicate with the 103/113 series of modem. 212A operates full duplex on two-wire systems. It supports either manual originate/answer or automatic answer.

For the 1200 bit/s option, the 212A modem uses the V.22 specification for 1200 Hz for the low channel and 2400 Hz for the high channel.

For the 300 bit/s, the 212A uses the FSK technique of the Bell 103/113 modems.

209A Series Modems

The 209A modem transmits and receives data at 9800 bit/s. It operates synchronously duplex over leased lines. It can also function as a multiplexer and allocate the bandwidth into smaller channels. It will accept serial data at 9600 bit/s or lower.

- one 7200 bit/s and one 2400 bit/s data streams
- two 4800 bit/s data streams
- one 4800 bit/s and two 2400 bit/s data streams
- four 2400 bit/s data streams

The 209A also has the following characteristics:

- synchronous formats
- private lines
- QAM
- automatic adaptive equalizer
- scrambling provided
- carrier frequency of 1650 Hz

Bell V.29 Modems

This popular modem (not compatible with the 209A) uses the V.29 specification described earlier. Please refer to V.29 for a description of this modem.

PHYSICAL LEVEL INTERFACES AND PROTOCOLS

**Section 8:
Interfaces for Digital Systems**

Section 8: Interfaces for Digital Systems

T1 Signaling

While analog signaling remains the prevalent signaling technique between DCEs (modems), the trend is toward increased use of digital signaling. This section expands the introductory material on digital systems, digital timing, and digital multiplexing (V.22). Owing to the wide use of the T1 carrier system (and its 56 Kbit/s "subrate"), it is used as a tutorial and example of a digital physical level interface. Moreover, this discussion also provides the more knowledgeable reader with references on T1 timing and framing conventions. This discussion is derived from [IEI87][1].

The T1 system is designed around a 1,544,000 bit/s rate. T1 carriers transmit 24 voice or data channels together in time division multiplexed frames. The T1 system provides the voice multiplexing by sampling the 24 channels at a combined rate of 192,000 times per second (8000 times per second per channel x 24 channels = 192,000). Figure 40a shows how the 24 channels are multiplexed into a frame. The frame contains one sample from each channel, plus an additional "sync" bit for frame synchronization. Thus, the complete frame is 193 bits (8 bits per channel x 24 channels + 1 sync bit = 193 bits). Since a frame represents only one of the required 8000 samples per second, a T1 system operates at 1,544,000 to accommodate all 8000 frames (193 bits per frame x 8000 frames = 1,544,000).

The details of the T1 physical level interfaces are described here with emphasis on the following concepts:

- alternate mark inversion (AMI)
- ones density requirements
- bit robbing
- binary 8 zero substitution (B8ZS)
- the framing bit

Alternate Mark Inversion (AMI)

The AMI concept is shown in Figure 40b. The T1 system requires that a 1 pulse must be sent as an opposite polarity from the preceding 1 pulse, regardless of the number of 0s in between the two 1s. The name, AMI, is derived from the use of alternating polarities to represent binary 1s, (marks).

Ones Density Requirements

T1 provides no separate physical-level clocking signal because the timing or clocking information is embedded in the data stream. At the receiving end, the clock is recovered from the data stream by the detection of 1 pulses. If the T1 data stream has insufficient 1 pulses embedded, the receiver can no longer produce reliable timing output.

To overcome this problem, a certain number of 1s must be present to ensure proper timing. This concept is called 1s density. The T1 facilities require that no more than

---

[1][IEI87]: "Digital Signalling with T1" is a lecture paper prepared by Information Engineering Inc, Falls Church, Virginia, June 1987.

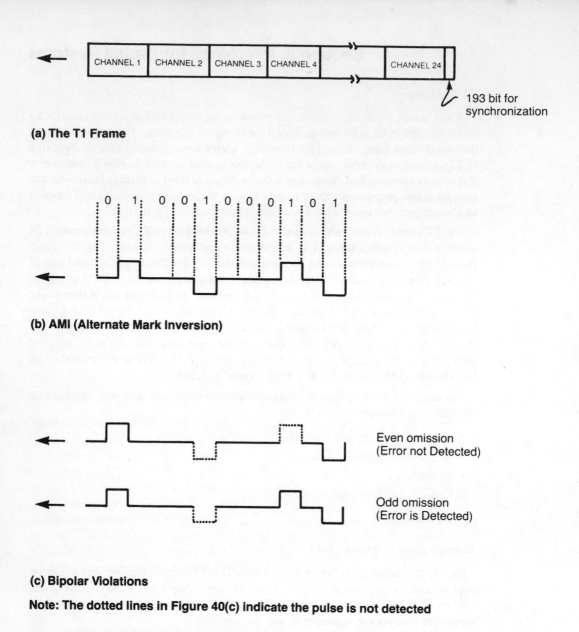

(a) The T1 Frame

CHANNEL 1 | CHANNEL 2 | CHANNEL 3 | CHANNEL 4 | CHANNEL 24

193 bit for synchronization

0 1 0 0 1 0 0 0 1 0 1

(b) AMI (Alternate Mark Inversion)

Even omission
(Error not Detected)

Odd omission
(Error is Detected)

(c) Bipolar Violations

Note: The dotted lines in Figure 40(c) indicate the pulse is not detected

Figure 40: Digital Framing and Timing

15 contiguous zeros shall be present in the frame. Each pulse helps keep the clock aligned to a mid-bit sampling to eliminate or reduce systematic and waiting-time jitter. This convention is adequate to keep the receiver and the repeaters synchronized.

Owing to noise, mechanical failures, etc., the bits may become distorted, which can cause a "violation" of the AMI rule. Bipolar violations or excessive errors are known as format errors because the errors are not in conformance with the required T1 format.

A bit distortion may not cause a format error. As Figure 40c shows, the nature of the error determines if the bipolar violation is detected. The bipolar signal is altered with errors of omission (pulses are deleted) or errors of commission (pulses are added). Not all possibilities are shown in Figure 40c.

- odd omission: creates a violation,
- even omission: does not create a violation,
- odd commission: creates a violation,
- even commission: does not create a violation, or creates two violations.

At best, only 50 percent of the errors can be detected. The percentage is even worse if the signal passes through certain equipment before reaching the receiver. To illustrate, a T1 multiplexer may multiplex together two signals in which a code violation exists in each. In effect, the two errors "mask" each other when the multiplexer logic combines the signals into a single multiplexed stream.

The signal can be tested, but the transmission line must be taken out of service. Moreover, the majority of errors are transient in nature and the testing routines often do not find any problem.

The errored bits cause problems in voice transmissions, especially if the frames control bits are corrupted. For data transmissions, the corruption is even more serious. Clearly, the problem begs for a solution, and later discussions in this section examine several enhancements to address this problem.

Bit Robbing

The earlier T1 channel banks use the eighth bit in every slot for control signaling. Examples of control signaling are off-hook, on-hook, ringing, busy signals, and battery reversal. When the 256-step quantizers were placed in operation, the use of the eighth bit to represent all possible 256-step values ($2^8 = 256$). During the development of newer systems, the designers recognized that every eighth bit was not needed for signaling and chose to minimize the number of bits required. Consequently, the channel banks designated as D2 (and later channel banks) use the eighth bit of every sixth and twelfth frame to provide signaling information. The least significant bit in these frames is overwritten with a signaling bit. This concept is called bit robbing and the respective sixth and twelfth robbed frame bits are called the A and B bits.

For the transmission of data, the eighth bit is unreliable. Consequently, most vendors have chosen to ignore this bit for data signaling. The majority of T1 and related systems use a 56 Kbit/s transmission rate instead of the 64 Kbit/s rate actually available.

B8ZS (Bipolar with 8 Zeros Substitution)

To establish 1s density in the T1 signal, a technique called B7 zero code suppression has been applied to several T1 systems. A binary 1 is substituted in a T1 frame to prevent an occurrence of more than 15 consecutive 0s. It is possible that this substitution can occur with any bit in the frame. A voice channel can tolerate the loss of the eighth bit to signaling and can even tolerate the loss of the seventh bit to B7 substitution. However, a data channel cannot operate with this arrangement.

Practically speaking, it is not necessary to rob bits in a data channel since there is no telephone signal. However, it is quite possible to have all 0s in a data channel. Therefore, the data could be corrupted by the B7 zero code suppression technique.

The insertion does not affect the voice channel but it certainly affects a data channel. To prevent this problem, a data channel generally only uses seven bits, and any 1 substitutions can be placed into the eighth bit. This prevents the B7 zero codes suppression from corrupting the data channel. This approach is undesirable and is being phased out with newer systems.

It is possible to provide more efficient capabilities with the older systems by changing the coding technique of the bipolar stream. The binary 8 zero substitution (B8ZS) has been applied to some of the older systems to address the all zeros word problem. The rules for BNZS are stated below and are illustrated in Figure 41:

- If a pulse preceding the all zeros word is positive (+), the inserted code is: 000 + – 0 – +.

- If a pulse preceding the all zeros word is negative (-), the inserted code is: 000 – + 0 + –.

If a system is using the B8ZS convention, the terminating device must be capable of monitoring the incoming signals, and upon detecting the B8ZS (bipolar violations in the fourth and seventh bit position), replace it with eight 0s.

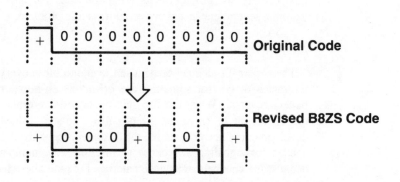

OR

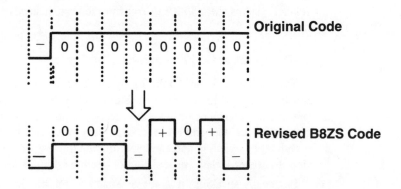

Figure 41: Synchronization of a Digital System with Binary & Zero Substitution (B8ZS)

The Framing Bit: 193rd Bit of the Frame

To decode the incoming data stream, a receiver must be able to associate each sample with the proper channel. At a minimum, the beginning and ending of the frame must be recognized. The function of the framing bit is to provide this delineation. This bit is located in the 193rd bit of each frame. It is not part of the user's information but added by the system for framing. The use of this bit varies significantly depending on the type of T1 and the age of the technology.

The original T1 channel bank (designated as D1) used the 193 bit each time to locate the beginning of the frame. Since the 1960s, the succeeding frame format of D1D, D2, D3, and D4 channel banks and the extended super frame format (ESF) have been used to improve the T1 systems, all using the 193rd bit.

The D1 approach used alternating 1s and 0s in the 193rd position of the frame. It was fast and inexpensive, but the D1 banks were very susceptible to frame loss in the presence of 1,000 Hz test tones. These tones created a perfect alternating 1 and 0 pattern in every 193 bits. This problem is called false framing and can cause the receiver to "lockup" on the wrong frame or not lockup on any frame. (Carriers have since migrated to a 1004 Hz test tone.)

The D2 channel banks had to deal with both the false frame problem and the A/B bit sequence. Consequently, D2 systems adapted a different sequence for the 193rd bit. Even though this technique was introduced with earlier D2 banks, today it is called the D4 frame format.

The D4 frame format is illustrated in Figure 42. The terminal framing (FT) bits are used to align the receiving channel bank onto the proper sequence of the 24 channels. The channel bank searches for the FT pattern to synchronize the incoming frames to the channel bank.

The signal framing bits or multiframe alignment bits (FS) indicate which frames are used for signaling bits (the robbed bits). They are also used to synchronize the timing between the channel bank multiplexer and the carrier's central office equipment.

The FT and FS framing bits are consolidated into the entire framing pattern that is used with a D4 channel bank. This composite framing convention, now known as the super frame (SF) format, is the D4 framing convention. This framing bit sequence repeats every 12 frames and constitutes the "super frame." To find the 193rd bit, the receiving channel bank looks for a repeating bit pattern of 100011011100.

The extended super frame (ESF) was introduced by AT&T to address several problems. The ESF provides additional signaling capabilities, more diagnostics, and even error detection. The ESF format is also shown in Figure 42.

The 193rd bit is now shared by (1) frame synchronization, (2) a data link control channel, and (3) a cyclic redundancy check (CRC).

The frame synchronization bits (F) occupy positions 4, 8, 12, 16, 20, and 24. They perform the combined functions of FT and FS and are coded as 001011. The six bits use 25 percent of the total numbered bits in the 193rd position of a 8000 frames per second system. Consequently, the F bit channel operates at 2 Kbit/s (8000 * 0.25 = 2000).

The data link control bits (DLC) are used to derive a time division multiplexed (TDM) channel of 4 Kbit/s. This channel can be quite useful for control and diagnostic activity without disrupting the user subchannels.

The DLC subchannel uses positions 1, 3, 5, 7, 9, 11, 13, 15, 17, 19, 21, and 23 for

Bit Value of 193rd Bit

Frame Number	F_T	F_s } →	SF	ESF
1	1		1	DL
2		0	0	CRC
3	0		0	DL
4		0	0	F = 0
5	1		1	DL
6		1	1	CRC
7	0		0	DL
8		1	1	F = 0
9	1		1	DL
10		1	1	CRC
11	0		0	DL
12		0	0	F = 1
13				DL
14				CRC
15				DL
16				F = 0
17	Repeat Every 12 Frames	Repeat Every 12 Frames	Repeat Every 12 Frames	DL
18				CRC
19				DL
20				F = 1
21				DL
22				CRC
23				DL
24				F = 1

F_T: Terminal Framing Bit
F_s: Multiframe Alignment Bit
   (Signal Framing Bit)
SF: Superframe
ESF: Extended Superframe

DL: Data Link Bit
CRC: Cyclic Redundancy Check Bit
F: F_T and F_s Functions

Figure 42: D4 and Extended Superframe Formats (193rd Bit)

a total of 12 bits, or 50 percent of the total number of the 193rd bit positions of the channel. Thus, it operates at a rate of 4 Kbit/s (8000 x 0.5 = 4000).

The data link subchannel typically uses a data link protocol such as HDLC or LAPB. The AT&T ESF system uses a simplified LAPB. The information (I field) is based on the telemetry asynchronous block serial protocol (TABS) protocol from AT&T.

The CRC capability is a significant enhancement to the T1 system. It occupies positions 2, 6, 10, 14, 18, and 22 and operates at 2 Kbit/s.

CRC essentially eliminates the false frame problem. The CRC provides a means to detect damaged bits. It then indicates an error, and the channel bank will be alerted to seek for a correct framing pattern. CRC is also used to evaluate the performance of the system. Since it detects logic errors instead of format errors, the line can be monitored for quality and performance.

Many varieties of digital level interfaces exist today. This discussion has focused on T1. The embryonic integrated services digital networks (ISDNs) use many of the ideas of the T1 system. As was stated earlier, digital physical level interfaces and protocols will grow in use, and some countries and standards groups have even stopped issuing physical level analog interface specifications. However, for the immediate future, the analog interfaces will remain as the more widely used approach.

Digital Data System (DDS)

Today, many organizations use digital lines and transmission schemes. One of the most widely used digital devices is AT&T's digital data system (DDS), generally implemented with the data service unit (DSU), and the channel service unit (CSU). In this section, we examine these devices and explain their principal characteristics.

The DSU and CSU

Digital transmission of data between computer and terminals occurs through devices known generally as customer premises equipment (CPE). In the 1970s and early 1980s, a user DTE was given an interface into a digital channel with a Western Electric 500A, a combined CSU and DSU, or a combination of the two (CSU/DSU) (see Figure 43). The DSU converts the DTE-oriented data signals into bipolar digital signals. The DSU also performs clocking and signal regeneration of the channel. The CSU performs functions such as line conditioning to keep the signal's performance consistent across the channel bandwidth; signal reshaping, which reconstitutes the binary pulse stream; and loop-back testing, which entails the transmission of test signals between the CSU and the network carrier's office channel unit (OCU). The CSU assumes other major responsibilities with the newer digital systems by using the ESF.

Figure 44 depicts the DSU which forms the basis for the DDS. The DDS channel is terminated at the user site, first by a CSU and then the DSU and at the other end by the OCU, usually located at the carrier's office. The purpose of the CSU is to provide a balancing and to equalize the loop. It also permits remote testing of the channel.

The customer interface is supported by EIA-232 at speeds of 2.4, 4.8, and 9.6 Kbit/s. At the 56 Kbit/s rate, the interface is implemented with the CCITT V.35. The subrate speeds use the conventional pin connector and the 56 Kbit/s service uses the 34-pin connector. The 56 bit/s unit differs from the subrate principally in that the clock of the data signals are balanced and DC coupled. This is in accordance with the CCITT recommendation V.35, which is discussed elsewhere.

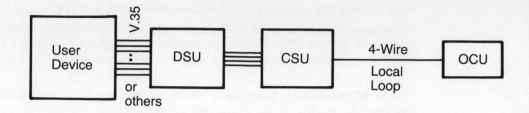

DSU: Data Service Unit
CSU: Channel Service Unit
OCU: Office Channel Unit

Figure 43: Digital Data System (DDS)

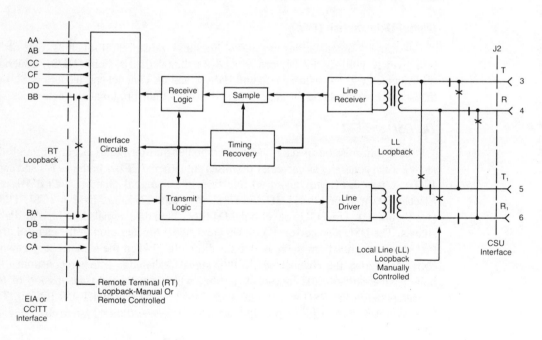

Figure 44: Data Service Unit (DSU)

DDS provides a full duplex, private line, two point, or multistation capability. It has no voice or alternate voice capability. Transmissions from the telephone office to the customers premises use baseband transmissions with nonloaded four-wire circuits. These circuits terminate first into the CSU. The CSU/DSU connection is achieved through a 15-pin connector.

The DSU is made up of two principal sections. The first section is called the channel interface. It provides the connection to the CSU as well as loopback testing. The second section is called the incoder/decoder. It contains the receiver and transmitter circuitry, as well as the clock recovery circuitry. It also contains the EIA and CCITT drivers. One of its principal functions is the conversion of EIA CCITT signals to the line baseband bipolar signals and vice-versa.

Tables 58 and 59 define the use of the 25-pin connector and 34-pin connector interfaces for the various data rates for the DSU. These pins are used generally in accordance with the EIA and CCITT specifications. However, the reader is encouraged to study the actual *Bell System Technical Reference Manual* for more detail (PUB 41450). The subrate speeds use EIA-RS-334 to describe the data and clock signals. They generally adhere to the 334 specification, except for the transmit clock, which has some variations on peak individual distortion.

The DDS provides for several options in the transmissions of duplex and half duplex systems. For these operations, there are minimum interface circuits defined. These circuits are summarized in Table 60.

The DSU also provides for loopback testing. Two loopbacks are available. Both can be operated manually at the local station, and one can be operated remotely from a test center. The first loopback is the local line (LL) loopback. Its function is to provide loopback testing between the DTE as well as CSUs. The second loopback is called the remote terminal (RT) loopback. If used, this procedure disconnects the customer equipment and does the loopback test toward the line at the interface connector. The use of the RT loopback with loopbacks available at the CSU enables a test center to isolate problems to the DSU or the local line.

Table 58: DSU 25-Pin Connector Assignments

Pin No. Destination	Function	EIA-232 Destination	CCITT
1	Protective Ground	AA	101
2	Transmitted Data	BA	103
3	Received Data	BB	104
4	Request to Send	CA	105
5	Clear to Send	CB	106
6	Data Set Ready	CC	107
7	Signal Ground	AB	102
8	Received Line Signal Detector	CF	109
9	Reserved for DSU Testing	–	–
10	Reserved for DSU Testing	–	–
11-14[1]	Not Used	–	–
15	Transmitter Signal Element Timing	DB	114
16[1]	Not Used	–	–
17	Receiver Signal Element Timing	DD	115
18-25[1]	Not Used	–	–

Note 1—These pins are left "floating" within the DSU. Any voltages on them are from coupling within the customer's interface cable.

Table 59: DSU 34-Pin Connector Assignments

Connector Pin	Function	EIA-232 Designation	CCITT
A	Protective Ground	AA	101
B	Signal Ground	BB	102
C	Request to Send	CA	105
D	Clear to Send	CB	106
E	Data Set Ready	CC	107
F	Received Line Signal Detector	CF	109
R	Received Data	BB(A)	104
T	Received Data	BB(B)	104
V	Receiver Signal Element Timing	DD(A)	115
X	Receiver Signal Element Timing	DD(B)	115
P	Transmitted Data	BA(A)	103
S	Transmitted Data	BA(B)	103
Y	Transmitter Signal Element Timing	DB(A)	114
AA	Transmitter Signal Element Timing	DB(B)	114
MM	Reserved for DSU Testing	–	–
H,J,K,L,M,N,U,W,Z	Not Used	–	–
BB-	Not Used	–	–
HH, JJ-LL	Not Used	–	–
NN	Not Used	–	–

Table 60: DDS Minimum Interface Circuits

	Interface Circuits				
Operation	Signal Ground	Transmit Data	Transmit Data	Transmit Timing	Receive Timing
Duplex	X	X	X	X	X
Half Duplex	X	X	X	X	X
Transmit-Only	X	X		X	
Receive-Only	X		X		X
*					

PHYSICAL LEVEL INTERFACES
AND PROTOCOLS

Section 9:
The Hayes Modems

Section 9: The Hayes Modems

Summary of the Hayes Products

The Hayes modems, developed by Hayes Microcomputer Products, Inc., have become a de facto standard for low- and medium-speed auto dialing modems. Hayes has several products available that connect directly to the telephone line, provide full and half duplex communications, originate and answer calls, and perform serial asynchronous transmission.

The Hayes modems were one of the first commercially successful efforts to "build" intelligence into a low-price modem.

The Hayes Smartmodem 300 is compatible with the Bell 103 type modem. The Smartmodem 1200 is compatible with the Bell 212A type modem, with the exception that the 1200 communicates only asynchronously. The Smartmodem 1200 is one of the biggest sellers in the history of the industry.

The newer Hayes modems are called the V Series Smartmodem 4800 and the V Series Smartmodem 9600. The V Series Smartmodem 4800 series is available in two options: as a stand-alone modem (4800) or as an inboard modem placed in an IBM PC compatible slot (4800B). The V Series Smartmodem 9600 is also available as a stand-alone modem or an inboard modem.

Both the 2400 and 9600 V Series modems offer error detection services. The technique is an automatic request for repeat (ARQ) protocol. This type of protocol automatically requests transmissions of corrupted data. The smartmodems also use a X.25 LAPB-like technique for achieving framing control. Both systems have dynamic data compression logic to provide compression of the data stream. The adaptive compression is completely automatic and does not require any user intervention. As with all the Hayes products, the EIA-232 interface is used between the modem and the user device.

The V Series Smartmodem 2400 supports speeds of 300, 1200, and 2400 bit/s. It can be used with synchronous or asynchronous transmission schemes. The asynchronous format can be either seven bits with MARK, SPACE even, odd, or no parity, or eight bits with no parity, and one or two stop bits. The 2400 series operates in full duplex mode. The 2400 is compatible with the Bell 103 for 300 bit/s, it operates at the 1200 bit/s rate by using the Bell 212A/CCITT V.22 specifications, and it uses the CCITT V.22 bis specification for the 2400 bit/s rate.

The V Series Smartmodem 9600 supports the following bit transfer rates: 300, 1200, 2400, 4800, and 9600 bit/s. It also supports asynchronous and synchronous transmissions. It uses the Bell 103 specifications for the 300 bit/s rate, the Bell 212A/CCITT V.22 specification for the 1200 bit/s, the CCITT V.22 bis specification for the 2400 bit/s specification, the CCITT V.32 specification for the 4800 bit/s rate, and the CCITT V.32 specification for the 9600 bit/s rate. In addition, the 9600 series performs trellis encoding on the 9600 bit/s signals. It operates at full duplex with speeds of 2400 bit/s and below. For higher speeds (9600 bit/s, 4800 bit/s), it uses a half duplex approach but simulates full duplex by using a ping-pong protocol for fast turn around to simulate the V.32 full duplex modem.

Hayes also offers the V series modem enhancer, which allows a user of the older Hayes Smartmodem 2400 and Smartmodem 1200 to take advantage of some of the technology described previously. The stand alone unit provides the ARQ error control, adaptive compression, and adaptive speeds. The characteristics of the Hayes modems are summarized in Table 61.

Table 61: The Hayes Modems

Smartmodem 300	Smartmodem 1200	Smartmodem 2400	Smartmodem 9600
300 Bit/s (Bell 103) Frequency Shift Keying (FSK) 1070 - 1270 Hz and 2025 - 2225 Hz	1200 Bit/s (Bell 212A and Bell 103 300 Bit/s) Phase Shift Keying (PSK) 1200 and 2400 Hz	300,1200,2400 Bit/s 300 Bit/s: Bell 103 1200 Bit/s: Bell 212A, CCITT V.22 2400 Bit/s: CCITT V.22 bis	300,1200,2400,4800,9600 300 Bit/s: Bell 103 1200 Bit/s: Bell 212A, CCITT V.22 2400 Bit/s: CCITT V.22 bis 4800 Bit/s: V.32 HDX 9600 Bit/s: V.32 HDX

Hayes Commands

The smartmodem provides a set of firmware commands that control the modem and allow it to manage remote communications. The commands are used to "adjust" the modem's behavior. The commands are coded as strings of ASCII characters.

The smartmodem is always in one of two functional states: local command state or on-line state. Whenever the power is turned on, the modem assumes the local command state; it then selects duplex mode of operation, sets registers, and changes parameters. The parameters also include the dial/answer commands that establish a remote connection and cause the modem to enter the on-line state.

The on-line state is used with two major modes: originate mode, when the modem originates a call, and answer mode, when it accepts an incoming call. Answer mode is also entered to initiate a call to an originate-only modem.

The Hayes modem accepts commands from the connected DTE under keyboard or program control and allows menu driven communications systems to be developed by the end user. The new package is called Smartmodem III and, like other of the Hayes systems, it is compatible with the IBM PC family and clones.

The commands allow the user to program the remote dialing systems, file retrieval, file transmittal, editing certain information, as well as actually creating messages. The software allows the user to establish terminal commands and modem settings.

The commands are used to direct firmware to control registers (UART registers) and buffers within the personal computer port and the modem. A summary of the commands for the Smartmodem 1200B are provided in Table 62, and some examples are provided here:

1. Commands to receive 2225 Hz MARK, 2025 Hz SPACE:

    ATS10 = 255C0H2D

    AT: Attention Code

    S10 = 255: Ignore carrier detect

    C0: Carrier off

    H2: Go off hook without closing auxiliary relay contacts

    D: Originate mode; go on-line

Table 62: Hayes Modem Commands

Command	Parameters	Function
	Dialing	
Ds		Dial
	s = 0..9 #	
	*	
	( ) - ./	
	p +	Pulse Dial
	R	Dial an "Originate-Only" Modem (Reverse Mode)
	T	Touch-Tone Dial
	,	Pause When Dialing
	;	Return to Command State after Dialing
A/		Repeat Command; Redial; the Only Command Neither Preceded by AT nor Followed by a Carriage Return
	Answering	
A		Answer Call Immediately
	Standard Operations	
En	n = 0,1	0 = No Echo 1 = Echo
Fn	n = 0,1	0 = Half Duplex 1 = Full Duplex
Mn	n = 0..2	0 = Speaker OFF 1 = Speaker ON until Carrier 2 = Speaker always ON
O		Return to On-Line State
Qn	n = 0,1	0 = Result Codes Sent 1 = Result Codes Not Sent
Sr?	r = 0..17	Read Register r
Sr = n	r = 0..17 r = 0..255	Set Register r to Value n
Vn	n = 0,1	0 = Digit Result Codes 1 = Word Result Codes
Xn	n = 0,1	0 = Basic Result Code Set 1 = Extended Result Code Set
Z		Reset
	Special Operations	
Cn	n = 0,1	0 = Transmitter OFF 1 = Transmitter ON
Hn	n = 0..2	0 = ON Hook (Hang Up) 1 = OFF Hook 2 = Special OFF Hook
In	n = 0,1	0 = Request Identification Code 1 = Request Check Sum

Note 1—AT is coded before each command; + + + changes modem from on-line to command state.

2. Commands to transmit 2225 Hz MARK, 2025 Hz SPACE:

    ATS10 = 255D

    > AT: Attention Code

    > S10 = 255: Ignore carrier detect

    > D: Originate mode, go off hook (key transmitter)

The newer Hayes products operate with a variety of systems, generally classified as data link control (DLC) protocols:

- XMODEM
- XMODEM CRC
- XMODEM-1K
- YMODEM
- YMODEM-G
- Kermit

The Hayes also will emulate the following terminals: TTY, VT52, VT102/100, and ANSI.SYS. The Hayes modems currently are operating with MS-DOS 2.0 through 3.3.

Hayes Modem and the IBM PC Interface

Figure 24 introduced the communications port. This section expands the examination of the port and describes the interface of the Hayes modem and the IBM PC communications port. For more detail, the reader is encouraged to obtain these specific vendors' products descriptions.

Figure 45 provides a simplified view of the IBM PC/Hayes modem of the physical level interface, primarily from the standpoint of the UART registers and the modem registers.

A PC communicates with the Hayes modem via the IBM PC bus, then through the PC UART, and then to the modem's microprocesser. The PC controls the transfer of information by reading and writing the UART registers. These registers reside at the port and are actually on the board of an in-board modem (our example). The IBM PC allows two I/O address spaces for two asynchronous devices in a typical configuration. The devices are designated COM1 and COM2. The Hayes modem occupies one of these addresses. COM1 and COM2 are controlled by their respective registers and are accessed by hexadecimal addresses (3F8-3FF for COM1 and 2F8-2FF for COM2).

PC UART Registers

The IBM PC UART registers are also illustrated in Figure 45. The interface uses the following registers (all registers are eight bits):

- line control register (LCR)
- divisor latch (DLL): least significant byte
- divisor latch (DLM): most significant byte
- line status register (LSR)
- modem control register (MCR)

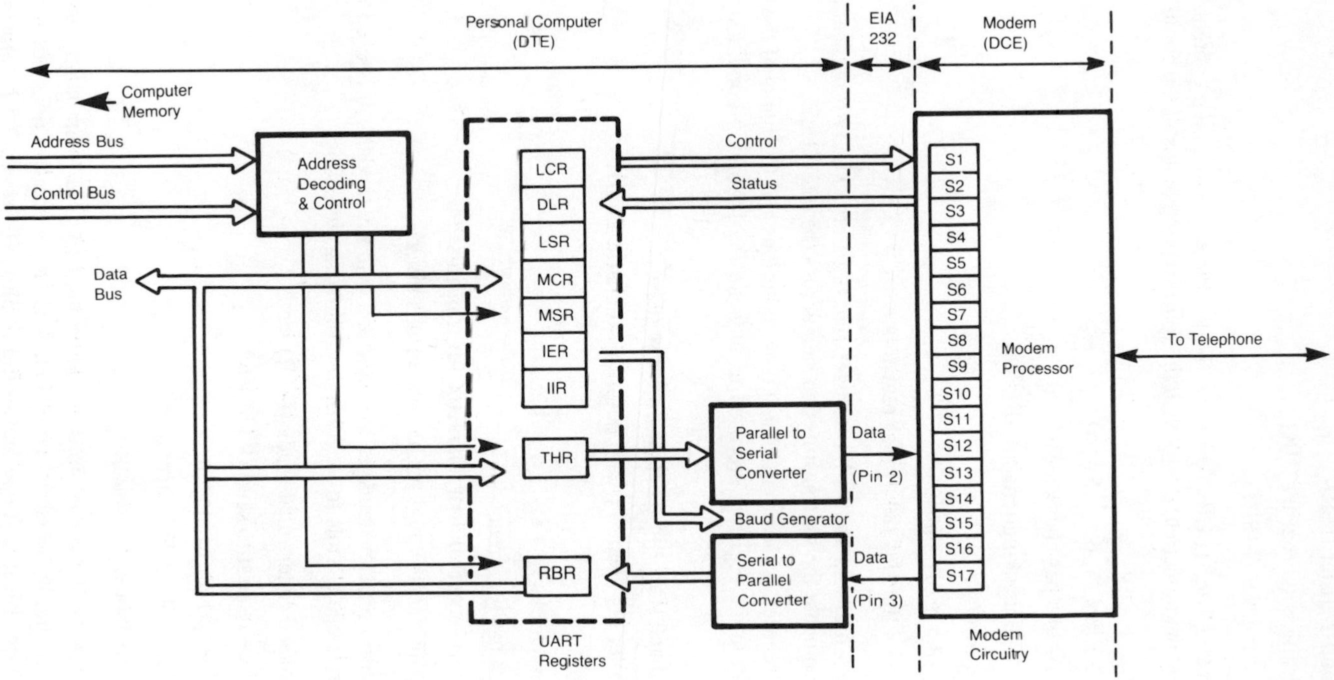

LCR: Line Control Register
DLR: Divisor Latch Registers
LSR: Line Status Register
MCR: Modem Control Register
MSR: Modem Status Register
IER: Interrupt Enable Register
IIR: Interrupt Identification Register
THR: Transmitter Holding Register
RBR: Receiver Buffer Register
S1-S17: Smartmodem Registers

Figure 45: The IBM PC and HAYES Modem Interface

- modem status register (MSR)
- receiver buffer register (RBR)
- transmitter holding register (THR)
- interrupt enable register (IER)
- interrupt identification register (IIR)
- modem speed register (MSR)

The line control register (LCR) describes the character format. It's contents are used by the PC and the modem to distinguish the following attributes of the communications interface:

- length of characters (5, 6 , 7, 8 bits)
- number of stop bits per character
- parity generation/checking (enable, disable)
- type of parity (even, odd)
- transmission of a break signal
- control of the bit transfer rate (bit/s) registers

The divisor latch registers are the bit transfer rate registers. The two registers are used together to compute the bit transmission rate across the interface.

The line status register is used to indicate error conditions and the status of the data registers. The bits in the registers are used to indicate the following conditions (or problems):

- data received and stored in receiver buffer register
- receiver register not cleared (read) before next character arrived
- parity problem
- received character lacks a valid stop bit
- a break signal has been received
- port is ready to accept another character for transmission
- last character in transmit register has been transmitted

The modem control register manages the interface with the modem. It is used with the EIA-232 interchange circuits to perform the following functions.

- enables/disables data terminal ready (DTR) lead
- enables/disables request to send (RTS) lead
- enables/disables power to modem
- enables/disables port-to-PC interrupts
- enables/disables loop-back testing

The modem status register is also used to control the EIA- 232 interchange circuits between the modem and the personal computer. The Hayes modem does not use all the bits in this register because it operates at full duplex. However, the PC port uses this register for the following tasks:

- enables/disables request to send (RTS) lead
- enables/disables clear to send (CTS) lead
- indication that modem has detected a ringing signal

- indication that a ringing signal is no longer on the line
- indication that modem has detected a carrier signal on the line

The receiver buffer register contains the incoming data. The transmitter holding register contains the next character to be transmitted. The "interrupt" registers control the use of interrupts across the interface. The interrupt enable and interrupt identification registers allow various types of interrupts to be enabled or disabled. They can also be set to control the priority of interrupt service.

Hayes Modem Registers

The Hayes modem uses several registers for physical level interface control. Their use depends on which Hayes modem is used. This section provides a brief summary of the functions of the registers.

The S0 register stores the number of rings at which the modem answers an incoming call. If the modem is not to answer a call, this register is set to zero.

The S1 register stores the number of ringing signals that have occurred. It is cleared after the last ring and after no ring has occurred for about 8 seconds. S1 is used in conjunction with S0.

The S2 register stores the escape code character ASCII value. The escape code returns the modem to the local command state from the on-line state. The S3 register stores the carriage return character, which is an ASCII value. The S4 register stores the ASCII value of the line feed character while the S5 register stores the value of the backspace character. This character is used for cursor control.

The S6 register stores the value to indicate how long the modem waits between acquiring the telephone line and dialing the first digit of the telephone number. It must be at least 2 seconds.

The S7 register stores the time for the modem to wait for the carrier signal from the remote modem. If the carrier is not received within the value designated in S7, the modem hangs up the line and returns a no carrier code to the personal computer.

The S8 register stores a pause time. This time is used to wait for a second dial tone when dialing through special telephone services or PBXs.

The S9 register stores the value for carrier detect time. This value determines how long a carrier must be detected to indicate a carrier detect across the EIA-232 interface.

The S10 register stores the period of time that a carrier can be interrupted or lost momentarily. If this register is set to 255, the modem assumes the carrier is always present.

The S11 register determines the duration and spacing of the dialing tones. Its default setting is 70 milliseconds, which establishes a dialing rate of 7.14 numbers per second. The value can be speeded up or slowed down by changing this register.

The S12 register stores the value of escape guard time. This determines the delay immediately before and after entering an escape code.

Hayes reserves registers S13 through S14, but their use is typically set up as follows.

The S13 register defines the use of odd or even parity, length of the character, and whether the eighth bit of a character is a SPACE or MARK.

The S14 register controls the use of local echo, whether pulse dials or touch tones are used, whether the speaker is enabled until a carrier is detected, and the use of the results codes.

Register S15 is set to establish the interface as originate or answer; half duplex or full duplex. It also stores information on the bit rate and the carrier on-or-off indication.

The S16 register controls the Hayes modem testing services. The testing features are not used if S16 is set to zero. Otherwise, the modem is enabled to perform self-testing.

The S17 register (also reserved) typically defines the following functions:

- modem on or off hook
- auto answer on or off
- carrier present or not present
- speaker on or off
- ring indicator true or false

Other registers are used with the newer modems.

The Hayes "Clones"

As with any successful product, less expensive systems emerge in the market place that clone the original. The Hayes 1200 modem is no exception. These clone modems are certainly less expensive than the Hayes modem, but the reader should check their capabilities very carefully. If they meet your requirements, they are good bargains. If they do not, they may cost more in lost productivity than was saved on the cost difference between the Hayes modem and the Hayes lookalike.

The following items should be checked, if they are deemed to be important:

1. Few clone makers offer the full Hayes command set. Since a user may not need the full Hayes command functionality, it may not be important. However, the clones should be checked if the full set is needed.

2. Make certain the EIA-232 connectors are compatible. Some clones use male connectors and others use female connectors.

3. Some clones do not support the range of communications packages supported by the Hayes modem. Others support a full range of programs.

4. The clones often do not implement all the smartmodems' registers (S registers).

5. The performance on noisy lines is yet another area that warrants investigation. Some clones perform quite well and others do not.

The National Software Testing Laboratories (NSTL) in Philadelphia, Pennsylvania conducts some excellent tests on communications products. The reader may wish to consult with the NSTL regarding specific evaluations.

PHYSICAL LEVEL INTERFACES AND PROTOCOLS

Section 10:
Example of a Parallel Interface: IEEE-488

Section 10: Example of a Parallel Interface: IEEE-488

The specifications and recommendations described in this book use serial transmission schemes. A brief description of a parallel interface is provided here in order to compare serial and parallel systems. Our example is the IEEE 488. For more detail, the reader should obtain IEEE Standard 728-1982.

The IEEE Standard 488-1975 standard digital interface for programmable instrumentation (otherwise known as the IEEE 488) was established to provide a physical level interface for instrumentation systems. However, the specification has also seen use in other kinds of systems such as user DTEs. The IEEE 488 provides interconnection for up to 15 devices on one local network. The channel can be extended to a length of 20 meters and support data rates of up to 1 Mbit/s.

The specification provides for "talkers." This describes a device that is enabled to send data over the IEEE bus. Likewise, it designates "listeners," which are devices enabled to receive data. The interface provides a contoller that designates which device is to talk and which is/are to listen. The controller is also capable of sending other types of control information and commands, and can also receive status information from the attached devices.

Figure 46 shows the IEEE specification. It is evident this interface differs from the other interfaces described in this guide, primarily because it is a parallel interface. The data lines, DIO1-IO8, are used to carry the user data in a bit serial fashion.

Figure 46 also illustrates the control lines for the interface. These are broadly classified as data byte transfer control and general interface management. Data byte transfer control uses three lines: DAV, NRFD, and NDAC. The general interface management uses five lines: IFC, ATN, SRQ, REN, and EOI.

The data byte transfer control lines perform the following functions. The DAV (data valid), which indicates the condition of the information on the DIO signal lines, stipulates the availability and validity of the DIO lines. Whereas the NRFD (not ready for data) indicates the readiness conditions of the devices attached to the bus, the NDAC (not data accepted) indicates the acceptance of data by the devices.

The general interface management lines perform the following functions. The IFC (interface clear) is used to place the system in a known quiescent state. This line is managed by the controller. The SRQ (service request) is used by the attached device to indicate a request for attention. It also can be used to request an interruption on the bus/line. The ATN (attention) is used by the controller to specify how the data on the DIO lines are to be interpreted by the devices. It indicates which devices are to respond to the data lines. The REN (remote enable) is also used by the controller to select alternate sources of devices. The EOI (end or identify) is used by a talker device to signify the termination of a transmission sequence. It is also used in conjunction with ATN by the controller to execute a polling sequence.

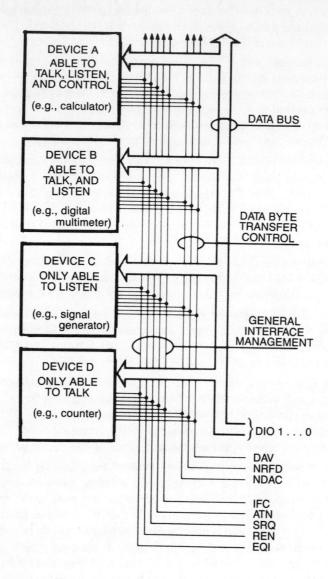

Figure 46: IEEE-488 Parallel Interface

PHYSICAL LEVEL INTERFACES AND PROTOCOLS

**Section 11:
Connecting DTEs Directly Together**

Section 11: Connecting DTEs Directly Together

User devices are often connected directly together, without the intervening modem and telephone channel. For examples, a personal computer is sometimes connected directly to an attached printer; a terminal may be attached directly to a PBX or a multiplexer; a terminal can be attached directly to a terminal cluster controller.

ISO TR 7477

In recognition of these requirements, the ISO provides specifications for direct connection between DTEs (ISO Technical Report [TR] 7477 - 1985 [E]). This report applies to DTEs conforming to the CCITT V.24 (X.24). It also applies to DTEs that employ the following CCITT specifications (and permit interconnection of these devices):

Speeds	CCITT Recommendations
up to 10 Mbit/s	balanced V.11 (X.27)
up to 100 Kbit/s	unbalanced V.10 (X.26)
below 20 Kbit/s	V.28

These interfaces also are applicable to the EIA specifications (EIA-232-D, EIA-449, etc.) and to the Bell interfaces that adhere to the CCITT recommendations. TR 7477 permits the DTE interconnection configuration to use the ISO 37, 25, or 15 pin connectors.

Tables 63 and 64 list the V.24 and X.24 circuits used for DTE interconnection and show the ISO connector pin numbers. For purposes of brevity and simplicity, the EIA-232-D/EIA-449 designations are not shown. Refer to Tables 18, 19, 20, and 21 to relate V.24 circuits to EIA-232-D/EIA-449 circuits.

The basic crossover arrangement is stipulated as (105/C and 109/I may be omitted)

DTE A	Crossover to	DTE B
103 or T		104 or R
104 or R		103 or T
105 or C		109 or I
109 or I		105 or C
102 or G		102 or G

The idea of ISO TR 7477 is that signals that are normally required by the DTE from the DCE are now provided by a connection to the complementary circuit of a DTE.

Direct Connection Using EIA Interfaces

We just learned that it is a common occurrence for two DTEs to communicate directly with others. For example, short distance connections do not need the DCEs and communications line.

The null modem is a very useful device for direct DTE-to-DTE connections and is readily available from most vendors. The reader might consider acquiring a shielded null modem as well. This may be necessary to meet regulations as well as to diminish the problems with noise.

The null modem comes in a variety of connection options. Table 65 shows some of the more common choices. These examples use the RS-232-C connector and not EIA-232-D.

On occasion, a user finds that connections through devices have either both male EIA or female EIA connectors. The answer to this problem is to install a gender changer (gender-mender). The gender changer can be placed between the two cables to solve either mismatch. In addition, most vendors provide connections for a variety of pin connections.

The reader is encouraged to check the vendor's guide very carefully because the use of the EIA pins and signals vary greatly among the many offerings. On numerous occasions, the author has spent many hours attempting to connect different terminals, personal computers, or printers together. In some instances, a special cable was needed; in other cases, special pin settings were required for the interface. An example of the problem is IBM's use of a DV-25 asynchronous board connector with male pins. Most other vendors place the male pins on the cable and the female sockets on the board.

Table 63: TR 7477 for ISO 4902 and ISO 2110 Connectors

V.24 Circuit No.	Interchange Points		ISO 4902 Pin No.	ISO 2110 Pin No.	Circuit Description/Remarks
	V.11	V.10			
–	–	–	1	1	Cable Shield (Note 1)
102	C - C′	C - C′	19	7	Signal Ground
103	A - A′ B - B′	A - A′ C - B′	4 22	2	Transmitted Data
104	A - A′ B - B′	A - A′ C - B′	6 24	3	Received Data
105	A - A′ B - B′	A - A′ C - B′	7 25	4	Request to Send (Note 2)
106	A - A′ B - B′	A - A′ C - B′	9 27	5	Ready for Sending
107	A - A′ B - B′	A - A′ C - B′	11 29	6	Data Set Ready
108	A - A′ B - B′	A - A′ C - B′	12 30	20	Connect Data Set to Line/Data Terminal Ready
109	A - A′ B - B′	A - A′ C - B′	13 31	8	Data Channel Received Line Signal Detector
113	A - A′ B - B′	A - A′ C - B′	17 35	24	Transmitter Signal Element Timing, DTE Source
114	A - A′ B - B′	A - A′ C - B′	5 23	15	Transmitter Signal Element Timing, DCE Source
115	A - A′ B - B′	A - A′ C - B′	8 26	17	Receiver Signal Element Timing

Note 1—Pin 1 is for connecting the shields between tandem sections of shielded interface cable.

Note 2—This circuit is optionally provided by the DTE.

Table 64: TR 7477 for ISO 4903 and ISO 2110 Connectors

V.24 Circuit No.	Interchange Points		ISO 4902 Pin No.	ISO 2110 Pin No.	Circuit Description/Remarks
	V.11	V.10			
–	–	–	1	1	Cable Shield (Note 1)
G	C - C'	C - C'	8	7	Signal Ground
T	A - A' B - B'	A - A' C - B'	2 9	2	Transmit
R	A - A' B - B'	A - A' C - B'	4 11	3	Receive
C	A - A' B - B'	A - A' C - B'	3 10	–	Control
I	A - A' B - B'	A - A' C - B'	5 12	–	Indication
S	A - A' B - B'	A - A' C - B'	6 13	–	Signal Element Timing (DCE Source)
B	A - A' B - B'	A - A' C - B'	7 14	–	Byte Timing (Note 2)
X	A - A' B - B'	B - B' C - B'	7 14	–	Signal Element Timing (DTE Source)

Note 1—Pin 1 is for connecting the shields between tandem sections of shielded interface cable.

Note 2—For DTEs using X.24 interchange circuits and requiring byte timing on circuit B, arrangement 6 of Figure 4 applies with the addition on an external source of byte timing.

Table 65: DTE-To-DTE Connections with EIA Pin Assignments

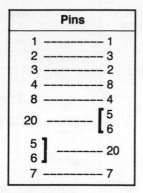
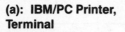

(a): IBM/PC Printer, Terminal

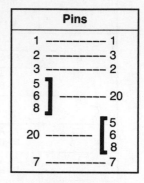

(b): Generic PC Printer, Terminal

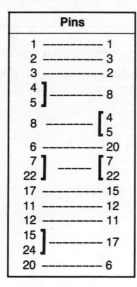

(c): Hewlett Packard #13232U

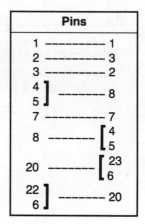

(d): DEC #H312A

PHYSICAL LEVEL INTERFACES
AND PROTOCOLS

Appendix A:
Addresses of Standards Organizations

Appendix A: Addresses of Standards Organizations

ANSI
American National Standards Institute
1430 Broadway
New York, NY 10018
Telephone: (212) 354-3300

EIA
Electronic Industries Association
2001 Eye Street, N. W.
Washington, DC 20006
Telephone: (202) 457-4966

FED-STD
General Services Administration
Specification Distribution Branch
Building 197
Washington Navy Yard
Washington, DC 20407
Telephone: (202) 472-1082

FIPS
U.S. Department of Commerce
National Technical Information Service
5285 Port Royal Road
Springfield, VA 22161
Telephone: (703) 487-4650

CCITT
Outside the United States
General Secretariat
International Telecommunications Union
Place des Nations
1121 Geneva 20, Switzerland
Telephone +41 22 995111

In the United States
United States Department of Commerce
National Technical Information Service
5285 Port Royal Road
Springfield, VA 22161
Telephone: (703) 487-4650

ISO
Outside the United States
International Organization for Standardization
Central Secretariat
1 rue de Varembe
CH-1211 Geneva, Switzerland
Telephone +41 22 34-12-40

In the United States
American National Standards Institute
1430 Broadway
New York, NY 10018
Telephone: (212) 354-3300

IEEE   The Institute of Electrical and Electronics Engineers, Inc.
                345 East 47th Street
                New York, NY 10017
                Telephone: (212) 705-7900

NBS   National Bureau of Standards
                Institute for Computer Sciences and Technology
                Technology Building, Room B-253
                Gaithersburg, MD 20899
                Telephone: (301) 921-2731

PHYSICAL LEVEL INTERFACES
AND PROTOCOLS

**Appendix B:
Codes**

Appendix B: Codes

Codes are the symbols used by the machines to direct their actions. The codes are based on binary numbers. Most of us are familiar with the decimal number system, consisting of the numbers 0–9. However, machines and the interconnecting channels are designed to support only two signal states: a 0 or a 1. For example, the binary equivalent of 394 is 110001010. Its decimal value can be established through positional notation:

$$1\times2^8 + 1\times2^7 + 0\times2^6 + 0\times2^5 + 0\times2^4 + 1\times2^3 + 0\times2^2 + 1\times2^1 + 0\times2^0$$

or $1 + 1 + 0 + 0 + 0 + 1 + 0 + 1 + 0$

or $256 + 128 + 0 + 0 + 0 + 8 + 0 + 2 + 0$

or 394_{10}

Each binary digit is called a bit. A group of eight bits make up a byte or octet (although in some systems, seven bits comprise a byte).

Binary numbers and codes are represented by several signaling techniques. The data can be represented by simply switching a current on or off; by changing the direction of current flow, or by measuring a current and its associated electromagnetic field. It is also possible to measure the voltage state of the line (such as on/off voltage, or positive or negative voltage) to represent binary 1s and 0s. Increasingly, optical fiber systems are used to transmit light pulses to represent binary 1s and 0s.

In addition to number representations, data communications systems must also represent other symbols, such as the letters of the alphabet or special characters (like the question mark, ?).

The early codes used in data communications were designed for telegraphic transmission. For example, the Morse code consists of dots and dashes in a particular sequence to represent characters, numbers, and special characters. The dots and dashes represent how long the telegraph operator presses the key on the transmitter to produce an electrical current.

Figures B-1 and B-2 are examples of two codes in wide use today. The EBCDIC code, developed and sponsored by IBM, and the ASCII code, published by the American National Standards Institute (ANSI). The ASCII code is an international standard, in that it is in conformance with the International Alphabet 5 or IA5. The EBCDIC is widely used primarily because of IBM's position in the industry. EBCDIC is an eight bit code. The bit positions in Figure B-1 are arranged to show the first four bits at the top of the table with the remaining four bits to the side of the table. The ASCII code is a seven bit code, although many vendors add an eighth bit for error-checking purposes. This bit is called a parity bit.

The codes perform the several functions. Table B-1 provides a summary and the interested reader can read the remainder of this appendix for a more detailed explanation of these codes.

- transmission control (TC)
- format effectors (FE)
- device control (DC)
- information separators (IS)
- data representation (DR)

Figure B-1: EBCDIC Code

Bits (8765) \ (4321)	0000	0001	0010	0011	0100	0101	0110	0111	1000	1001	1010	1011	1100	1101	1110	1111
0000	NUL	SOH	STX	ETX	PF	HT	LC	DEL			SMM	VT	FF	CR	SO	SI
0001	DLE	DC$_1$	DC$_2$	DC$_3$	RES	NL	BS	IL	CAN	EM	CC		IFS	IGS	IRS	IUS
0010	DS	SOS	FS		BYP	LF	EOB	PRE			SM			ENQ	ACK	BEL
0011			SYN		PN	RS	UC	EOT				DC$_4$	NAK			SUB
0100	SP										c	.	<	(	+	|
0101	&										!	$	*	)	;	¬
0110	−	/										,	%	−	>	?
0111											:	#	@	,	=	"
1000		a	b	c	d	e	f	g	h	i						
1001		j	k	l	m	n	o	p	q	r						
1010			s	t	u	v	w	x	y	z						
1011																
1100		A	B	C	D	E	F	G	H	I						
1101		J	K	L	M	N	O	P	Q	R						
1110			S	T	U	V	W	X	Y	Z						
1111	0	1	2	3	4	5	6	7	8	9						□

Figure B-2: ASCII Code

Bit Positions (4321) \ (765)	000	001	010	011	100	101	110	111
0000	NUL	DLE	SP	0	@	P	\	p
0001	SOH	DC1	!	1	A	Q	a	q
0010	STX	DC2	"	2	B	R	b	r
0011	ETX	DC3	#	3	C	S	c	s
0100	EOT	DC4	$	4	D	T	d	t
0101	ENQ	NAK	%	5	E	U	e	u
0110	ACK	SYN	&	6	F	V	f	v
0111	BEL	ETB	'	7	G	W	g	w
1000	BS	CAN	(	8	H	X	h	x
1001	HT	EM	)	9	I	Y	i	y
1010	LF	SUB	*	:	J	Z	j	z
1011	VT	ESC	+	;	K	[	k	{
1100	FF	FS	'	<	L	/\/	l	:
1101	CR	GS	−	=	M	]	m	}
1110	SO	RS	.	>	N	∧	n	~
1111	SI	US	/	?	O	−	o	DEL

Table B-1: Use of Codes

DC_1	Turns-On or Starts an Ancillary Station or Other Control Functions
DC_2	Turns-On or Starts an Ancillary Station or Other Control Functions
DC_3	Turns-Off or Starts an Ancillary Station or Other Control Functions
DC_4	Turns-Off or Starts an Ancillary Station or Other Control Functions
BEL	BELL: Controls Alarm or Other Attention-Getting Devices
ESC	ESCAPE: Used to Provide a Code Extension
SI	Shift In: Used with ESC to Extend a Code Extension
SO	Shift Out: Used with ESC to Reinstate the Standard Meanings of a Code
US	Variable Use; Usually Delimits a Data Unit Called a Unit
RS	Variable Use; Usually Delimits a Data Unit Called a Record
GS	Variable Use; Usually Delimits a Data Unit Called a Group
FS	Variable Use; Usually Delimits a Data Unit Called a File
BS	Backspace: Moves a Cursor or a Printing Mechanism Backwards
CR	Carriage Return: Moves a Cursor or a Printing Mechanism to the Beginning of the Same Line
FF	Form Feed: Moves a Cursor or a Printing Mechanism to the Next Form or Display
HT	Horizontal Tab: Moves a Cursor or a Printing Mechanism to a Next Assigned Position (or "Tab")
LF	Line Feed: Moves a Cursor or a Printing Mechanism to the Beginning of the Next Line
VT	Vertical Tab: Moves a Cursor or a Printing Mechanism to an Assigned Line
CAN	Cancel: Indicates Preceding Data Are to Be Ignored
SUB	Substitute: Used in Place of a Character That Is Invalid or in Error
SP	Space: Used to Separate Characters or Words on a Cursor or Printing Mechanism
DEL	Delete: Obliterates Unwanted Characters (e.g., Previous Mistakes)
NUL	Null: No Character Indicator. Used as a Time-Fill or Media-Fill
ACK	Positive Acknowledgment: A Positive Response by a Receiving Station to the Reception of Data or a Control Data Unit
DLE	Data Link Escape: Changes the Meaning of a Succeeding Character or Characters
ENQ	Enquiry: A Request for a Response
EOT	End of Transmission: Indicates the End of Transmission of Data (Some Vendors Use as a Negative Acknowledgment)
ETB	End of Transmission Block: Signifies End of a Block of Data
ETX	End of Text: Indicates the End of Transmission of Data That Was Initiated with STX (Start of Text)
NAK	Negative Acknowledgment: A Negative Response by a Receiving Station to the Reception of Data or a Control Data Unit
SOH	Start of Heading: Indicates the Start of a Header
STX	Start of Text: Indicates the Start of User Data (Text)
SYN	Synchronous or Idle: Used to Synchronize Sending Station's Transmission with the Receiver
EM	End of Medium: Used to Identify the Physical End of a Medium, Such as a Tape File

The transmission control characters facilitate the communications between stations. For example, the code ACK conveys that data was received, checked for errors, and determined to be error-free. The transmission control characters are: ACK, DLE, ENQ, EOT, ETB, ETX, NAK, SOH, STX, SYN, and EM.

Format effectors control the display functions of a device. For example, BS can backspace a printer head or a CRT cursor to a preceding space on a line.

These codes were developed several years ago before the advent of intelligent terminals. These earlier terminals had no cathode ray tube (CRT) screen, and were primarily paper-oriented printers. Consequently, the device-control functions are fairly limited. As the industry developed more sophisticated devices, the control codes were insufficient to provide all of the necessary device-control commands. To address this situation, ANSI now publishes codes to extend the basic code. ANSI X3.41 and X3.64 use the ESC character to "arm" subsequent control characters to provide additional functions. Specifically, X3.41 defines the command set for ASCII code extension and X3.64 defines the specific actions that the codes actually initiate on the device. For example, the three symbols of ESC 6 C instruct a terminal to move its screen cursor forward by six positions.

The format effector characters are BS, CR, FF, HT, LF, VT, CAN, SVB, SP, DEL and NUL and are described in Table B-1.

The device control characters are intended to control a station on the link. They are similar to the transmission control characters. They are DC1, DC2, DC3, DC4, BEL, ESC, SO, and SI.

The information separators are used to separate data logically. For example, the separators can be used to define data elements belonging to a logical user record; records comprising a group; and groups comprising a file or database. They are US, RS, GS, and FS.

The fifth function is to actually convey or represent data. For example, the letter C is represented as 11000011 in EBCDIC and 1000011 in IA5/ASCII. The IA5/ASCII figure is read as follows for C (column 4, row 3):

b7	b6	b5	b4	b3	b2	b1
1	0	0	0	0	1	1

The b1 position is the low-order position.

The binary signals are represented by some type of electrical, optical, or radio signal. A common convention (protocol) is to represent a zero with a positive voltage and a one with a negative voltage. In the old days (1960s/1970s) paper tape was used to represent codes. A perforation in the tape (MARK) represents a one and no perforation a zero (SPACE).

PHYSICAL LEVEL INTERFACES
AND PROTOCOLS

Glossary

A

Abbreviated dialing: A feature of some telephone switches that permits users to establish calls by entering fewer digits than would otherwise be required.

Access line: Part of a leased telephone line that permanently connects the user with the serving central office.

ACD (automatic call distributor): A switching system that automatically distributes incoming calls in the sequences they are received to a centralized group of receivers without human interface. If no receivers are available, the calls will be held until one becomes free.

AC/DC ringing: Telephone signaling wherein alternate current is used to operate a ringer and direct current is used to activate a relay which stops the ringing when called party answers.

Acoustic coupler: A device that allows a telephone handset to be used for access to the switched telephone network for data transmission; digital signals are modulated as sound waves. Used with portable devices usually.

Active line: A line that is ready and available for data transmission; usually held in active state through continuous transmission of special signals.

ACU: See automatic calling unit.

A/D (analog-to-digital) conversion: Translation of an analog signal to an intelligible representation in digital form.

Adaptive equalization: A modem feature that allows a modem to automatically compensate for distortions on the line.

Adaptive speed: See autobaud.

Address: In data communications, a sequence of bits, which identifies a station, user, or application; in telephony, the number entered by the caller that identifies the called party.

Aerial cable: Communications wires or cables connected to poles, towers, or similar overhead support structures.

Alias: In digital pulse code modulation (PCM) systems, a spurious signal that is a result of energy between the signal frequencies and the sampling frequency.

Alternate mark inversion (AMI): A digital signal that is represented by alternate polarities.

AM: See amplitude modulation.

Ambient noise: Interference that is present in a communications line at times when a signal is present.

Amplifier: A component that boosts the strength or amplitude of a transmitted analog signal; equivalent to a repeater (or regenerative repeater) in digital transmissions.

Amplitude: The size or magnitude of a voltage or current waveform.

Amplitude modulation (AM): Transmission method in which variations in the voltage waveform of a carrier signal determine encoded information. Also called AM.

Amplitude variation (ripple): Unwanted variation of signal voltage at different frequencies on a communications line.

Analog loopback: Technique for testing transmission equipment. Isolates faults to the receiving or transmitting circuitry; where a device sends back a signal that is then compared with the original signal.

Analog transmission: In communications, a continuous and periodic nondiscrete signal represented by continuously variable physical qualities. Contrast with digital transmission.

ANSI (American National Standards Institute): A coordinating organization in the U.S. for numerous other standards groups.

Answerback: The response of a device to transmitted control signals; typically part of handshaking between devices.

Answering tone: A signal sent by the called modem (the "answer" modem) to the calling modem (the "originate" modem) to indicate the called modem's readiness to accept data.

ASCII (American national standard code for information interchange) (X3.4): The standard, 7-bit (8 bits, with parity) character code used for data communications and data processing. Conforms to international alphabet #5 (IA #5), or ISO V.3. Also called USASCII.

ASCII terminal: A terminal that uses ASCII; usually synonomous with asynchronous terminal.

Asynchronous: Transmission that is not related to the timing of the transmission facility. Transmission characterized by individual characters, surrounded by start and stop bits, from which a receiver derives the necessary timing for sampling the data stream. Also see start-stop transmission.

AT&T (American Telephone and Telegraph Company): The predominant carrier in the United States.

Attenuation: Reduction or loss of signal strength; loss of communications signal energy. Attenuation increases with both frequency and cable length. Contrast with gain. Also see loss.

Audio frequencies: Frequencies that can be heard by the average human ear— between 15 and 20,000 Hz.

Auto-answer: Automatic answering; capability of a device to respond to an incoming call on a dial-up line and to establish a data connection with a remote device, without operator intervention.

Autobaud: The capability of a device to adjust to variable transmission speeds on a channel. A process by which a receiving device determines the speed, code level, and stop bits of incoming data by examining the first preselected sign-on character. Also called adaptive speed.

Auto-dial: A modem that automatically originates calls (dials the desired number).

Automatic calling unit (ACU): A device or circuitry within a modem that dials and answers calls on a switched telephone circuit.

AWG (American wire gauge): See gauge.

B

Background noise: See thermal noise and noise.

Backward channel: A channel used for sending low speed data in the opposite direction of the primary (forward) channel. Also see reverse channel.

Balanced (to ground): The impedance-to-ground on one wire equals the impedance-to-ground on the other wire of a two-wire circuit. Contrast with unbalanced (to ground).

Balancing network: A system of circuit elements designed to simulate the impedance of uniform cable or open-wire circuits.

Balun: Balanced/unbalanced, an impedance-matching device used to connect balanced twisted-pair cabling with unbalanced coaxial cable.

Band splitter: A multiplexer designed to divide the composite bandwidth into several independent, narrower bandwidth channels.

Bandwidth: The difference, expressed in Hertz (Hz), between the highest and lowest frequencies of a transmission channel; that is, the range of frequencies in the channel. Also see frequency band. Also called frequency range.

Baseband: The band of frequencies occupied by a signal below the point that the signal is modulated as an analog carrier frequency; in modulation, the frequency band occupied by the aggregate of the transmitted signals when first used to modulate the carrier; or, an unmodulated signal.

Baud: A measurement of the signaling speed of a data transmission device; equivalent to the maximum number of signaling elements, or symbols, per second that are generated. Also called modulation rate.

Bellcore (Bell Communications Research): Organization established by the AT&T divestiture, representing and funded by the BOCs and for establishing telephone-network standards and conducting research; includes some of former Bell Labs.

BER: See bit error rate.

BERT (bit error rate testing): Testing a data line with a pattern of bits that are compared before and after the transmission to detect errors.

Bias: Communications signal distortion with respect to bit timing, or bit sampling; also occurs when certain electrical specifications (capacitance) are not met.

Bipolar: A signaling method used for digital transmission services, in which the signal carrying the binary value successively alternates between positive and negative polarities.

Bit: Binary digit contraction. The smallest unit of data communications information, used to develop representations of characters or bytes.

Bit duration: The time that it takes one encoded bit to pass a point on the transmission medium. Also see bit time.

Bit error: The value of a bit is changed in transmission and interpreted incorrectly by the receiver.

Bit error rate (BER): The percentage of received bits that are in error, relative to a number of bits received; usually expressed as a number referenced to a power of 10 (e.g., 1 in 10 or 1:10) also referenced to a fraction (e.g., $1:10^{-1}$).

Bit error rate testing (BERT): Testing a data line with a pattern of bits that are compared before and after the transmission to detect errors.

Bit rate: The rate at which bits are transmitted over a communications path. Normally expressed in bits per second. The bit rate is not to be confused with the data signaling rate (baud), which measures the rate of signal changes being transmitted. Also see BPS, and bit/s.

Bit/s (bits per second): Unit of measure for data transmission speed. The following terms are used with bit/s: Kbit/s, or kilobit/s = thousands of bits per second; Mbit/s, or megabit/s = millions of bits per second; Gbit/s, or gigabit/s = billions of bits per second; Tbit/s, or terabit/s = trillions of bits per second. Also see BPS and bit rate.

Bit time: The length of time a bit manifests itself on a communications channel. Also see bit duration.

Board: An informal term describing the circuitry that provides the interface of a communications channel to a device, such as a DTE, a DCE, or a DSE. Also called circuit board, serial board, or communications interface adapter.

BOC (Bell Operating Company): One of the 22 local telephone companies divested from AT&T; now reorganized into seven regional Bell holding companies.

Boot strap: A technique, usually used on a computer, to bring a system into a desired state by means of its own action, usually by execution of the first few instructions of a loading routine, which loads the rest of the system.

BPS (bits per second): The basic unit of data communications rate measurement. Usually refers to rate information bits are transmitted. Also see bit/s and bit rate.

Branch cable: A cable that diverges from a main cable to reach some secondary point.

Break: A signal used to "break in" when the opposite party or unit is sending. Also a space condition that exists longer than one character time. Often used by a receiving terminal to interrupt the sending device's transmission.

Breakout box: A test device used for monitoring and inserting signals at the EIA-232-D and other physical interfaces.

Broadband: Transmission systems that support a wide range of electromagnetic frequencies. The transmission medium and radio frequency carrier signals are in the 50-to-500-MHz range. Any communications channel having a bandwidth greater than a voice-grade telecommunications channel. Also called wideband.

Buffer: A storage area for data.

Bus: A single connective link between multiple devices or sites; any of the processing sites can transmit to any other. Usually used in describing a local, parallel link.

Byte: Some set of contiguous bits that make up a discrete item of information. Also see octet and character.

C

Call forwarding: Calls to one station can be automatically switched to another specified station.

Call setup time: The overall length of time required to establish a switched call.

Camp-on: A feature of a switching system that notifies a calling station that a called station is busy and allows the calling station to wait and later connects when the line becomes free.

Card module: A printed-circuit board that plugs into equipment.

Carrier: An analog signal that is modified by information (changes to frequency or amplitude or phase or combinations of amplitude and phase) to represent the information in a communications system.

Carrier: A continuous signal modulated with a second baseband signal.

CCITT (International Telegraph and Telephone Consultative Committee): (from the French, Comite Consultatif International Telegraphique et Telephonique). An influential international standards setting organization.

Central office (CO): In telephony, the phone company facility, usually an end office, at which subscribers' local loops terminate. Handles a specific geographic area. Identified by the first three digits of the local telephone number. Also see end office.

Centronics: Printer manufacturer that set the de facto interconnection standards for parallel printers.

CEPT: Conference of European Postal and Telecommunications (PTT) Administration

Channel: See line; also called link.

Channel bank: Equipment that performs multiplexing of lower-speed, digital channels into a higher-speed composite channel.

Character: A language unit composed of a group of bits. Also see byte and octet.

Character code: A set of binary representations for the alphabet, numerals, and common symbols, such as ASCII, EBCDIC, and V.3.

Character parity: A technique of adding an overhead bit to each character to provide error-checking at the receiver.

Character synchronization: The process wherein a receiving device determines which bits, sent over a data link, should be grouped together into characters.

Check bit: See parity bit.

Circuit: The path that provides communications between two or more locations.

Circuit board: See board.

Circuit load: A percentage of maximum circuit capacity reflecting actual use during a span of time. Also called line load.

Circuit switching: A method of communications whereby an electrical connection between calling and called stations is established on demand (for exclusive use of the caller) until the connection is released.

Clear to send: See CTS.

Clock: A signal that provides a timing reference for a transmission link. Used to control functions such as sampling interval, signaling rate, and duration of signal elements.

Clocking: Time synchronizing of communications information.

Clock pulse: A clock signal used to synchronize the transmission signal of one device to another.

CO: See central office.

Coaxial cable: A transmission medium consisting of one or more central wire conductors (two in the case of twin axial cable) surrounded by a dielectric insulator and encased in either a wire mesh or extruded metal sheathing. Sheathing prevents electromagnetic leakage.

Code: A group of bits that are predefined to represent characters, numbers, and special characters. Rules specifying how data are represented.

Codec (coder/decoder): Performs a specific analog-to-digital conversion.

Common battery central office: A telephone central office that supplies power to its associated stations.

Communications: Transmission of intelligence between two points.

Communications interface adapter: See board.

Communications line: Any medium, such as a wire, telephone circuit, or satellite channel that connects to devices, such as a terminal and a computer.

Complex wiring: Multiline, nonresidential telephone wiring inside user premises. Since 1983, this wiring is deregulated only for wiring done after fall 1983. Also called intrasystem and multiwiring. Contrast with simple wiring and embedded wiring.

Common carrier: Any supplier of transmission services to the general public authorized by the appropriate regulatory authority and bound to adhere to applicable operating rules, such as making services available at a common price and on a nondiscriminatory basis.

Composited circuit: An older term describing a circuit used for telephone and telegraph simultaneously by frequency division.

Compromise net: In a telephone line, a network used in conjunction with a hybrid coil to balance a subscriber's loop.

Conditioning: A technique of applying electronic elements to a communications line to improve the capability to support higher and better quality transmission rates. Also see equalization.

Connecting block: A cable termination block where access to circuit connections is available.

Connector: A physical interface, typically with male and female components.

Control line timing: Clock signals between a DCE and a DTE.

Controlled carrier: A feature of a DCE that allows the carrier signal to be turned ON or OFF under command of the DTE. Controlled carrier is required on multipoint lines.

CPE: See customer premises equipment.

CPS (characters per second): A data rate unit.

Crosstalk: Transference of electrical energy from one transmission medium to another (usually adjacent) medium; generally in the voice-grade frequency range and typical of unshielded twisted pair wires.

CSDC (circuit switched digital capability): Older name for AT&T-designed service, implemented within the BOCs, that offers users a 56-Kbit/s digital channel on a user-switchable basis. Uses same local loop as for analog voice, but without loading coils. Now called accunet switched 56 service or 56 Kbit/s switched digital service.

CSU (channel service unit): A component of customer premises equipment (CPE) used to terminate a digital circuit at the customer site. Performs certain line conditioning functions and responds to loopback commands from central office; also, ensures proper 1s density in transmitted bit stream and performs bipolar violation correction.

CTS (clear to send): A control line and signal between a DCE and a DTE.

Current: The amount of electrical charge flowing past a circuit point measured in amperes.

Current loop: An interface in which the absence or presence of current flow (as opposed to voltage levels) is used to provide signaling between devices.

Customer premises equipment (CPE): Communications equipment located on customer's premises. CPE is unregulated and can be obtained on a competitive basis.

Cycle: An interval of space or time in which an event is completed; describing a complete oscillation of an analog waveform.

Cycles per second: The number of oscillations in one second of the analog waveform. See also hertz (Hz) and frequency.

CXR carrier: A communications signal used to indicate the intention to transmit data on a line.

D

DAA (data access arrangement): A telephone system protective device used to attach nonregistered equipment to the carrier network; slowly being phased out of industry.

DACS (digital access and cross-connect system): AT&T-manufactured central office switching equipment; allows a T1 carrier facility, or subchannels to be switched, or cross-connected to another T1 carrier.

Damping: A characteristic designed to prevent unwanted oscillatory conditions in a circuit.

Data: Represented images to convey intelligence, including voice, text, facsimile, and video.

Data circuit-terminating equipment: See DCE.

Data communications: The transmission and reception of data. Data transfer between source and destination via one or more data links.

Data link: A direct data communications transmission path between two adjacent nodes or devices.

Data service unit: See DSU.

Data set: An electronic terminating unit for analog lines that is used for data signal modulation and demodulation. Also see modem.

Data set clocking: A time-based mechanism furnished by the data set for regulating the bit rate of transmission.

Data switching exchange: See DSE.

Data terminal equipment (DTE): Typically, an end-user device, such as a terminal or computer.

Data transfer rate: The number of bits, characters, or blocks per unit of time transferred from one site to another.

dB (decibel): A unit of measurement used to express the ratio of two values equal to 10 times the logarithm derived from a ratio of the two levels.

dBm: Decibel referenced to 1 milliwatt. Relative strength of a signal, calculated in decibels, when the signal is compared in a ratio to a value of 1 milliwatt. At 0 dBm, a signal delivers 1 milliwatt to a line load, while at - 30 dBm a signal delivers 0.001.

dB meter: A meter having a scale calibrated to read directly in decibel values at a specified reference level, usually dBm.

DCE (data circuit-terminating equipment): In a communications link, equipment that is either part of the network or an access point to the network. In the case of an EIA-232-D connection, the modem is usually regarded as DCE, while the user device is the DTE, or data terminal equipment. In this case, the DCE is at the physical level. In a CCITT X.25 connection, the network access and packet-switching node is viewed as the DCE and is considered to be at the network level.

DDD: See direct distance dialing.

DDS (dataphone digital service): Private-line digital service offered by BOCs and AT&T Communications, with data rates at 2.4, 4.8, 9.6, and 56 Kbit/s.

Decay: See attenuation and loss.

Decibal: See dB.

Dedicated line: A communications line that is not dialed; may be privately owned. See also leased line, private line, and nonswitched lines.

Delay: A period of time that elapses between the end of one event and the start of another.

Demodulation: The extraction of transmitted information from a modulated carrier signal.

Demodulator: A functional section of a modem that converts the received analog line signals back to digital form.

Diagnostic modems: Modems that communicate with each other over a low-speed channel for the purposes of communicating control and diagnostic information.

Diagnostics: The process of detecting errors, "bugs," or deficiencies in a system.

Dial pulse: An interruption of the direct current (dc) loop of a calling telephone. The current is interrupted once for each unit of value in the dialed digit.

Dibit: A group of two bits used often in modulation where each possible dibit (00,01,10,11) is encoded and modulated on to the carrier.

Digital loopback: Technique for testing the digital processing circuitry of a communications device; may be initiated locally or remotely via a telecommunications circuit.

Digital transmission: Techniques where information is encoded as either a binary "1" or "0." The representation of information in discrete binary form in contrast to the analog representation of information in variable, continuous waveforms. Contrast with analog transmission.

DIP (dual in-line pins): Term to describe the pin arrangement on an integrated circuit (IC).

Direct distance dialing (DDD): Dialing without operator assistance; common term used in North America's dial telephone network.

Direct inward dialing: An external caller can call an extension without going through an operator.

Direct outward dialing: An internal caller at an extension can dial an external number without going through an operator.

Disconnect: In communications, to disengage a device used in a connection; for example, a telephone call.

Distortion: The unwanted modification or change of signals from their true form by some characteristic of the communications line or equipment being used for transmission (e.g., delay distortion, amplitude distortion).

Distribution frame: A structure for terminating telephone wiring, usually the frame is at the telephone central office or the user's office.

Double-current signaling: A MARK is represented by current in one direction and a SPACE by current in the other direction.

DOV (data over voice): On voice telephone lines, sending modulated data by using carrier frequencies above the voice band.

Driver: A module that manages an I/O port to an external device, such as a serial EIA-232-D port to a modem; also describes a module that manages a group of software subroutines.

Drop: Refers to the place on a multipoint line where a tap is installed so that a station can be connected.

Dropouts: Cause of errors and loss of synchronization with telephone line data transmission when the signal level drops at least 12 dB for more than 4 milliseconds. Bell standard allows no more than two dropouts per 15-minute period.

DSE (data switching exchange): A device that routes or switches data from input to output lines.

DSU (data service unit): A DCE-type device that transmits and receives digital signals across a communications link. Now generally combined with a channel service unit (CSU); performs conversion of customer's data stream to bipolar format for transmission.

DTE (data terminal equipment): Typically, an end-user device, such as a terminal or computer.

DTMF (dual tone multi-frequency): The push-button, or touch-tone, signaling method where each depressed key on a telephone generates two audio output ones. The combination is unique for each of the 12 keys. Contrast with rotary dial.

DTS (digital termination system): A method of bypassing local loop service. May use either microwave or fiber-optic cable.

Dual tone multi-frequency: See DTMF.

Duplex: See full duplex (FDX).

Duplexed system: Two or more distinct and separate sets of facilities, each of which is capable of assuming the function of the other.

DUV (data under voice): On communications links where the low-frequency bands are used for data. The higher-frequency bands are used for voice; hence, data are "under" voice.

E

Echo cancelation: A technique that isolates and cancels unwanted signal energy from the primary signal.

Echo suppressor: A device installed in long-distance telephone lines for eliminating echo back to the speaker. It blocks the receive side of the line during the time the transmit side is in use.

EIA (Electronics Industries Association): A U.S. trade organization that issues its own standards and contributes to ANSI.

Embedded wiring: Multiline telephone wiring installed by the telephone company in user's premises before fall 1983. This wiring remains regulated and under tariff. Contrast with complex and simple wiring.

Encoding/decoding: The process of reforming data into a format suitable for transmission and then reconverting it after transmission.

End office: The first telephone office that a data line is connected to over the local subscriber loop or access line. The end switching office for a dialed connection; also a class 5 telephone central office, at which subscribers' loops terminate. See also central office.

Envelope delay: An analog line impairment wherein a variation of signal delay occurs across the frequencies in the data channel bandwidth.

Equalization: The spacing and operation of amplifiers so that the gain provided by the amplifier, for each frequency, coincides with the signal loss at the same frequency. Also, circuitry that compensates for the differences in attenuation at different frequencies, usually a combination of adjustable coils, capacitors, and/or resistors. See also conditioning.

Equalizer: A device to compensate for distortions on telephone lines.

Exchange: The local telephone central office or the local area that a caller may place a call without incurring an extra charge.

Exchange carrier: After 1984 divestiture, the local telephone company. Contrast with interexchange carrier.

External modem: A stand-alone modem, in contrast to a modem within a device, which is called an inboard modem.

F

F1F2: A type of modem that operates over a half duplex line (two-wire) to produce two subchannels at two different frequencies for low-speed full duplex operation. Also see reverse channel and backward channel. Contrast with forward channel.

Fading: A phenomenon in microwave or radio transmission, where atmospheric, electromagnetic, thermal, or gravitational influences cause a signal to be deflected or diverted away from the target receiver.

Far-end crosstalk: Crosstalk that travels along a circuit in the same direction as the signals in that circuit.

FCC (Federal Communications Commission): Commissioners appointed by the President under the Communications Act of 1934; regulates all interstate telecommunications in the United States.

FDM: See frequency-division multiplexing.

FDX: See full duplex.

Federal Communications Commission: See FCC.

Federal Information Processing Standard: See FIPS.

Filter: Electronic circuitry that blocks some components of a signal while allowing other components to pass through uniformly. For example, a high-pass filter blocks all frequencies in a signal that are below a specified frequency.

FIPS (Federal Information Processing Standard): A U.S. government standard promulgated by the National Bureau of Standards.

Fixed equalization: A simple equalization technique for modems where the amount of compensation is preset in the modem, usually by the manufacturer.

Forward channel: The communications path carrying data or voice from the call initiator to the called party. Contrast with reverse channel, F1F2, and backward channel.

Four-wire circuit: A circuit that consists of two twisted pair cables. A four-wire circuit provides two separate circuits between stations. This facilitates communications in both directions simultaneously.

Four-wire repeater: A device used in a four-wire circuit consisting of an amplifier servicing one direction of the circuit and an amplifier for the other direction.

Fox message: A diagnostic test message that uses all the letters and numbers: "The quick brown fox jumped over a lazy dog's back 1234567890."

Framing: A control procedure used with multiplexed digital channels, where bits are inserted so that the receiver can identify the time slots that are allocated to each subchannel.

Frequency: The number of repetitions per a unit of time of a waveform; the number of complete cycles per unit of time, expressed in hertz (Hz). Also see hertz and cycles per second.

Frequency band: Portion of the electromagnetic spectrum within a specified upper- and lower-frequency limit. Also see bandwidth. Also called frequency range.

Frequency-division multiplexing (FDM): Sharing a transmission channel where carrier signals of different frequencies are transmitted simultaneously; each user is assigned to a different carrier frequency.

Frequency modulation (FM): Encoding a carrier wave by varying the frequency of the transmitted signal. Also see frequency shift keying (FSK).

Frequency offset: Analog line frequency changes; one of the impairments encountered on a communications line.

Frequency range: See frequency band and bandwidth.

Frequency shift keying (FSK): A form of frequency modulation in which the carrier frequency is made to vary or change in frequency at the instant when there is a change in the state of the signal being transmitted. Also see frequency modulation.

FSK: See frequency shift keying.

Full duplex (FDX): Operation of a communications link where transmissions travel in both directions at the same time between devices. Also called two way simultaneous (TWS) and duplex.

Full/full duplex: A protocol that, when operating on a multidrop line, is capable of transmitting from the master location to one of the slave sites. At the same time, the master location can receive a transmission from a different slave site on the same line.

G

Gain: The degree to which the amplitude of a signal is increased. The amount of amplification realized when a signal passes through an amplifier, repeater, or antenna. Normally measured in decibels. Contrast with loss and attenuation.

Gauge: Wire size standard used in communications line media descriptions. Also called AWG (American wire gauge).

Giga: Designation for one billion.

Gigahertz (GHz): An analog frequency unit equal to one billion Hertz.

Ground: An electrical connection or common conductor that connects to the earth.

Guardband: The unused frequency band between two channels; provides separation of the channels to prevent mutual interference.

Guard frequency: A single-frequency carrier tone used to indicate that the analog line is prepared to send data. Also, the frequencies between subchannels in FDM systems used to guard against subchannel interference.

H

Half duplex (HDX): A communications line where transmission occurs in both directions, but only one direction at a time; transmission directions are alternately switched to accommodate two-way data flow. Also called two-way alternate (TWA).

Hard wired: A communications link that permanently connects two nodes, stations, or devices. Circuitry that performs fixed operations by unalterable circuit layout rather than under stored-program control.

Harmonic telephone ringer: A ringer that responds to alternating current only within a narrow frequency band. Different frequency ringers are employed for selective ringing on a multiparty telephone line.

Hertz: Internationally recognized unit of measure for electrical frequency. The number of cycles per second. Abbreviated Hz. Also see frequency and cycles per second.

High pass: A frequency level, above which an analog filter will allow all frequencies to be passed.

Hiss: See thermal noise and noise.

Hybrid: An inductive device that converts a two-wire circuit into a four-wire circuit or a four-wire circuit into a two-wire circuit.

Hz: See hertz.

I

Idle character: A character transmitted on a communications channel that does not produce output at the receiver; often used to keep channel in some preferred type of condition such as an "idle state."

IEEE: The Institute of Electrical and Electronics Engineers, Inc.

Inboard: A device, typically a modem, that is located inside the cabinet of another device, typically a DTE.

INTELSAT (International Telecommunications Satellite Organization): An international organization of over 100 countries that administer, use, and share revenue from satellite services.

Interchange circuit: In a physical interface, a circuit with an associated pin assignment on the interface connector.

Interexchange carrier: After 1984 divestiture, the long distance carrier furnishing service between local telephone companies. Contrast with exchange carrier.

Interface: A shared boundary; a point of demarcation between two devices, where signals, connectors, timing, and handshaking are defined.

Intermodulation distortion: An analog line impairment where two frequencies create an erroneous frequency, which in turn distorts the original data signal representation.

International Standards Organization: See ISO.

International Telecommunications Union: See ITU.

Interoffice trunk: A direct circuit between telephone central offices.

Intrasystem wiring: See complex wiring.

IRC (International Record Carrier): One of a group of common carriers that, in the past, carried traffic from gateway cities in the United States to locations abroad and overseas.

ISDN (integrated services digital network): The CCITT standardization for a network that allows a variety of mixed digital transmission services.

ISO (International Standards Organization): A voluntary standards organization responsible for the promulgation of the widely known seven-layer open systems interconnection (OSI) model.

ISU (integrated service unit): A device that combines the functions of both a CSU and a DSU.

ITDM (intelligent TDM): A digital multiplexer that assigns time slots on demand rather than a fixed scanning basis. Also called statistical TDM.

ITU (International Telecommunications Union): The telecommunications agency of the United Nations. Provides standards for communications and coordinates worldwide frequency allocations and radio regulations.

IVDT (integrated voice data terminal): Devices that feature a terminal keyboard and display as well as a voice telephone instrument.

J

Jumper: A patch cable or wire used to establish a circuit for testing.

K

K (kilo): Notation for one thousand (e.g., kilobit/s).

K: Expression for 1024; standard quantity measurement for disk and diskette storage, and semiconductor circuit capacity; e.g., a Kbyte of memory equals 1024 bytes.

L

Leased line: A communications line, usually a four-wire circuit, for voice and/or data, leased from a communications carrier on a monthly basis. See also private line, dedicated line, and nonswitched line.

Limited distance modem (LDM): A modem that can operate properly over relatively short distances (up to about 20 miles or 32 km). LDMs must operate over metallic wire circuits (nonloaded). Also called short-haul modem.

Line: Usually refers to a communications circuit or path for voice or data of any media (wire, optic, etc.). Also called link or channel.

Line driver: A device that allows two or more devices to communicate over twisted pair cable. The twisted pair cable is driven in a balanced line configuration, which provides high immunity to electrically noisy environments.

Line group: A set of communications lines of the same type; for example, satellite links/lines.

Line hit: Electrical interference causing undesirable signals to be introduced onto a circuit.

Line Load: See circuit load.

Line speed: The rate at which data are sent over a data link. Line speed is usually measured in bits per second and abbreviated as bit/s or BPS.

Line turnaround: The delay in a half duplex communications link between the time one frame of data has been sent and received and the next frame transmitted; in EIA-232-D connections, the delay after request to send (RTS) has been signaled and a clear to send indication (CTS) is received.

Link: See line; also called channel.

Loaded line: A telephone line equipped with coils (called loading coils) that minimize voice-frequency amplitude distortion.

Loaded wire: Refers to local loops that have loading coils installed.

Loading: Adding inductance to a transmission line to minimize amplitude distortion; accomplished with loading coils. Also placing a software program or a database into a computer.

Loading coil: An induction device employed in telephone company local loops (greater than 18,000 feet in length) that compensates for wire capacitance and boosts voice-grade frequencies; often removed for new generation of high-speed local-loop data services.

Local analog loopback: A loopback test that forms the loop at the line side (analog output) of the local modem.

Local loop: The access line from either a user terminal or a computer port to the first telephone office along the line path. Also called subscriber loop.

Long lines: A communications line in which facilities of a long distance carrier are used. The former term used to describe AT&T long-haul facilities and organizations; after divestiture, renamed to AT&T Communications.

Loopback: Diagnostic procedure used for transmission devices; a test pattern is sent to a device, then sent back to the originator, and compared with the original pattern.

Loop current: A terminal-to-line interface that involves switching an electrical current on and off to represent data bits of 1 and 0.

Loop start: Method of signaling off-hook condition between a phone and a switch. Picking up the receiver closes a loop, allowing dc current to flow, which is interpreted as a request for service.

Loop transmission: A mode of multipoint operation where the network is configured as a closed loop, and each station receives, regenerates, and retransmits data until it arrives at its destination station.

Loss: Reduction in signal strength. Also see attenuation. Also called decay. Contrast with gain.

Low pass: A specific frequency level below which an analog filter will allow all frequencies to pass.

M

M (Mega): Designation for one million.

m (milli): Designation for one-thousandth (0.001).

Magnetic delay line: A communications line described by the propagation time of its magnetic waves.

MARK: The condition of the data line when sending a logic one. In telegraph communications, a MARK represents a closed condition with current flowing. Contrast with SPACE.

Master clock: The central source of timing signals, which stations use for synchronization.

Megabyte (Mbyte): 1,048,576 bytes, equal to 1024 Kbytes; usually rounded to 1,000,000.

Megahertz (MHz): A unit of analog frequency equal to 1 million Hz.

Metallic circuits: Circuits that use metal wire (copper) from end to end. Implies that no loading coils or other devices are interposed between the ends of the circuit.

Metallic facility terminal: A telephone company device which may only be connected to another device through a metallic wire (no microwave, optical fiber, etc.).

Microsecond: One-millionth of a second (0.000001).

Microwave: Part of the electromagnetic spectrum above 890 megahertz; including line-of-sight open air microwave transmission and satellite communications.

Milliampere (mA): Electric current measurement unit.

Millisecond: One-thousandth of a second (0.001).

Milliwatt (mW): A power unit of measurement equal to 0.001 watt.

MIL-STD 188: A military standard interface similar to RS-232 between a DCE and a DTE.

Modem: An acronym taken from functions the unit performs by modulating and demodulating the digital information from a terminal or computer port into an analog carrier signal to be sent over an analog line. See also data set.

Modem eliminator: A device that allows two DTE devices to be connected together without using modems.

Modem sharing unit: A device that allows several terminals or other devices to share a single modem.

Modulation: Changing the properties of a signal to encode and convey information such as voice or data images.

Modulation rate: See baud.

Modulator: The sending function of a modem.

Multidrop line: See multipoint line.

Multiplexing: Combining of multiple data channels onto a single medium; user data are interleaved on a bit, byte, or block basis (time division) or separated by different carrier frequencies (frequency division).

Multipoint line: A line interconnecting several stations. Also called multidrop. Contrast with point-to-point.

Multiwiring: See complex wiring.

Nanosecond: One-billionth of a second (0.000000001).

Narrowband: Subvoice-grade channels; data speeds from 100 to 200 bit/s.

Near-end crosstalk: Energy transferred from one circuit to an adjoining circuit; occurs at the end of the transmission link where the signal source is located; caused by high-frequency or unbalanced signals and insufficient shielding.

Network: An interconnected group of nodes; a series of points, nodes, or stations connected by communications channels.

Node: A point where one or more devices interconnect into a transmission line. A physical device that allows for the transmission of data within a network.

Noise: Extraneous signal disturbances in a communications link; electromagnetic interference; random variations in signal voltage or current. See also thermal noise. Also called background noise or hiss.

Noise suppressor: Circuitry in a receiver or transmitter that reduces noise.

Nonswitched line: A direct connection between two stations. A connection established without dialing. See also leased line, private line, and dedicated line.

Normal contacts: The circuit contacts of an access jack that are normally closed when a plug is not inserted into the jack and are interrupted by plug insertion.

NTIA (National Telecommunications and Information Administration): Agency of the U.S. Department of Commerce concerned with the development of communications standards.

Null modem: A device to interface two asynchronous DTEs or DCEs.

O

Octet: A set of contiguous eight bits that make up a discrete item of information. Also see byte and character.

Off-hook: Condition indicating the active state of a subscriber's telephone circuit. It signals a central office that a user wants service. Contrast with on-hook.

Off-line: Condition in which a user, terminal, or other device is not connected to a computer or is not actively transmitting via a network.

On-hook: A subscriber's telephone circuit, where the telephone or circuit is not in use. Contrast with off-hook.

On-line: A direct connection between a remote terminal and a central processing site.

On-line testing: Testing of a station concurrently with the station's ongoing communications process.

Open air transmission: A transmission that uses no physical communications medium other than air.

Open wire transmission: Communications lines mounted on aerial crossarms on utility poles; supported above the surface of the ground on insulators.

Originate and answer: A procedure whereby two modems transmit and receive with complimentary frequencies. One modem's transmit frequencies are the other's receive frequencies and vice versa.

Oscillator: An electronic device used to produce repeating signals of a given amplitude or frequency.

Oscilloscope: An instrument, typically used in communications systems diagnostics, that displays visually a signal's characteristics, such as current and voltage.

OSI (open systems interconnection): OSI reference model, a seven-layer network architecture being used for the definition of network protocol standards.

Out-of-band: The use of separate channels for the data signals and control signals (example: EIA-232-D interfaces).

P

Parallel: Describing the simultaneous occurrence of two or more related acitvities.

Parallel transmission: Data transfer in which all bits of a character are sent simultaneously, either over separate communications lines or circuits or over a single channel by using multiple frequencies. Contrast with serial transmission.

Parity bit: An additional non-user bit appended to a group of bits, typically to a seven- or eight-bit byte, which indicates whether the number of 1s in the group of bits is an odd or even number; mechanism for error checking a transmission. Also called check bit.

Parity check: Process of error checking using the parity bit.

Parity error: An error that occurs in data where extra bits are sent with the data based on a calculation made at the transmit end. The same calculation is performed at the receive end. If the results of both calculations do not agree, a parity error has occurred.

Pass-band filters: Filters that allow only the frequencies within the communications channel to pass while rejecting all frequencies outside the pass band.

Patching jacks: Access devices used to patch around faulty equipment by using spare units.

PC (phase corrector): A function of synchronous modems that adjusts the local data clocking signal to match the incoming data.

Phantom circuit: A superimposed circuit derived from two suitably arranged pairs of wires called side circuits; the wires are circuits unto themselves but also act as one conductor for the phantom circuit.

Phase: Describing the point an analog signal has reached in its cycle.

Phase hits: A sudden electrical disturbance on a communications line that causes the phase of the carrier signal to change. This causes bit errors on the data line.

Phase jitter: An analog line impairment caused by power and communications equipment along the line, shifting the signal phase relationship.

Phase modulation (PM): Changing the phase of an analog signal in such a manner to represent binary data. Also see phase shift keying.

Phase shift keying (PSK): The phase-modulation encoding technique used by many modems. Also see phase modulation.

Physical layer: Within the OSI model, the lowest level of processing. It is concerned with the electrical, mechanical, and handshaking procedures over the interface that connects a DTE to a DCE.

Physical unit (PU): In IBM's SNA, the component that manages the resources of a node.

Picosecond: One-trillionth of a second; one-millionth of a microsecond (0.000000000001).

Ping-pong transmission: A technique wherein one device transmits traffic, then stops intermittently to receive traffic from another device; since transmission can occur at a very high data rate, it gives the appearance of full duplex transmission.

Plug board: A panel into which plugs are placed for control (such as patching) of devices and equipment.

PM: See phase modulation.

Point of presence (POP): The access point within a LATA of a long-distance and/or inter-LATA common carrier. The local telephone company terminates subscribers' circuits for long-distance dial-up or leased-line communications at the POP.

Point-to-point: A communications line connected directly from one point to another. Contrast with multipoint lines.

Polarity: Referring to two opposing charges, such as positive and negative.

Port: A point of access into a computer, a network, or other device.

Port sharing unit: A device that allows multiple terminals, computers, or telephones to share one or more ports.

Postal, Telegraph, and Telephone Ministry: See PTT.

Power level: The measurement of the power in a channel; usually measured in decibels.

Private line: A line reserved for the exclusive use of one or several parties. Also see dedicated line, leased line, and nonswitched line.

Protocol: A formal set of conventions governing the control of inputs and outputs between the two communicating processes.

PSK: See phase shift keying.

PSTN (public switched telephone network): Same as the dial-up phone network.

PTT (Postal, Telegraph, and Telephone Ministry): Government authority or agency that operates the public telecommunications network, sets standards and policy, and negotiates communications issues internationally for a particular country; not found in the United States, or Canada, and PTT structure has changed in the United Kingdom and Japan.

Public switched telephone network: See PSTN.

Public network: A network established and operated by communications common carriers or telecommunications administrations for service to the public.

Q

QAM (quadrature amplitude modulation): Modulation technique using variations in signal amplitude, and phase that allows data-encoded symbols to be represented as any of 8, 16, 32, 64, or 128 different states. Used to increase the number of bits per baud (signaling change).

Quad: A cable consisting of two twisted pairs of conductors, each separately insulated.

Quadbit: A group of four bits used often in modulation where each possible combination of the bits is encoded and modulated on to the carrier.

Quadrature amplitude modulation: See QAM.

Quadrature distortion: Analog signal distortion frequently found in phase modulation modems.

R

Recommended standard (RS): A term used to describe standards published by groups such as CCITT and the EIA. Called "recommended" because these groups are not enforcing bodies.

Reference edge: The edge of a data carrier used to establish measurements in or on the data carrier.

Reference noise: The level of noise that will produce a reading equal to that produced by 1 picowatt (-90 dBm) of electric power at 1000 Hz.

Remote station: Any device that is attached to a controlling unit by a data link in contrast to a local computer channel attachment.

Request to send: See RTS.

Reverse channel: An optional feature provided on some modems that provides simultaneous communications from the receiver to the transmitter on a two-wire channel by the use of two subchannels. See also F1F2 and backward channel. Contrast with forward channel. Also called split channel modem.

Ring down: A method of signaling subscribers and operators with a special signal.

Ring network: A network topology in which each node is connected to two adjacent nodes to form a circle or hub.

Rotary: A facility installed at a computer facility to allow dial up calls to be switched to an available port at a computer, multiplexer, or front-end processor.

Rotary dial: In a dial network, a method of creating a series of pulses to identify the called station. Each dialed number is represented by a code of pulses created as the dial of the telephone returns to its original position. Contrast with DTMF.

Rotary line group: A group of lines that are identified by a single symbolic name or number; upon request, connection is made to the first available line.

RS: See recommended standard.

RS-232-C: A standard interface between a DTE and a DCE at the ISO physical level. Sponsored by the EIA (Electronics Industries Association). RS-232-C is being replaced with EIA-232-D.

RTS (request to send): Part of DTE handshaking to a DCE. Signal notifies DCE that DTE wishes to send traffic.

S

Sealing current: A current used by the local telephone company to provide better contact of switches in their office. The current is used to burn away impurities that develop over time on the switch contacts.

Selector channel: A channel designed to operate with only one I/O device at a time. Once the I/O device is selected, a complete record is transferred one byte at a time.

Serial board: See board.

Serial transmission: The sequential transmission of the bits over a circuit. Contrast with parallel transmission.

Shielding: Protective enclosure surrounding a transmission medium to minimize electromagnetic leakage and interference from other signals and noise.

Short-haul modem: See limited distance modem.

Signal-to-noise ratio: Ratio of the magnitude of a transmission signal to the noise of a channel. The relative strength of the desired signal compared to the strength of unwanted noise; usually measured in dB.

Simple wiring: One or two line wiring in residences and small businesses. If installed by telephone company, it remains the property of the telephone company unless bought by the user. Any inside wiring other than complex wiring. Contrast with complex wiring and embedded wiring.

Simplex: One-way data transmission.

SPACE: The condition on a data line when sending a logic zero. In telegraph communications, a SPACE represents an open condition with no current flowing. Contrast with MARK.

Split channel modem: See reverse channel.

Start bit: In asynchronous transmission, the start bit is appended to the beginning of a character to provide timing.

Start-stop transmission: A transmission technique where each character is preceded by a start bit and followed by a stop bit. See also asynchronous.

Stop bit: In asynchronous transmission, the stop bit is appended to the end of each character. It sets the receiving hardware to a condition where it looks for the start bit of a new character.

Subscriber loop: See local loop.

Switched line: Communications link in which the physical path may vary with each use.

Switched service: A common carrier communications service, which requires that call establishment take place before a data link can be established. For example, DDD is a switched service.

Synchronous transmission: A technique wherein messages are sent in blocks and all characters are sent contiguously. No start or stop bits are appended to each character.

T

Tail circuit adaptor: A device commonly used to connect two synchronous devices; often used to interface an analog facility into a digital facility.

Tandem office: A phone company switching center for the telephone network; interconnects central offices when direct inter-office trunks are not available.

Tariff: The rates, rules, and regulations concerning specific equipment and services provided by a communications carrier.

TDMA (time-division multiple access): A satellite transmission technique in which several earth stations have use of total available transponder power and bandwidth, with each station transmitting in short bursts in sequence or under the control of a reference station.

Telco: Informal abbreviation for telephone company.

Telegraphy (or telegraph): An older data transmission technique with signaling wherein the direction, or polarity, of dc current flow is reversed to indicate bit states.

Telephony: Term describing voice telecommunications using telephone technology.

Terminal: A point in a network at which data can either enter or leave; a device, usually equipped with a keyboard, often with a display.

Terminated line: A telephone circuit with a resistance at the far end equal to the characteristic impedance of the line. No reflections or standing waves occur when a signal is entered at the near end.

Terrestrial circuits: Use of nonsatellite channels.

Test board: Switchboard equipment with testing apparatus; connections can be made to telephone lines or equipment for testing purposes.

Test center: A facility for detecting and diagnosing faults and problems with communications lines and the equipment attached to them.

Test tone: A tone used in diagnostics and troubleshooting.

Thermal noise: A type of electromagnetic noise produced in conductors or in electronic circuitry that is proportional to temperature. See also noise. Also called background noise or hiss.

Tie line: A dedicated telephone circuit that links two points together without using the switched telephone network.

Time-out: A protocol procedure requiring a device to make some response to a command or frame within a certain period of time. If the response does not occur within that period of time, a time-out condition occurs.

Tip: The end of the plug used to make circuit connections in a manual switchboard. The tip is the connector to the positive side of the battery that powers the equipment.

Toll center: A class 4 telephone central office circuit switching facility where time and distance based toll charge information is collected.

Transceiver: Any device that can both transmit and receive.

Transducer: A device that converts energy from one form to another.

Transients: Intermittent, signal impairments lasting a short time.

Transmission: The sending of a signal.

Trellis encoding: A forward error correction (FEC) technique that detects damaged bits and attempts to correct them.

Tribit: A group of three bits often used in modulation where each possible combination of three bits is encoded and modulated onto the carrier.

Trunk: A multiple line circuit that connects two switching or distribution stations or centers. Also a circuit from a PBX to a class 5 telephone office.

Trunk exchange: A telephone exchange dedicated to interconnecting trunks.

Trunk group: Multiple trunk circuits between the same two switching centers.

Turnaround time: The time required to reverse the direction of transmission, over a half duplex channel. Also, the elapsed time between submission of a transaction, or job, and the return of processed output.

TWA: See two-way alternate and half duplex.

TWS: See two-way simultaneous and full duplex.

Twinaxial cable: A shielded coaxial cable with two central conducting leads.

Twisted Pair: Two wires wrapped around each other in staggered twists in order to improve the electrical characteristics and signal quality.

Two-way alternate (TWA): See half duplex.

Two-way simultaneous (TWS): See full duplex.

Two-wire circuit: Circuit consisting of two insulated electrical conductors, typical of most local loops or subscriber loops.

U

Unbalanced: In a two-wire circuit, the two wires have different impedance to ground. In a coaxial cable, a center conductor carries the signal and the shield is at ground potential.

Unbalanced (to ground): In a two-wire circuit, the impedance-to-ground on one wire is different from the other. Contrast with balanced (to-ground).

USTA (United States Telephone Association): A professional association of telephone carriers and venders.

W

Wait state: The condition of a task that is dependent on one or more events in order to proceed.

WATS (wide area telephone service): A flat rate or measured bulk rate long-distance telephone service provided on an incoming or outgoing basis. OUTWATS permits a customer, by use of an access line, to make telephone calls to any dialable telephone number in a specific zone for an hourly rate. INWATS permits reception of calls from specific zones over an access line in like manner but the called party is charged with the call.

White noise: See thermal noise.

Wideband: See broadband.

Wiring closet: Termination point for customer premises wiring, offering access to service personnel.

Wraparound: The continuation of sequencing of traffic, going from the maximum allowed number back to zero.

X

XOFF/XON (Transmit OFF/transmit ON): A commonly used peripheral device flow-control protocol. Implemented with characters of a code, typically the ASCII DC1 for XON and DC3 for XOFF.

Z

Zero code suppression: The insertion of a "one" bit to prevent the transmission of number of consecutive "zero" bits.

Zero transmission level point (0 TLP): A reference point for measuring the signal power gain and losses at which a zero dBm signal level is applied.